KU-709-385

Beyond the Cold War

FROM THE PUBLIC AFFAIRS CONFERENCE CENTER

OF THE UNIVERSITY OF CHICAGO

Beyond the

Essays on

in a

ESSAYS BY

CHARLES BURTON MARSHALL

ROBERT E. OSGOOD

HERMAN KAHN

LAWRENCE W. MARTIN

PHILIP E. MOSELY

TANG TSOU

MYRON RUSH

GREGORY GROSSMAN

ROBERT J. ALEXANDER

LEONARD BINDER

ERICH HULA

Cold War

American Foreign Policy
Changing World Environment

EDITED BY
ROBERT A. GOLDWIN

RAND McNALLY & COMPANY • CHICAGO

940.55 G02

38779

RAND MᶜNALLY PUBLIC AFFAIRS SERIES, Robert A. Goldwin, editor
America Armed: Essays on United States Military Policy
A Nation of States: Essays on the American Federal System
Why Foreign Aid?
Political Parties, U.S.A.
100 Years of Emancipation

RAND MᶜNALLY POLITICAL SCIENCE SERIES
BARBER, *Power in Committees*
BAYLEY, *Political Liberties in the New States*
BECKER, *Political Behavioralism and Modern Jurisprudence*
BOBROW, ed., *Components of Defense Policy*
CLEMENS, ed., *Toward a Strategy of Peace*
DIAMOND, GARFINKEL, and FISK, *The Democratic Republic: An Introduction to American National Government*
ELDERSVELD, *Political Parties: A Behavioral Analysis*
FROMAN, *Congressmen and Their Constituencies*
GOLDWIN, ed., *Beyond the Cold War*
GOLEMBIEWSKI, *Behavior and Organization: O & M and the Small Group*
GRODZINS, *The American System*
HAIGHT and JOHNSTON, eds., *The President: Roles and Powers*
HANNA, ed., *Independent Black Africa*
LONG, *The Polity*
MILBRATH, *Political Participation: How and Why Do People Get Involved in Politics?*
___ *The Washington Lobbyists*
PEABODY and POLSBY, eds., *New Perspectives on the House of Representatives*
PRESS AND WILLIAMS, *Democracy in the Fifty States*
SCHMIDHAUSER, ed., *Constitutional Law in the Political Process*
SINGER, ed., *Human Behavior and International Politics: Contributions from the Social-Psychological Sciences*
SCHUBERT, ed., *Judicial Behavior: A Reader in Theory and Research*
STEINER, *Social Insecurity*
STRAUSS, *The City and Man*
STRAUSS and CROPSEY, eds., *History of Political Philosophy*
ULMER, ed., *Introductory Reader in Political Behavior*
WILLIAMS and PRESS, eds., *Democracy in Urban America: Readings in Government and Politics*

083697218X

COPYRIGHT © 1963, 1965 BY THE PUBLIC AFFAIRS CONFERENCE CENTER.
THE UNIVERSITY OF CHICAGO

ALL RIGHTS RESERVED
PRINTED IN U.S.A. BY RAND MCNALLY & COMPANY
LIBRARY OF CONGRESS CARD CATALOGUE NUMBER 65:18590

EDITOR'S INTRODUCTION

THE PROCESS THAT PRODUCED THIS VOLUME OF ESSAYS ON UNITED *States foreign and military policy began in November, 1962, with a letter, from Thomas J. Watson, Jr., addressed to me in my capacity as Director of the Public Affairs Conference Center of The University of Chicago. That the writer of the letter was gravely disturbed by the Cuban missile crisis of October, 1962, was made evident in his opening sentence:*

"The events of the last few weeks — while heartening from the point of view of the willingness of this country to stand up for its rights in the Western Hemisphere — have emphasized once more to anyone who lives in the United States and thinks about the situation that we are indeed living on a tinderbox."

The letter went on to pose an arresting question: Although the nation and the world had come through the Cuban crisis still in one piece, what hope was there for the survival of civilization if this sort of nuclear confrontation occurred several more times, even if infrequently, over the next decade or two? Mr. Watson proposed that a conference be held, and that papers be written by foreign policy and military experts, to explore the possibilities of a "basic solution of the problems between the East and West." After many conversations and some modifications, the proposal was agreed to.

Ten papers were commissioned, each author writing within his own area of special competence but with a general theme in mind. As director of the conference and editor of the papers, I wrote to each author to set forth the conference topic:

The general task of this conference will be consideration of the prospects for basic improvements in the international situation during the next decade or so. We are asking each author to keep two standards or goals uppermost in his mind while writing: (1) to advance the interests, broadly conceived, of the United States and its allies without increasing the danger of global nuclear war; and (2) to decrease the likelihood of nuclear war without endangering the vital interests of the United States and its allies.

The papers were written and the conference — all of the authors and about a dozen others attended — was held in October, 1963. Three days of discussion

Editor's Introduction

revealed an underlying question in the minds of the authors and many of the other participants: Is the Cold War approaching its end? This question was not "assigned" as a theme of the conference, but it seemed to spring up and dominate our discussions no matter which one of the essays was being considered. There was, of course, no unanimity among us in our answers. But all seemed to see it as a question worthy of very serious consideration, because its answer seemed to be the foundation of almost all other policy decisions.

About a month after the conference ended, while the authors were still making rather limited revisions of their papers, prior to publication, President John F. Kennedy was assassinated. In addition to the dismay and sorrow that all Americans experienced at this shocking event, we realized that many of the original papers, written as analyses of the policies of the Kennedy Administration, would have to be revised extensively. Rewriting began early in 1964, but once the original momentum was lost the project moved forward very slowly, and sometimes not at all during that election year. Many of the papers were rewritten in the form of advice to the new Johnson Administration, but one delay and another made that approach, too, obsolete.

Finally, early in 1965 I wrote to the authors asking them to recast their papers to address themselves to the great theme we had discovered in common late in 1963: Looking ahead a few years at least, are there signs that we are approaching a new era in which it might be said that the Cold War has either ended or been transformed? If so, what are the signs, what policies are appropriate to the developing situation, and what problems and opportunities can be anticipated "beyond the Cold War"?

The volume you now hold is the response of the several authors to that final editorial request. One paper on Communist China, by Professor Tang Tsou, who was present at the conference, has been added to the original conference papers.

Robert A. Goldwin

Chicago, Illinois
October, 1965

CONTENTS

●

CASTRO, LATIN AMERICA AND UNITED STATES POLICY
Robert J. Alexander

THE NEW STATES IN INTERNATIONAL AFFAIRS
Leonard Binder

THE UNITED STATES AND THE UNITED NATIONS
Erich Hula

THE AUTHORS

•

ROBERT A. GOLDWIN

is Lecturer in Political Science and Director, Public Affairs Conference Center, University of Chicago, and Editor of the Rand McNally Public Affairs Series. He has edited *Readings in World Politics*, 1959; *Readings in American Foreign Policy*, 1959; *Readings in Russian Foreign Policy*, 1959; *America Armed*, 1963, and *Why Foreign Aid?*, 1963.

CHARLES BURTON MARSHALL

is Research Associate, Washington Center of Foreign Policy Research. He is the author of *The Limits of Foreign Policy*, 1954, and *The Exercise of Sovereignty*, 1965.

ROBERT E. OSGOOD

is Professor of American Foreign Policy, The Johns Hopkins University, and Research Associate, Washington Center of Foreign Policy Research. His books include *Ideals and Self-Interest in America's Foreign Relations*, 1953; *Limited War*, 1957; and *NATO: The Entangling Alliance*, 1962.

HERMAN KAHN

is Director of the Hudson Institute and the author of *On Thermonuclear War*, 1960; *Thinking About the Unthinkable*, 1962; and *On Escalation: Metaphors and Scenarios*, 1965.

LAURENCE W. MARTIN

is Woodrow Wilson Professor of International Politics, University of Wales, and was formerly Associate Professor at the Johns Hopkins School of Advanced International Affairs. His books include *Peace without Victory: Woodrow Wilson and the British Liberals*, 1958, and (joint author and editor) *Neutralism and Nonalignment: The New States in World Affairs*, 1962.

PHILIP E. MOSELY

is Director of the European Institute, Associate Dean of the Faculty of International Affairs, and Professor of International Relations, Columbia University. He is the author of *The Kremlin and World Politics,* 1960, and the editor of *The Soviet Union, 1922-1962,* 1963.

TANG TSOU

is Associate Professor of Political Science, University of Chicago. His special fields of study are Chinese-American relations and contemporary Chinese politics. He is the author of *The Embroilment Over Quemoy: Mao, Chiang, and Dulles,* 1959, and *America's Failure in China,* 1963.

MYRON RUSH

is Professor of Government, Cornell University, and a former senior staff member of The RAND Corporation. He is the author of *The Rise of Khrushchev,* 1958; *Political Succession in the USSR,* 1965, and *Strategic Power and Soviet Foreign Policy* (co-author, Arnold Horelick, to be published February, 1966).

GREGORY GROSSMAN

is Professor of Economics and Chairman of the Center for Slavic and East European Studies, University of California (Berkeley). His special field of study is the Soviet economy and Soviet economics. He is the author of *Soviet Statistics of Physical Output of Industrial Commodities,* 1960.

ROBERT J. ALEXANDER

is Professor of Economics, Rutgers University. He is the author of *Today's Latin America,* 1962; *The Venezuelan Democratic Revolution,* 1964, and *Latin American Politics and Government,* 1965.

LEONARD BINDER

is Chairman of the Department and Professor of Political Science and a Member of the Committees on Near Eastern Studies, South Asian Studies, and for the Comparative Study of New Nations, University of Chicago. His published works include *Religion and Politics in Pakistan,* 1961, and *Iran: Political Development in a Changing Society,* 1962.

ERICH HULA

is Professor of the Graduate Faculty, New School for Social Research. His special fields of study are international organization and international law. His writings include "Four Years of the United Nations," 1950; "The Evolution of Collective Security under the United Nations Charter," 1959; and "United Nations in Crisis," 1961.

Beyond the Cold War

IN THIS INTRODUCTORY ESSAY, CHARLES BURTON MARSHALL EMBARKS *on a discussion of the highest level of foreign policy — commonly called strategy. Mr. Marshall begins by commenting on the newness of this word, strategy, in the vocabulary of foreign-policy makers and the significance of its adoption from military terminology.*

Why is there a need for strategy? Most simply because no nations, not even the greatest superpowers, have sufficient means to accomplish all of their goals in world politics. Every government must make choices and establish priorities among competing desirable goals. The circumstances of the Cold War and the age of nuclear weapons tend only to emphasize the limitations of power of all nations in our time. And these limitations, which prevent any nation from achieving every good thing it desires for itself, force every nation to choose.

Strategy, as defined by Mr. Marshall, is concerned primarily with choosing. The strategist must choose "which areas to yield, to contest, or to overrun." The strategist must appraise "what initiatives in coercing others or for winning their support may help or hinder the broad cause."

As the argument develops, it becomes clear that strategy cannot be guided solely by analysis of the objective circumstances. For American strategists, there can be no systematic choice among competing goals without the guidance of an understanding of our nation's highest goal, a grasp of our most fundamental national purpose.

When we turn to this question, a paradox is at once encountered. Mr. Marshall finds in our national heritage, in our two most fundamental documents, the Declaration of Independence and the Constitution, strong contrast, at least, if not direct opposition. The main theme of the Declaration, he maintains, is the unity of mankind and the derivative mission of the people of the United States, in proclaiming their nationhood, to serve as an example for all men in the pursuit of universal goals. But in the Constitution of the United States, which formed the government embodying the principles of the Declaration, he finds that "no universals are proclaimed," and the language of a world mission is dispensed with.

The difference between the Declaration and the Constitution, according to Mr. Marshall, is reflected in our conduct of foreign policy and the formulation of strategy. One part of our "national psyche" desires to transcend the diversity of men separated into nations and make the unity of mankind paramount. And this inclination exists side by side with the strong desire to promote the national interest of the United States. Our policy "remains faithful to the spirit of the Declaration of Independence. At the same time, policy-makers are oath-bound to the Constitution. . . ."

Whether these dual tendencies can be made compatible depends on the quality of our understanding of ourselves. And, as Mr. Marshall shows, however the configurations of the international situation may be altered in the future, these characteristics of American foreign policy strategy will persist.

Charles Burton Marshall

•

STRATEGY AND PURPOSE
IN UNITED STATES FOREIGN POLICY

A LITTLE MORE THAN FIVE DECADES AGO A WRITER NAMED HOMER LEA
was widely derided as heretical, deluded, irrelevant, and mischievous
for attempting to deal with the United States' relations to its environment in such martial terms as radiuses of attack, comparative resources for levying war, states of military proficiency, and looming
conflicts of dominion. Such ideas—so the critics' argument went—
had no bearing on the American future. Even after the advent of
World War II, John Nicholas Spykman's *America's Strategy in World
Affairs*[1] incurred wide skepticism for its disposition to view concern
with the geography and technology of security as a thenceforth
abiding aspect of national life rather than a passing abnormal
necessity due to be alleviated upon defeat of the moment's adversaries.

Attitudes so recently regarded as exceptional have come to be
taken generally for granted. The circumstance undoubtedly has
much to do with a now quite common practice, of using the term
strategy to denote enduring and engrossing considerations relevant
to foreign policy. The key word is by origin a military expression
cognate with the Greek *strategos,* signifying a general or one in
supreme command and relevant to generalship at its most recondite
level, and, by strict standards of meaning authorized by the dictionary, remains exclusively such.

I. THE MEANING OF STRATEGY

THE PRACTICE OF APPLYING STRATEGY VIRTUALLY AS A SYNONYM OF
higher policy is of fairly recent origin. I first became aware of the
usage in an official context fourteen years ago in connection with

[1]John Nicholas Spykman, *America's Strategy in World Affairs* (New York: Harcourt,
Brace, 1942).

production of a basic paper regarding national security — NSC 68 — whose contents were then closely guarded but have since become widely known. That same year, as I recall, the Secretary of State used the phrase "Strategy of Peace" as a title for a major speech on foreign policy. A decade later the aspiring Senator John F. Kennedy applied the same phrase to a book consisting of his collected addresses on world affairs. Subsequently, during his tragically shortened tenure as President, the key word used to turn up often in his discourses at press conferences and on more formal occasions. Others widely echo the use. Various institutions focusing on foreign policy purport to be strategic in intent and adopt the word in their names.

Maybe the usage is here to stay, notwithstanding the restrictiveness of the dictionary definition. In part the vogue may be a matter of style. The term sounds big. Individuals sometimes invoke it to vest their ideas with thoughtfulness, dimension, and authority, without attention to its meaning. In part, however, the vogue has a measure of validity due not only to steady concern with security considerations in foreign policy under present conditions, but also to ideas implicit in the term but not so clearly derivable from the companion word *policy*. *Strategy* suggests the idea of discriminating choices. More dimensions are implicit in it than in the other word. Any response or purpose might qualify to be called a policy, but a strategy seems to suggest deliberateness, scope, and complex calculation. So probably the prevalence of the term reflects a sense of our having gone beyond the simplicities characteristic of earlier times in world affairs.

Testing the appropriateness of the term in application to national undertakings in the broad calls for taking into account some characteristics of warfare. Its nature is obscured by a current tendency to refer to a type of conflict as limited war — implicitly as if some contrasting sort of war were infinite. All wars are limited. No war, whether experienced or merely notional, presents infinite possibilities. Wars vary not between being finite and measureless but in the manner of their finiteness.

The phenomenon of war occurs when adversary political societies or groups of such, disposing armed forces, seek to resolve conflicting purposes by acting upon each other's wills through effecting a determinative shift of relative capabilities for bringing force to bear — each side to its own advantage and to the disadvantage of the antagonist. To that end, as an essential part of the process, they use their armed forces to expend energy destructively upon the respective adversary establishments. The numbers of political entities drawn in on either side, the purposes put at issue in combat, the levels of force

3

capabilities generated, the areas chosen for destructive expenditure of energy, the range of devices used, the intensity of the destructive expenditure, the amounts of materiel and of manpower committed to the effort, and the time entailed — such are the interdependent variables, directly or inversely related according to circumstances, involved in the measurement and therefore in the management of warfare.

Strategy concerns calculation of interrelations among such factors. How, in broadest terms, to interweave potential and purposes is its focus. Strategy relates to the establishment and application of a pattern of ends and a framework of means whereby to assess tactical opportunities, to choose which areas to yield, to contest, or to overrun, and to appraise what initiatives in coercing others or for winning their support may help or hinder the broad cause. The occasion for strategy is a situation of choice — to wit, a situation of having means enough to afford some exercise of preferences but lacking such abundance as to be able to effectuate every desire. Strategy involves renunciation and deferment as well as pursuit and achievement of ends. It entails choice among purposes brought into conflict because of limitation of means.

The strategic content of thinking involved in planning and levying war varies from one instance to another. In uncomplicated cases, as for example between antagonists so inherently incommensurate in capabilities as to spare one side appreciable need to calculate the interrelated magnitudes and to afford the other side little opportunity to do so, the management of war may be mostly a matter for tacticians. The closer the two sides are to being even in potential, the greater becomes the requirement of systematic calculation of the interacting factors of magnitude: the greater, in other words, the role of strategy.

The prominence of the term owes something also to an awareness of our being in a phase of pervasive and unremitting contest in world affairs. The main elements of changed circumstance accounting for this intensification of concern about external affairs can only be named here, for each is so complex as to deserve book-length explanation. They are:

1. The establishment of positions of great scope and importance — namely the Soviet Union and the Chinese People's Republic and appurtenant areas — for revolutionary purposes in world affairs.

2. The emergence of weapon systems characterized by prodigious destructive capabilities and instant readiness for delivery over spans of thousands of miles.

3. The sharing of pre-eminence in such weapons by two societies —one the United States, the other the Soviet Union—based beyond the confines of what used to be the central theater of military significance and political importance in world affairs, namely Central and Western Europe.

4. The progressive disappearance—a major phenomenon of our times—of the Europe-based, inequalitarian imperial order once serving as a framework of relationship between economically and politically advanced societies and the less-developed and tradition-bound lands and peoples.

5. As a corollary, the proliferation of juridically independent new states, entering into the public life of the world often without having as yet established adequate bases of public life within themselves and participating in the making of history without, in many instances, canons of relevant historic experience of their own.

6. As a further corollary, the approach to universalization of the equalitarian usages of diplomacy in succession to the inequalitarian arrangements of empire.

7. The existence and continuous activity of an institution—to wit, the United Nations—now also approaching universality and designed for and devoted to what is called parliamentary diplomacy.

Some of these developments were never willed by the United States and have been thrust upon its consciousness by forces and events beyond its ordaining. Others, though encouraged by the United States, differ widely in actuality from the hopes which prompted sponsorship. In sum, they illustrate the inherent adventitiousness of foreign affairs and the limitations on power of even a first-rank government for affecting its environment. In consequence of them, attending to the external concerns of the United States has become a hugely more involuted and rigorous business than it was in previous epochs. The inherent necessity of choice and renunciation in exterior relations is borne in upon general and official consciousness constantly rather than being a point of intermittent concern, as in earlier and less exacting stages of national experience. The margin for error has shrunk. Interactiveness among the globe's quadrants has become increasingly manifest. A need for seeing the world steadily and whole has become patent. Foreign policy itself has no traditional terms for distinguishing readily between pervasive and lasting considerations and immediate and local problems. The borrowing of a discriminating analogy from military discourse is natural and convenient.

Charles Burton Marshall

II. Two Basic Views of National Purpose

HOWEVER NOVEL SOME FEATURES OF THE SITUATION IN WHICH THE United States now defines the purposes of policy, the basic premises from which it conceives those purposes are part of a memory reaching back to the national origins. In some degree, the premises tend to come into contradiction. Policy must strive to maintain a workable compatibility between them. In this sense, policy is a matter of making ends meet. Contrasting premises about the character and role of the American nation in relation to other peoples are most fundamental in this regard. These premises reflect divergent perspectives about societies and their origins and courses.

One outlook may be described as rooted in Genesis, in the Book of Daniel, and in the Book of Revelation. Medieval theocratic thought was preoccupied with it. The Anabaptists in the sixteenth century and Levelers and the Fifth Monarchy sect in the seventeenth century implicitly reflected it. The view has counterparts in some respects in the assumptions of Karl Marx and of the Darwinists. I refer here to the notion of humankind as unified in origin and in the pristine situation. "God . . . hath made of one blood all the nations of men," as the Apostle Paul put the notion at Mars Hill. Notwithstanding divergence into variant cultures in consequence of having wandered afar from the original base, mankind remains inherently a unity according to this view. Such institutional structures as governments are seen as divisive of mankind. In this vein, as a contemporary example, George F. Kennan, in *The Realities of American Foreign Policy,* speaks of "these unsatisfactory but indispensable arrangements we call governments" and describes peoples as "separated from one another" by them.[2]

According to this outlook, moreover, the apparatus of governments is in a sense aberrant. The existence of politics is due to accidents of diversity among human societies. Mankind has the potential—indeed, the destiny—of being reunified at some climax lying ahead. A vision of this is conveyed in Chapter 21 of Revelation: a new Jerusalem, an end of conflict, a final heightening of enlightenment and prosperity, a falling away of particularism, with all the nations transcended and paying homage. For men involved in the vicissitudes and uncertainties of temporal experience, no idea has had more pervasive and compelling appeal than the idea, in its various versions, of a new Jerusalem. "Earth at last a warless world, a single race, a single tongue—" in Tennyson's summation.

[2]George F. Kennan, *Realities of American Foreign Policy* (Princeton: Princeton University Press, 1954), p. 49.

Strategy and Purpose in United States Foreign Policy

By a contrasting perspective, diversity has been characteristic of the human situation back as far as the evidence is adducible. Societies took shape at diverse points, in diverse times, and under divergent circumstances. As the matter is put in Bertrand de Jouvenel's *On Power:*

> It is no longer treated as proved that there was only one primitive society; now, on the contrary, it is readily admitted that different groups of men have from the beginning presented different characteristics, which, as the case might be, either caused them to develop differently or prevented them from developing at all . . .[3]

According to this concept, such order, security, and continuity of authority as men have achieved have been realized by the combined efforts of particular groups in particular localities by dint of getting and maintaining control of territory. The limited monopolies of force called governments, however imperfect and contingent, form the basis of whatever experience men have had in living together in peace. Governments, by this view, are not divisive of mankind but afford such opportunity as there is, limited as it may be, for men to live peaceably together. A group living an established existence under one span of government identified with some marked-off area of the earth's surface has interests of its own and a legitimate right as well as an inherent necessity to uphold them; and if such a group is unable or indisposed to fend for its own interests, then surely no one else will.

Diversity is what makes political relationships necessary. Community makes them possible. Any version of policy which seeks to renounce and to transcend the differences represents a flight into Utopia. Any version which undertakes to make an absolute of diversity amounts to a declaration of war against or an instrument of secession from mankind in the large. Community and diversity are thus complementary characteristics, each varying in degree from one relationship to another. It is not my purpose here to choose between these two concepts — to try to make an absolute case for either relative notion. My point pertains only to noting their place in our national habits of thinking about world relations, for these two contrasting notions are crystalized in the American store of ideas by the two founding documents — the Declaration of Independence and the Constitution.

[3]Bertrand de Jouvenel, *On Power* (New York: Viking Press, 1949), p.65.

Charles Burton Marshall

III. World Mission and National Interest

IN AN EXCELLENT BOOK, *To the Farewell Address*,[4] FELIX GILBERT examines the substantive links between the Declaration of Independence and the ideas about foreign policy publicized in the months preceding the Declaration in Thomas Paine's *Common Sense*. The pattern calls not only for separation from the Crown but also for renunciation of all political alliances. Force may be necessary to sunder the ties, but thereafter it can be dispensed with as an instrument of policy. The connections with England are perceived as making the colonies heirs to the enmities of the motherland. Freed from those ties, the colonies, as states, will enjoy a universal friendship latent in relations among nations. As unencumbered market places, they will serve commercial interests of all nations. Their security will be founded on their detachment. By avoiding discriminations, they will find a response in a harmony of interest inherent among all nations. A general interest will be caused to flourish merely by avoidance of alignment with particular interests. Independence is postulated not merely for particular advantage but as fulfillment of a duty to all mankind. It is to be an action of withdrawal into autonomy only in a juridic sense. In practice, the action will set a republican example due to receive general emulation. Implicitly, power will not have to be sought or husbanded. It will come in consequence of being eschewed; it will come through rational purpose and good example.

The Declaration of Independence itself is essentially a document concerning foreign relations. It presents a demand for entry into the nexus of diplomacy — assuming "among the powers of the earth . . . separate and equal station" — rather than continuing to acquiesce in the management of American relationships with the exterior world under the vicarious and inequalitarian usages of empire. The statement solicits sympathy and support for the cause among other societies. In doing so, it postulates rationality as a general characteristic — premising "truths to be self-evident" to the world at large. The Declaration postulates a norm for relationships among diverse peoples and areas.

The Declaration stands as an expression of universalizing ideas. It was not inescapably necessary for it to have been of that character. The men who led the way in cutting the leading strings to the imperial base might simply have aired particular grievances and have emphasized the impracticability of the exercise of rulership across the sea. In-

[4]Felix Gilbert, *To the Farewell Address*, (Princeton: Princeton University Press, 1961), pp. 36-43.

stead, in keeping with the intellectual style of the times, they postulated universal principles.

The truths proclaimed are asserted as unexceptionably valid rather than being merely applicable in the particular case. Absentee sovereignty is declared abhorrent to basic laws of the universe. Americans are portrayed as claiming the due of all men everywhere. The new nation is thus implicitly an exemplar for all mankind — a nation with a world mission, the guide to a new Jerusalem. The document conveys to us ideas of the Enlightenment — universal rationality, harmony of interests, the feasibility of new beginnings, men's boundless capacities for transforming conditions of existence.

It would be an exaggeration to portray the Constitution as representing an order of thought entirely antithetic to the Declaration, for both documents are products of the same society within a short span of time, enjoying the support of the same men in large numbers. Yet surely one can properly describe the second as contrasting with its precursor.

The national leadership is now less hortatory. Maintaining a going concern is seen to require more than declaratory purposes. Independence is seen implicitly as entailing a capacity to meet obligations. The nation must put itself in position to perform on contracts if it is to be a respectable entity in a world of states. Nothing comes automatically. It is not enough just to keep attuned to a hypothetical universal harmony of interests. The new nation has to put itself in position better to look after its own concerns.

The Constitution represents an attempt to come to terms with particular actualities — an attempt not so much to transform a situation as to manage it. The language of a world mission is dispensed with. No universals are proclaimed. The nation's purposes focus on perfecting the union of states. They are concerned with justice within. The tranquility which the document seeks to ensure is domestic. The common defense which it undertakes to provide for means security for a national base. The welfare postulated as a purpose of government is that of the generality of Americans. The blessings of liberty to be secured are for "ourselves and our posterity." These are all domestic purposes. The preoccupation is with the homeland.

On the one hand is the concept of a nation founded upon and exemplifying universally applicable principles, taking the lead in a new order of the ages, portraying for others what their future is to be like, setting an example for all to follow; on the other hand is the concept of a nation, in Alexander Hamilton's phrase, "likely to experience a common portion of the vicissitudes and calamities which have fallen to the lot of other nations" and constrained therefore to do what it can to fend off trouble and to look out for itself.

IV. Power and Responsibility

At the moment of the American challenge for independence the world situation represented order in an appreciable degree. The governments — mainly, indeed almost exclusively, European — participating in the world's public life had learned long since to desist from interference in each other's domestic arrangements, accepting each other's autonomy and confining their quarrels to marginal issues. In the main, each participant could look ahead with solid assurance against destructive violence and change. The tenor was interrupted by two decades of turmoil prompted by the French Revolution. A century of order, apparently more engrossing and solid than ever before, succeeded.

External problems did not press heavily on the United States then. The country could even afford the luxury of a massively violent internal division without incurring lasting and serious disadvantages in the environment. With respect to the world at large, Paine's prophecies of the universal efficacy of the American example were far from vindicated. The sweeping propositions of the Declaration retained vitality, however, in the national consciousness. A dialogue between the two contrasting ideas of universal mission and national interest persisted through the nineteenth century. It would oversimplify and overclarify matters to represent the dialogue as having been developed with studied logic and by consistent proponents. The nation was portrayed at once as standing apart from the world and yet as affecting it pervasively. The nation was destined to be puissant, but it was to eschew power — an echo of ideas underlying the Declaration. "I hope our wisdom will grow with our power, and teach us that the less we use our power, the greater it will be," ran Thomas Jefferson's formula in answer to a nice question as to how to be both self-denying and self-aggrandizing.

Yet it was mostly a rhetorical dialogue rather than a debate about actual policy choices. Jefferson, for example, giving counsel for dealing with what he called the enmities of Europe, might foretell a time "at no distant future" when "we may shake a rod over the heads of all, which may make the stoutest tremble" and assert that "even should the cloud of barbarism and despotism again obscure the science and liberties of Europe, this country remains to preserve and restore light and liberty to them." Walt Whitman, moreover, might turn recurringly to a theme of America ascendant in the world and bearing the destinies of all nations. For all practical intents, nevertheless, the United States followed the counsel of George Washington's Farewell Address, abiding by the more restricted and less lofty policy concepts of the Constitution as distinguished from the Declaration, and being preoccupied with filling out and consolidating a continental position.

It is not enough merely to call that position unique. All national positions are so. It is necessary to understand its particular combination of characteristics—a generally healthful land of great range and endowment, generally accessible in all its parts, located in both the northern and the western hemispheres, and facing both upon the Atlantic and the Pacific. In earlier but still recent times it was possible still to speak cogently of that position as a basis for a policy of standing apart. Thus Samuel Flagg Bemis, closing his distinguished *Diplomatic History of the United States* in 1936, wrote:

> The continental position has always been the strength of the United States in the world. American successes in diplomacy have been based on a continental policy. The interests of the United States today rest on the same support. It is a safe ground on which to watch and wait for a better world. A *continental* policy was instinctive with the Fathers. Its pursuit has been most consonant with the genius and the welfare of the American people. Where they have left it, to "become of age" or "to take their place"—on other continents— among the great powers of the world, they have made their mistakes. Where they have followed it, they have not gone astray.[5]

The words seem to belong to another age rather than to a time less than three decades ago. There is no question now of watchfully waiting for the emergence of a better world—no question, moreover, of whether or not to stand among the great powers, for pre-eminence in that respect has been thrust upon the United States by events. The nation is involved in an endless discourse with itself, growing out of consciousness of this pre-eminence and a contrasting awareness of its having been first among the once colonial peoples beyond Europe to seek successfully both a place in the nexus of diplomacy and the prerogatives of a history-maker. While engrossed in the affairs of the northern hemisphere, its people and its officials still retain habits of thinking of the United States as being located in the western hemisphere in a way more intimate and basic than in the northern. Thus the President and the Secretary of State are wont to say "this hemisphere" in referring to the Americas. The dialogue between the

---

[5]Samuel Flagg Bemis, *Diplomatic History of the United States* (New York: Holt, 1936), p. 809.

concept of a world mission—that is, the view of the nation as the bearer of universal values destined to prevail at large in the future—and the concept of the nation as a finite entity constrained to look to its own interests is no longer one merely of academic or literary interest separate from the practical issues of policy. Rather, it involves issues of continuous exigent concern.

V. The Short Run and the Long

UNDERTAKING WAR AGAINST SPAIN IN HOPE OF CLEARING UP A NUISANCE near the national periphery, the Congress re-enunciated the grand propositions of the Declaration of Independence. Pondering whether to make avail of opportunity to take over the Philippines, President McKinley implored divine guidance and then explained the action in terms of universal altruism. In a series of actions relevant to the traditional policy known as the Monroe Doctrine, the United States government adopted a posture described as follows by Dexter Perkins in *The United States and Latin America:*

> ... it is remarkable how little emphasis was placed ... on ... national safety. No doubt the foreign offices of all countries indulge in high sounding generalities.... But this fact is conspicuously true in ... American diplomacy. Again and again ... the emphasis is on ideology, rather than on security....[6]

Invoking war against Germany in 1917, the United States was not content to rest its cause upon the security issues involved but was constrained—borrowing a phrase from a British publicist, H. G. Wells—to "make the world safe for democracy." Interposing American resources against the Axis a generation later, Franklin D. Roosevelt propounded an Atlantic Charter with its four freedoms, all universal.

Reviewing the many such instances, a skeptic might well agree with Perkins:

> ... American statesmen have believed, and acted on the belief, that the best way to rally American opinion behind their purposes is to assert a moral principle. In doing so, they have often gone far beyond the boundaries of expediency. And perhaps it is fair to say that in underemphasizing security, they have helped to form a national habit which unduly subordinates the necessities of national defense to the assertion of lofty moral principles.[7]

[6]Dexter Perkins, *The United States and Latin America* (Baton Rouge: Louisiana State University Press, 1961), pp. 18-19.

[7]*Ibid.,* p. 19.

Strategy and Purpose in United States Foreign Policy

The record reflects more than merely the rhetoric of policy propaganda, however. The universalistic assumptions of the Declaration are fixed in conscience as well as consciousness. The Enlightenment is echoed to us in our great normative document and with it an age-old assumption about the original and inherent unity of mankind. Under a deep national predisposition, actions in world affairs undertaken in pursuance of the more finite purposes of the Constitution are not *ipso facto* justified but require vindication consonant with a universal scheme of good. Like Thomas Paine, this part of the national psyche —of which I personally do not completely partake—feels better in identifying national purposes with service to all mankind.

This attitude dwells upon ultimate goals and conceives them as including resolution of all differences and harmonization of all interests—in sum, the transcending by policy of politics among nations. This view tends to assume the omnipotence of mankind for solving all problems. It subscribes to the feasibility of new starts. It puts great store by the power of example alone. It places great confidence in the power of documents to transform situations and to enter into the general conscience—an understandable assumption in view of the efficacy of the Declaration in affecting our own national approach.

The repeated invocations of this frame of thought in regard to external affairs are not a mere matter of presidential guesswork as to what will go over with the public. The makers of policy—that is, successive Presidents and their spokesmen and principal counselors— do not simply humor these preconceptions but, in the usual case, share them in some significant portion. The relevant notions are essential to a framework for justifying policy undertakings to those themselves in charge and are not a mere device for persuasion.

As a world power, the United States states its case and vests its ultimate hopes in propositions which guided it at the beginning of its national history, back when this country was the ugly duckling among states. Centrally involved in trying to create the conditions of a new order in world affairs, the nation abides by the discourse of times when it stood afar from the centers of the world's political concerns and enjoyed the benefits of an order largely maintained by others.

True to the frame of thought of the Declaration, national policy is steadfast in devotion to universalizing of independence. It abides by Paine's postulate of the inherent incapacity for justice in all rulerships exercised from afar. It has been, and continues, assiduous in establishing self-determination as a political absolute of our time. The inherent capacity of any people in whatever area to find within itself the canons of nationhood and to make its way as a going concern is taken for granted. The faith has shifted somewhat from Wilsonian premises of the efficacy of democratic forms and institutions in ensuring success. Emphasis, for the time being, is on economic factors as the key to the venture. A span of time and a proper level of investment will bring everything around.

The community of nations, along with an inherent community of interests among nations, is premised. The universalizing of independence, the introduction of increasing diversities into the nexus of diplomacy, is seen as helping community along to full realization. The ease, the virtual automaticity, of the process of bringing community into play is not assumed as it was in Paine's discourse. More time and more organizing effort are seen as required, but the reconciling end is sure and will enfold even our adversaries. Fending off a cliché about having a no-win policy, the Secretary of State has countered with a cliché about having a set of purposes by which everybody will win.[8] Thus also the Assistant Secretary of State in charge of policy planning postulates hope in encouraging Communist governments "to perceive that the world we ... are trying to create ... has a place of dignity for all nations which pursue their national interests with integrity, which respect the hard imperatives of interdependence and the rights of other nations and peoples."[9] It is as if conciliation were awaiting the reassertion of irreproachable abstractions, as if divisive issues were rooted in miscomprehension, and as if indeed an inherent unity of purpose needed only right modes of expression to become revealed and made operative.

A danger of sorts inheres in uncritical acceptance of the optimistic postulates of the eighteenth century reflected in the Declaration. The case for universal independence, for example, poses diversity as right, proper, good—along with the assumptions of inherent harmony of interest and community among nations. Opposed qualities are thus placed in apposition. The case for freedom, stated by its most committed proponents, is linked to a concept of historical momentum amounting to an ineluctable force. Free will is seen as borne along toward triumph by deterministic currents. The danger is one of logical contradiction, but this troubles the discourse of policy no more than it did the Enlightenment. Community and diversity come on the same package, like Gold Dust twins.

We are out to promote them both, along with a theory combining the best parts of two other opposed ideas, freedom and determinism.

[8]*The Department of State Bulletin,* Vol. 47, p. 343.
[9]*Ibid.,* Vol. 47, p. 682.

Strategy and Purpose in United States Foreign Policy

In the late President Kennedy's words, "No one who examines the modern world can doubt that the great currents of history are carrying the world . . . toward the pluralistic idea . . . No one can doubt that the wave of the future is . . . the liberation of the diverse energies of free nations and free men."[10] An Under Secretary of State has added a gloss: "Free will, not historical determinism, is the credo of free men." Free will, in his version however, becomes indistinguishable from historical determinism: "This is the only acceptable working hypothesis for free men today: We are on the side of history, and the trends are running our way."[11]

Community and authority, linked and mutually supporting, pervade the world in the proffered American solution for the dilemma of armaments. All disputes over particulars are engrossed in a general agreement on global conditions of legitimacy, documented and made contractually binding. The agreement becomes by stages a basis for a world monopoly of coercive power subservient to no national or regional interest but responsive only to the general good and irresistible when brought to bear on malefactors threatening the general security. Such is the main proposition of the United States' plan for general and complete disarmament in a peaceful world, published under the title *Blueprint for the Peace Race.*[12] Subsumed into a general legitimate order, intimidated by a force irresistible by definition, and no longer possessing weapons effective beyond their bounds, the nations will become secure, tame, and inoffensive, as in Paine's vision of the future. Disarmed, the structures of particular governments will no longer be divisive of mankind. On the grand scale will be established one span of community and authority such as traditionally imagined to have obtained at the outset of human experience.

For the long run, policy remains faithful to the spirit of the Declaration of Independence. At the same time, policy-makers are oath-bound to the Constitution and to the more immediate and limited obligations laid upon them by it in the world as it is in distinction from what, in views of some, the world ought to be and even might conceivably become someday. This, the world as it is, presents quite another scene. No frame of universal legitimacy has been agreed upon. Governments all prefer peace to war, but the conditions of peace as a reliable, enduring order, commonly accepted as legiti-

[10]*Ibid.,* Vol. 46, p. 617.

[11]*Ibid.,* Vol. 47, p. 9.

[12]United States Arms Control and Disarmament Agency, *Blueprint for the Peace Race: Outline of Basic Provisions of a Treaty on General and Complete Disarmament in a Peaceful World* (Washington: U.S. Government Printing Office, 1962).

mate, remain obdurately at issue. Governments invoke the concept of community as a matter of habit, but community remains an uneven reality—fairly strong as between some and almost nonexistent as among others. International authority has no autonomous and continuously effective existence but is at best a contingent factor subject to being contrived issue by issue. High levels of armament are at once decried and maintained, because the great adversary nations lack the bond of mutual trust enabling them to disarm with assurance and are at odds on the conditions of legitimacy integral to such trust.

Such is the sort of world anticipated in Leopold Schwartzchild's *World in Trance,* written in 1942:

> Never again can we believe that any new magic can achieve what we ourselves must achieve by hard work. Mankind is not capable of sudden rebirths .... There are good reasons for the fact that the millenium has never materialized .... Against the eternally lurking jungle, weapons and compulsion are always the only defense and nothing liberates us from the duty of doing the utmost for ourselves .... And if the great powers have a common will, everything is well. If not, there is no collectivity, and once again we are alone; with our nearest friends we are thrown back on our resources. We must always be prepared for that eventuality ....[13]

Policy must come to terms with such a world every day. This is the world of the short run, which, like the long, is with us now and will linger on indefinitely. There means are never quite in balance with demands, and so strategy must operate. There is where national purpose is tested, where destiny is determined; for destiny, as Cassandra observes in Jean Giraudoux' *Tiger at the Gates,* "is simply the relentless logic of each day we live."

[13]Leopold Schwartzchild, *World in Trance* (New York: L. B. Fischer, 1942), p. 415.

IN THE PRECEDING ESSAY, THE INHERENT AMBIGUITIES OF AMERICAN foreign policy were explored. One of Charles Burton Marshall's specific examples serves admirably as an introduction to this essay: "High levels of armament are at once decried and maintained." Robert E. Osgood, in this essay, accepts the challenge in that paradox of American military and disarmament policy by attempting to explain and even to defend both the decrying and maintaining of high levels of armament.

Mr. Osgood begins by itemizing the constructive functions and destructive tendencies of the arms race that have been major features of the Cold War. Has the nuclear arms race increased or diminished the likelihood of nuclear war? If the arms race tends, on balance, to encourage caution and restraint, should it be decried?

Even those who are convinced that the arms race between the U.S. and the U.S.S.R. has had a "stabilizing, moderating, and pacifying effect," looking beyond our experience to probable developments in the next decades, when the most dangerous arms may be in the hands of many other nations, "must seriously consider adopting any measures that might prevent or mitigate these dangers." For "if war were to occur, it could be catastrophic." We must consider seriously any and every disarmament proposal.

But Mr. Osgood suggests that every such proposal must be evaluated by its effectiveness in lessening the one greatest danger: sudden catastrophic war. Because of the uncertainty that any partial plan can perform that task reliably, men have turned to "general and complete disarmament," which has been, since 1959, Mr. Osgood points out, "the ostensible end result of the principal official disarmament plan in both the United States and the Soviet Union."

Programs of arms reduction and arms control are considered insufficient because they can have little more than "marginal effect" in preventing sudden catastrophic war. General and complete disarmament is thought to avoid this major inadequacy of the partial plans. But does it? Mr. Osgood argues that general and complete disarmament must itself be considered only a partial disarmament program in the nuclear age, because there is no way to eliminate the capacity to rearm suddenly and decisively. What would be the effect on all nations of this capacity, which no scheme can eliminate, in a disarmed world?

With a description of the dangers and crises of a totally disarmed world, Mr. Osgood concludes by suggesting a long-range armament and disarmament policy calculated to balance security and international responsibility, no matter how the face of the Cold War may be altered.

ROBERT E. OSGOOD

•

THE PLACE OF DISARMAMENT
IN AMERICAN POLICY

WHATEVER OTHER PROBLEMS OF FOREIGN POLICY THE UNITED STATES
may have to deal with in the next decade or so, the problems of
disarmament will continue to command a major share of the attention
of American statesmen. For the emergence of disarmament as one of
the primary concerns of governments in the past century reflects
basic conditions of international life which are not likely to abate in the
foreseeable future. The principal material condition is the cataclysmic
increase in the destructive capacity of states to wage war. The
principal political condition is the existence of unreconcilable conflicts of national will and interest for which sovereign states might be
willing to fight. These conditions endanger the interests of virtually all
states because few could avoid catastrophic losses if a war were fought
with the most powerful weapons, and there is no warrant in history
for supposing that such a war can be avoided forever merely by a
balance of fear among adversaries.

This is not to say that disarmament can overcome or even
mitigate the danger of catastrophic war. It is only to say that without
disarmament the danger, in some form and degree, is bound to
persist as long as international politics among sovereign states persist.
Therefore, successfully or in vain, tactically or in earnest, governments must continually ponder, propose, and parley about methods
of regulating the instruments of their potential destruction. For this
reason it behooves the United States to have a sound view of the utility
of disarmament as a means of protecting its multiple interests in
security, a congenial international order, and peace.

By disarmament I mean all measures taken by formal international agreement to control, limit, reduce, or eliminate the development, manufacture, deployment, transfer, possession, or use of weapons and of military facilities, resources, and personnel. Clearly, this
embraces a great variety of measures, some of which raise different

18

kinds of policy considerations than others. One of the objects of this paper is to fit the proper policy considerations to distinct kinds of disarmament measures. But first it is necessary to put the general problem of disarmament in the broad context of international politics and in the particular context of the modern arms race.

COERCION, COMPETITION, AND EQUILIBRIUM

THE PROBLEM OF DISARMAMENT IS PART OF THE PROBLEM OF RESTRICTing the competition for power in an anarchical system of sovereign states.

The central political facts of international relations are: (1) The dominant units of organized human activity and loyalty are sovereign states, among whom the bonds of sentiment and interest are weak and transitory compared to exclusive national concerns, and (2) among these states there is no supranational body with the authority and the preponderance of power to determine and enforce a general will, a transcendent system of order and justice.

The intensity of national feelings, the clash of transcendent ideologies identified with national purposes, the diversity of national political systems and material circumstances, and the massive mobilization of collective pride, ambition, and fear create serious conflicts among states, which cannot be resolved by the fragile and rudimentary means of peaceful settlement. Therefore, the ultimate means by which a nation-state can achieve its will is its power to coerce opponents, singly or in concert with like-minded nations. Because of the atomistic, anarchical nature of international society, the power of physical coercion, whether it is used or merely implied, pervades international relations to an extent far exceeding the role of coercion among competing groups within a well-governed state with a virtual monopoly of physical coercion.

Given the dependence of states upon their own will and power, together with their material *inter*dependence, the power of armed coercion necessarily becomes a value in itself, for which some states must continually compete with their opponents. In this situation, even if all states aimed for nothing more ambitious than the preservation of their territorial security, the security of one state would tend to create insecurity for another, thus driving many states into a competition for relative armed power, which itself must jeopardize their security.

Yet the competition for military power is seldom unlimited. The material limits upon independent power in a system of states, the hazards of unrestrained competition, and the interference of this

Robert E. Osgood

competition with foreign and domestic interests, have ordinarily led states to restrict their ambitions and their pursuit of power. The principal instrument of restriction is countervailing military power. Throughout the history of international relations some states have combined to keep the power of other states within tolerable limits. The resulting deterrence or frustration of extreme power and ambition has periodically produced a degree of equilibrium, moderation, and regularity in national competition based upon reciprocal restraints, which at least the major powers have found an interest in preserving.

Yet in time, under the impact of new material and political conditions, changes in internal regimes, and the challenges of dissatisfied powers, every period of relative international order has degenerated, often in the wake of extreme violence. Indeed, it would seem that no configuration of countervailing power can sustain a permanent equilibrium unless states are willing to subordinate their particular interests, including their immediate security, to the preservation of some international system of mutual restraints. But, as the fate of the eighteenth-century balance of power, Metternich's Concert of Europe, and Woodrow Wilson's vision of collective security demonstrates, this is precisely what states have not been willing to do.

Nevertheless, the cycle of equilibrium and violent disorder might be tolerable forever were it not for the fact that the instruments of countervailing power have become progressively more destructive, until now we have reached a point at which their unrestricted use would be truly self-defeating for the belligerents and perhaps catastrophic for humanity. Yet we have *not* reached a point at which national security and a modicum of international order and peace can be preserved without the exercise of countervailing military power by sovereign states.

This is the most important reason for seriously considering methods of directly restricting weapons by international agreement. But before we examine the utility and feasibility of various kinds of restrictions we should appreciate the constructive functions as well as the dangers of the distinctive contemporary form of armed competition: the arms race.

THE ARMS RACE

SINCE THE LATTER PART OF THE NINETEENTH CENTURY THE SO-CALLED arms race has become the dominant form of competition for military power. Along with military coalitions it has become the principal means by which the major powers have exercised countervailing power. Through arms races satisfied states have tried to check the extreme ambitions of states that would drastically upset the distribution of power: dissatisfied and expansionist states have sometimes acquiesced. Lacking the capacity to achieve a preponderance of power, states have, at times, been content to pursue their interests within an equilibrium of power sustained by an arms race.

An arms "race" — strictly speaking, a somewhat misleading metaphor — is a competitive advancement in the type, quality, and quantity of military technology among opposing states. As a major feature of international politics, it is a relatively recent phenomenon, beginning in the last third of the nineteenth century with the rapid acceleration of innovations in military and civilian (especially transportation and communication) technology, the spectacular development of heavy industry and mass production, the creation of material and financial abundance, and the state's systematic mobilization of economic and material resources for military preparation, along with the mass conscription of manpower. The Anglo-French naval race from 1866 to about 1898 was the first sustained increase in arms expenditures and levels that was accompanied by a series of major technological innovations producing significant tensions and insecurities among the participants. In the Cold War, one of the most prominent features of the arms race, stemming from the experience in World War II and the new importance of forces-in-being, is the comprehensive mobilization of scientific research as well as technological development to sustain a process of constant innovation in weapons systems. Thus the modern arms race is, in reality, a multiplicity of overlapping qualitative and quantitative advancements in a constantly changing variety of weapons which are continually coming into operation and growing obsolete.

The special importance of the arms race lies not only in its possible dangers but also in the fact that it supplants some of the previous and now obsolete nonmilitary methods by which states have adjusted their relative power; for example, countervailing shifts of alliance, dynastic marriages, territorial compensations, and colonial exploitation. Most important, the arms race tends to supplant war, historically the principal means of altering or protecting the political *status quo* and the distribution of power.

In a constantly shifting field of interests and power, if states cannot satisfactorily adjust their power and accommodate conflicting interests by peaceful means, they will be inclined to seek their ends by war. The fact that the arms race has become the principal medium for

Robert E. Osgood

the peaceful change of power in a dynamic field of power and interests has a strong bearing upon the utility and feasibility of disarmament measures which are intended to restrict this medium.

Since World War I, which was generally attributed largely to the arms race that preceded it, one of the primary avowed purposes of disarmament has been conceived to be the prevention or restriction of arms races. Before World War I the chief liabilities of arms races were believed to be their great expense, the encouragement of militarism, and the development of inhumane weapons. After World War I, and, even more markedly, after World War II, disarmament advocates became more concerned with counteracting the purported tendency of arms races to aggravate international tensions and incite general wars.

This shift of emphasis springs from an historical exaggeration of the effect of arms races upon the outbreak of war, but it correctly reflects the growing danger that arms races may create weapons that make war catastrophic. Therefore, we should distinguish between the effects of the race, or competition, as such and the effects of the arms that the race produces. Some argue that these two aspects of arms races are practically inseparable. Nevertheless, different kinds of disarmament are intended to deal more with one than with the other. Thus one kind of disarmament would deliberately preserve the competition in arms while making it more stable. Another kind aims to diminish the destructive potential of arms while permitting a balanced competition to continue. Still another finds safety from the destructiveness of arms only in abolishing the arms race itself.

In large part, the controversies among these different "schools" of disarmament policy turn upon different views concerning the nature and effects of the current arms race. Therefore, before considering the efficacy of different kinds of disarmament it is necessary to distinguish more precisely between the positive functions and the particular dangers of this arms race.

THE STABILIZING EFFECT OF ARMS RACES

IT IS GENERALLY ACKNOWLEDGED THAT THE FUNDAMENTAL CAUSE OF tension and war lies in the conflicting aims and special interests of states, which cause states to arm against each other. Yet it is also true that competition in armaments may aggravate tensions and help incite war. All competition for military power is bound to be provocative in so far as it threatens the security and other vital interests of adversaries. On the other hand, arms competition may also enforce caution and restraint on adversaries. The provocative effect of arms races, like other forms of international competition, should therefore be weighed against their moderating and deterrent effect.

The history of arms races demonstrates that they have been provocative (notably, the Anglo-German naval race of 1898-1912) but that, considered within the context of the whole range of international competition, they have had only a slight, indirect effect in causing war.[1] Among the general causes of World War I the preceding arms races had much less influence than the network of alliance commitments, the nature of mobilization plans, and the confidence of statesmen and military staff officers in military victory. Furthermore, arms races have usually been self-limiting and have often exerted a deterrent or stabilizing effect. Their expense and their aggravation of tensions and insecurity have induced competing states to keep arms races limited. The ability of *status quo* powers to confront expansionist states with a disadvantageous balance of power by a continual advancement in the quality and quantity of their arms has helped maintain peace. Thus some arms races have ended because they outlived their apparent usefulness or because political circumstances changed, and others have led to political settlements and truces. The outbreak of World War II marked the failure of deterrence not because of an arms race but because the opponents of aggression engaged in an arms race too late with too little.

The history of prenuclear arms races suggests that a prudent pursuit of countervailing power through quantitative and qualitative advances is, on balance, a moderating influence upon the continual competition for power among adversaries. This is not surprising, since the arms race has helped states to maintain their security by internal means without resorting to the unsettling territorial transfers and acquisitions, the contests for allies, and, most important, the military interventions which were common devices for achieving a favorable distribution of power in the eighteenth and nineteenth centuries.

Undoubtedly, the current US-USSR arms race has aggravated the tensions that spring from the political and ideological conflicts of the Cold War. Yet America's maintenance of vast military strength throughout a broad spectrum of continually changing technology, especially in nuclear striking power, has also been an indispensable deterrent to Soviet and Chinese military adventures. The US-USSR arms race, far from being an unlimited and increasingly provocative

[1]See Samuel P. Huntington, "Arms Races: Prerequisites and Results," *Public Policy*, eds. Friedrich and Harris (Cambridge, Mass.: Harvard Univ. Press, 1958).

Robert E. Osgood

competition, has by reciprocal limitation settled into a dynamic equilibrium maintained by somewhat reduced expenditures and based on an approaching parity of Soviet and American capacities to devastate each other in response to a direct attack. Contrary to past expectations that a nuclear stand off would encourage overt non-nuclear aggression, limited military actions above the level of "unconventional" or "internal" war seem securely deterred by the risk of "escalation" and some improvement in the conventional resistance capacity of the United States and its allies.

The relative limitation and stability of this arms race is fostered by three technical characteristics, which reinforce the notable caution of the participants:

(1) The extreme, virtually self-defeating destructiveness of any war in which the nuclear powers were to use their most powerful weapons against each other, together with the prospect that these weapons *would* be used if the United States and the USSR and their allies became involved in direct combat, gives these adversaries unprecedented incentives to avoid direct combat, as long as the United States and the USSR retain a minimum capacity to inflict intolerable damage upon each other regardless of what military initiative the other might take.

(2) The maintenance by the United States and the USSR of a very great number of weapons, especially nuclear weapons, means that a given relative advance in the quantity or the offensive or defensive quality of one adversary's weapons is not likely to give him a sufficient military advantage to reduce his inhibitions against resorting to war. Beyond the minimum capacity of each side to inflict intolerable retaliatory damage upon the other, one side would have to achieve a revolutionary technological breakthrough or a tremendous quantitative superiority in order to undermine the security of the other.

(3) The fact that the US-USSR arms race is a collection of many arms races throughout a wide variety of rapidly changing weapons diminishes the chances that any single innovation or series of innovations or any numerical superiority in a particular weapon achieved by one side will upset the military balance enough to raise the incentives for war before the other side redresses the balance with its own innovations.

For these reasons the balance of deterrent over provocative effects in the current arms race seems even greater than in previous arms races. The current arms race seems inherently more stable and less prone to war than previous races (for example, the naval races before and after World War I) in which a relatively small quantitative

24

superiority of arms could give one adversary a significant military advantage. Like previous arms races, the current one is substantially limited by the inability of either participant to gain a decisive superiority at a cost that will not jeopardize competing objectives requiring money, material, and manpower. It is true that the characteristics of some nuclear weapons have created a novel danger that warfare might result from a technical accident, the unauthorized use of weapons, or a false apprehension of sudden attack: but this danger has been reduced to minimal proportions by unilateral safeguards and the development of relatively invulnerable missiles.

The New Dangers of Arms Races

On the other hand, when one thinks not of the stability and the deterrent effect of the present military equilibrium but of the consequences of warfare if, somehow, war did occur, the US-USSR arms race seems anything but beneficient. It seems, in fact, far more dangerous than any armed competition in history. This is because, by all odds, the greatest danger of the current arms race lies in the awesomely destructive weapons the race has fostered and will evidently continue to foster. The arms race may make war unlikely, but if war were to occur, it could be catastrophic. Considering the whole history of international relations, it is difficult to imagine the most powerful adversaries forever remaining in such a stable military equilibrium and indefinitely pursuing their competing interests with such caution and foresight as to avoid war with each other. It is unlikely that such a war would be significantly limited.

The current arms race also poses another novel, though more speculative, danger: the prospect that additional states will acquire nuclear and other catastrophic weapons. It now seems unlikely that any states who have not already achieved nuclear explosions will have sufficient incentive to acquire nuclear weapons in the next decade, although perhaps a dozen states have the capability. But this would be a rash prediction to make for subsequent decades if the process of nuclear diffusion is not stopped by international agreement. If India were to follow China's example, or if Israel were to decide to produce nuclear weapons, a chain effect might rapidly set in.

So far, the remarkable stability of the US-USSR arms race has depended a great deal upon several unique circumstances: There have been only two major participants, and they have enjoyed a preponderance of power in the world; both have developed a vast, diversified panoply of military power at a roughly equal pace; the defensive participant acquired nuclear weapons first and maintained nuclear superiority during the transitional period to stable parity; the leadership of both participants has been disinclined to pursue its foreign interests by military means. Under different circumstances, prospective arms races among additional nuclear powers, especially among states who are not subordinate members of the Soviet or American blocs, are likely to be far more provocative. This prospect is already unsettling to the existing nuclear powers and to the non-nuclear powers who wish to remain so. Their apprehensions may spring only from the natural distaste for changing the nuclear *status quo* on the part of those with a special interest in perpetuating it, but they may also be farsighted intimations of a period of acute international tension and disorder that would follow the end of an exclusively bilateral nuclear balance.

It is impossible to predict in detail the consequences of nuclear diffusion, because one cannot foresee exactly which nations will acquire nuclear weapons, what kinds of nuclear capabilites they will acquire, when and in what sequence and pace they will acquire them, how they will seek to exploit their capabilities in their foreign relations, or how the original nuclear powers and the remaining non-nuclear powers will react to these contingencies. Quite possibly the introduction of nuclear capabilities into some international rivalries and animosities would be stabilizing for some of the same reasons that have restrained the United States and the USSR from coming to blows, but one cannot reasonably suppose that this would be the universal effect of nuclear diffusion. More likely, a number of conditions would aggravate international conflicts and greatly increase the danger of nuclear exchanges: the uneven development of nuclear capabilities among adversaries, the incautious approach of some regimes to new-found destructive power, their lack of safeguards against unauthorized and accidental use together with the possibilities of ambiguous national responsiblity for nuclear blows, the incentive for great powers to intervene preventively in small nuclear powers' conflicts, and the fragmentation of NATO—hence, the weakening of mutual defense commitments and the undermining of deterrence—under nuclear separatism.

For these reasons I reach the conclusion that the arms competition between the United States and the USSR exerts, on the whole, a stabilizing, moderating, and pacifying effect on the general competition for power that springs from the political and ideological conflicts of the Cold War, but that the kinds of weapons this competition has already produced and is likely to produce in the future and the prospect that additional states will acquire them are so dangerous to the United States and to humanity that we must seriously consider adopting any measures that might conceivably prevent or mitigate these dangers. Among such measures, disarmament has attracted ever-increasing attention in this century.

All prospective disarmament agreements, however, raise three crucial questions: (1) the question of utility: Would disarmament mitigate the dangers of the arms race without weakening national security? (2) the question of mutual acceptability: Would states see a mutual interest in disarming? (3) the question of continuity: If so, would they continue to share this interest and observe the agreement in good faith?

The answers to these questions with respect to a particular disarmament agreement would constitute an assessment of its value. I shall consider the questions in a general way with respect to three different kinds of disarmament measures, which I call arms reduction and limitation, limited arms control, and general and complete disarmament.

ARMS REDUCTION AND LIMITATION: UTILITY

THE AGREED REDUCTION OR LIMITATION OF ARMS IS INTENDED TO stabilize, freeze, or eliminate some elements of the over-all military competition while maintaining a military equilibrium that does not disadvantage any signatory. This type of disarmament includes many kinds of measures, intended to achieve a variety of purposes, and involving different kinds of considerations.

Before the nuclear age several disarmament agreements restricting the number, kind, and location of weapons and military facilities were signed and put into effect, ranging from zonal restrictions on fortifications and military deployments to limitations upon the production and possession of capital ships. A nuclear test ban is also an arms restriction, but with the substantial difference that it would limit the kinds of weapons available to states by restricting their development instead of their production, possession, or deployment.

Arms reductions and limitations have been justified on a number of different grounds, apart from the purely pacifist and socio-political arguments against arms and the military establishment. The principal objectives espoused before World War II were, first, to avoid the great expense of an arms race that did not promise to improve and might actually diminish the security of its participants

Robert E. Osgood

and, second, to avoid the animosities and provocations to war which an arms race might stimulate. Governments also proposed and agreed to restrictions upon arms and military activities in particular zones, not so much to restrict an arms race as to pacify particular points of potential provocation and war. Finally, some proposed restrictions were intended to make war less inhumane by prohibiting certain kinds of weapons, notably, at the Hague Conferences, dumdum bullets, asphyxiating gas, and air-dropped bombs.

In the nuclear age three other objectives have been adduced for arms restriction: (1) the elimination or the reduction of war's immense destructive potential; (2) the prevention or retardation of the spread of nuclear weapons to additional states; (3) the prevention of radioactive damage to civilian life from nuclear testing.

The first question to ask about any kind of disarmament is whether it would actually achieve its ostensible objectives without undermining national security if states complied with it.

In the past, some formal arms reductions and limitations have succeeded in saving money and mitigating provocative tensions without damaging the security of the signatories: for example, the Rush-Bagot Treaty of 1817, which limited the construction, number, and type of naval vessel on the Great Lakes; and the Argentina-Chile convention of 1902, which limited and reduced the production, possession, and transfer of some kinds of war ships and prohibited others. More debatably, one can argue that the comprehensive Washington Naval Treaties of 1921 temporarily stabilized an existing distribution of power in the Pacific and need not have weakened American security if the United States had built up to the treaty limits and otherwise remained vigilant against Japanese expansion.

The utility of disarmament, of course, depends crucially upon the nature of the foreign policies, intentions, and military capabilities of the states whose relative power it affects, as the British promotion of disarmament in the face of German rearmament after World War I demonstrated. For this reason arms reductions and limitations are most likely to be effective when they are associated with a mutually satisfactory resolution of political disputes and rivalries and accompanied by credible defense commitments capable of preserving a balance of power.

Judging from the history of disarmament, there is no inherent reason why arms reductions and limitations could not serve the mutual interests of the major opponents in the Cold War. Yet it is quite doubtful that disarmament treaties analogous to the naval agreements of the interwar period would serve the same purposes under the conditions of modern military technology. For technological innovations and improvements now take place at such a rapid pace and throughout such a broad spectrum of weapons that restrictions upon one or only a few kinds of weapons merely rechannel the arms race (as, indeed, the restrictions upon battleships in the Washington Treaties were followed by accelerated competition in cruisers and submarines). Rechanneling an arms race may be useful for other reasons, such as limiting deployment of peculiarly destructive or provocative weapons, but it does not necessarily save money or help stabilize a military equilibrium.

Arms restrictions in particular geographical zones, however, are a somewhat different matter. In the past, zonal disarmament has proved useful in pacifying particular areas of potential military competition and war while satisfying or accommodating the security interests of the signatories. The Rush-Bagot Treaty and its extension to the United States-Canadian border are examples. So are the demilitarization of the Norway-Sweden boundary in 1905, the conventions of 1923 and 1936 concerning fortification and passage of warships in the Turkish Straits, and the demilitarization of the Antarctic in 1959. In the future this kind of agreement, especially when accompanied by a political agreement, might be useful where border maneuvers and deployments still have military significance, as between militarily weak states outside Europe. Generally, however, between states with modern arms of great range and speed, territorial demilitarization or arms restriction would no longer help to prevent wars. This is the case in Europe. In Berlin the withdrawal of American and Soviet contingents without a secure settlement of the division of Germany would tend to disturb, not pacify, a local area of potential armed conflict.

Perhaps in the future, space may become a new zone of military competition and potential war, more significant for the major powers than territorial zones. If so, there may be useful analogies to the Antarctic treaty in that the advanced technological powers may find in this relatively unexplored zone a common interest in channeling the arms race around areas of potential competition by refraining from expensive; provocative, or accident-prone military tests and deployments from which neither seems likely to benefit. Here a nuclear test ban could be a precedent.

In the past, weapons prohibitions or restrictions which were undertaken in peacetime for purely humanitarian reasons have generally been violated if they conflicted with military necessity in war. Sadly, one must recognize that humanitarian restraints on the

Robert E. Osgood

manufacture and use of weapons have grown much weaker since World War I (although gas and biological weapons do suffer a peculiar stigma). Restrictions on the manufacture of particularly odious weapons, even if they could be policed, would be more likely to weaken the deterrent threat of counteruse than to reinforce humanitarian revulsions. On the other hand, when the very process of developing weapons may harm civilian life in *peacetime*, as in the case of atmospheric nuclear testing, there may be useful restrictions upon development which are compatible with military security. The same can be said of weapons tests that would be a great nuisance or that would be difficult to distinguish from hostile use—as in the case of weather control, for example.

In the future, however, the utility of all kinds of agreed reductions and limitations of arms must depend chiefly on whether they can eliminate or mitigate the catastrophic nature of war and prevent or retard the spread of catastrophic weapons to additional states, since these have become the most serious dangers in the arms race.

Theoretically, the best and perhaps the only way to get rid of the danger of sudden catastrophe is to get rid of the weapons that could cause it. But, questions of practicability aside, the trouble with this solution is that if it worked it would destroy the present basis of military equilibrium and security, which lies in the capacity of the principal adversaries to inflict intolerable retaliatory damage upon each other. To be sure, with major adjustments of relative non-nuclear power, another military equilibrium might conceivably be reached, but only at the price of reverting to a prenuclear military balance in which the inhibitions against going to war would be much weaker.

Reducing the sudden destructive potential of forces-in-being might be worth the price of increasing the likelihood of a major war except for the virtual certainty that once the principal technological powers became engaged in such a war, if not during the preceding tension, they would quickly rearm to regain the most destructive weapons. Possibly the fear of counter-rearmament would either deter these states from engaging in war or restrain them from using the catastrophic weapons during war, but it is much more probable that, in the absence of a high-level balance of destructive power-in-being, the rearming belligerents would be virtually compelled to use their most powerful weapons before their adversary could threaten proportionate destruction.

Can disarmament mitigate the danger of nuclear proliferation? A universal nuclear production cut-off, a complete nuclear test ban, and nondissemination and nonacquisition pledges would probably discourage proliferation if there were no strong national incentives to acquire nuclear weapons. But no state, like France or China, which regards an independent nuclear force as a vital instrument of power and policy can be expected to sign or to be bound by nonproliferation agreements. Rather, they will regard such agreements as discriminatory devices intended to preserve the preponderence of the super-powers. The superpowers can retard and in some cases prevent nuclear proliferation by refraining from economic, technical, and material assistance to nuclear aspirants, but international agreements would probably add little except political embarrassment and problems of inspection to existing informal restraints of this nature. International agreements would pose special problems within NATO. Here the price of formal pledges of nuclear abstinence by allies who are actual or potential nuclear aspirants seems likely to be compensatory nuclear assistance and even the transfer of nuclear weapons by the nuclear to the non-nuclear allies. In any case, if a nuclear ban were to be applied to her allies, the United States would have to seek the long-run advantages of inhibiting nuclear proliferation at what might be a high political price of formally perpetuating American preponderance. Nuclear guarantees and various forms of nuclear sharing on a multilateral basis seem much more promising methods of discouraging proliferation, especially among allies, than formal agreements, which in fact are likely to be incompatible with such methods.

Arms Reduction and Limitation: Mutual Acceptablity

THE VALUE OF ARMS REDUCTION AND LIMITATION, OF COURSE, CANNOT BE judged simply by its possible utility without regard for the probability of states reaching and keeping agreements of mutual interest. If the abstract utility of disarmament were the overriding consideration, disarmament proposals and discussions would not have produced such disproportionately meager results in comparison to the attention they have commanded.

One fundamental reason that governments have not reached disarmament agreements more readily is simply that some states have been dissatisfied with the existing distribution of military power while other states have been unwilling to change the distribution to satisfy them. Furthermore, the hardest thing for states with seriously conflicting policies to agree upon is the relative military power upon which their ability to support these policies must depend. For military power is a general asset that is crucial to the pursuit and protection of a whole range of particular interests. Thus even states who do not see

31

themselves as adversaries or potential belligerents must be extremely wary about formally restricting their pre-eminent means of pursuing an independent and successful policy in the future.

The more states a disarmament agreement would include, the less likely these states are to agree upon a mutually satisfactory distribution of power between them, since the agreed distribution must accommodate a greater number of divergent, interacting policies and interests. On the other hand, a disarmament agreement that proposes a satisfactory ratio of power between two or only a few states may be unacceptable because it creates unsatisfactory military ratios with nonsignatories.

Nevertheless, states with no serious conflicts of interest and states who are not dissatisfied with their relative military power would have much less difficulty in reaching a formal arms limitation representing a mutually satisfactory distribution of military power at a lower level of armament if it were not for the ambiguity of military power—that is, the great practical difficulty of knowing exactly what constitutes sufficient military power. The ultimate test of sufficiency is successful combat; but as the constituents of military power have become more diverse and complex and the destructive potential of military power has grown immensely, the outcome of war has become harder to calculate while the penalties of miscalculation have become much more severe. Nor is it much easier to judge the sufficiency of military power by its psychological effects—whether deterrent, intimidatory, or otherwise—since the complex interactions of the many factors affecting the behavior of states render the cause-and-effect relationship quite obscure.

Given the ambiguity of military power, statesmen are naturally reluctant to commit their countries in a solemn treaty to a judgment of sufficiency that may turn out to be wrong—or at least look wrong. On the other hand, disarmament, by revealing and prescribing legitimate armaments, may hinder governments from capitalizing upon the ambiguity of their military power by extracting from the uncertainty of other governments' estimates some increment of security, influence, or prestige that the realities of power might not justify. In any case, statesmen who are faced with doubts about the sufficiency of their military power are inclined to seek a compensatory margin of safety in disarmament agreements that others are, for similar reasons, unwilling to grant. Thus governments that would be quite content with a particular ratio of power which they were free to estimate and change unilaterally might be absolutely opposed to signing an arms agreement which formally limited them to this ratio.

The Place of Disarmament in American Policy

Perhaps the most familiar practical obstacle to disarmament, as revealed in all disarmament negotiations, is the difficulty of measuring military power and comparing the power of one state with that of another. Sometimes this difficulty is mitigated by limiting arms at an existing ratio that competing states find satisfactory. But even then agreement upon an equitable definition of the categories and the quantities of weapons and forces that compose a ratio presents formidable problems. Proposed changes in the level or composition of military power complicate the problem of agreement, since they will almost certainly alter the military significance of any numerical ratio of arms.

These and other difficulties of measurement and comparison are so well known from experience and analysis that I need not elaborate them. It should be noted, however, that since the brief age of battleship primacy in the arsenals of great powers these difficulties have been immensely compounded by the growing diversity and interdependence of weapons and the unequal increments of military power that contemporary weapons contribute to the armaments of states in divergent geographical, material, and political conditions.

The political and technical difficulties that impede states from agreeing upon formal arms restrictions are magnified in proportion to the extent these restrictions alter existing categories and quantities of armaments. Yet the interdependence of weapons systems may pose a serious obstacle to confining agreed restrictions to a single or to only a few weapons in the total arsenals of states.

The ambiguity created by the dynamism of military technology now poses a special obstacle to disarmament. A disarmament treaty restricts the freedom of states to adjust their military power to unforeseen developments which may upset the original basis of agreement. Gradual developments may sometimes be accommodated by amendment, but now the normal process of technological innovation may substantially alter the material foundation of an agreement every few years. The more comprehensive the restrictions and the lower the level of armament, the more likely any particular innovation will be to upset the balance of power. The disadvantaged state can then redress the balance only by violating or abrogating the treaty when renegotiating it is apt to be tedious and futile.

The rapid obsolescence of arms agreements under the impact of technological innovation virtually rules out comprehensive and substantial disarmament as a practical or effective restriction upon arms races, unless the process of innovation can itself be drastically restricted, which would be extremely difficult to achieve or enforce. It need not, however, rule out the feasibility of disarmament that restricts a single weapon or only a small part of the total military technology available to competing states (as in the nuclear test ban) in order to seal off particular areas of potential development. Indeed, in one respect a partial disarmament agreement of mutual interest is more feasible now than before the nuclear age: When the US and the USSR have a surplus of destructive capacity within a parity of strategic retaliatory power, there is more room for arms restrictions that do not enable one side to gain a sudden or irrevocable advantage by a technological development.

Demilitarization or partial disarmament in territorial zones may avoid many of the ambiguities that afflict general restrictions of weapons, since the determinants of military power are relatively well defined by the local situation. Here the practical obstacle to disarmament lies not so much in estimating its impact upon the military balance as in satisfying the political interest of the states that would be affected. In general, a mutually acceptable change in the local military balance by formal agreement presupposes a formal accommodation of the political differences that led to that balance.

ARMS REDUCTION AND LIMITATION: CONTINUITY

THE SAME FACTORS THAT MAKE DISARMAMENT AGREEMENTS HARD TO achieve may also make them prone to violation or abrogation. Thus continual changes in the configurations of power and interests in international relations, and, especially, unpredictable technological developments, will tend to undermine the original bases of agreement, while the formal restrictions on unilateral adjustment to these changes may foster dangerous insecurities, tensions, and frustrations. In such cases national security and international order may best be served by revising or abrogating the treaty. Yet complicated arms restrictions, adopted only after months and years of hard bargaining, are likely to have an inertia that prolongs them beyond their usefulness.

In the United States we have been preoccupied with the problem of preventing the violation of an arms agreement, but we have paid little attention to the problems arising from the tendency of such an agreement to become obsolete. Verification procedures cannot provide a safeguard against the obsolescence of an agreement; they can only detect and discourage one method of redressing obsolescence: clandestine violation. Furthermore, verification procedures, and,

most notably, complicated inspection systems, are themselves susceptible to technological obsolescence.

Not that clandestine violation and, therefore, verification procedures are unimportant. On the contrary, they have assumed unprecedented importance since World War II, because the development,
production, and deployment of postwar weapons are much more
susceptible to concealment and dissimulation. It is now virtually
impossible to verify restrictions on the development and production
of a number of weapons and weapons components without the kind
of extensive international ownership, supervision, and licensing that
was considered essential in the case of nuclear material even in 1946.
The Soviet Union has special internal as well as military reasons for
opposing the kind of comprehensive inspection that would be required to give us reassurance against violation of substantial disarmament, but it is doubtful that the United States would really tolerate
some of the measures she has urged in the confidence of Soviet
rejection. Moreover, quite apart from inviting international interference in domestic affairs, comprehensive inspection procedures may
jeopardize some kinds of military concealment — for example, Polaris
submarines — that are as important to American as to Soviet security.

Of course, the adequacy of verification methods is a matter of
degree and judgment related to other factors, such as the effect of
undiscovered violations on the military balance. Thus the more
comprehensive and the larger the reductions and restrictions of arms,
the more nearly perfect verification must be, since an undiscovered
violation would be a proportionately serious threat to the military
balance. Correspondingly, the best protection against serious violations of disarmament may lie not so much in the technical perfection
of the inspection system as in a relatively high level of arms and an
active weapons development program throughout a broad spectrum
of technology.

THE VALUE OF ARMS REDUCTIONS AND LIMITATIONS

COMPREHENSIVE AND EXTENSIVE ARMS REDUCTIONS AND LIMITATIONS, I
conclude, are neither desirable nor feasible. Partial arms reductions
and limitations within territorial zones of potential conflict among
lesser powers might be useful and feasible in conjunction with political settlements, but among major military powers they would no
longer perform their historic function. Limitations on the development, production, and deployment of arms could be desirable and

practicable if they contributed to the following two objectives without significantly affecting the existing level, structure, and distribution of military power: (1) preventing or retarding the development and deployment of certain kinds of weapons which would be particularly expensive, destructive, prone to accident, provocative, or inconvenient and unhealthy to civilian life; (2) preventing or retarding the spread of nuclear weapons to additional states. But for these purposes unilateral or reciprocal informal restraints seem more promising.

The necessary military condition of any useful disarmament agreement is a stable military equilibrium favorable to American interests. Under foreseeable political and military circumstances, this presupposes, among other things, a virtual parity of US-USSR strategic retaliatory power at a high level of destructive capacity, based on a broad spectrum of technology within a continuing arms race marked by a rapid rate of innovation and obsolescence. Hopefully, in this situation, which is approximately the existing state of affairs, arms efforts will remain at a fairly constant plateau of expenditure by virtue of mutual recognition that an intensified race would only create expenses and trouble without increasing security.

LIMITED ARMS CONTROL

IT IS EVIDENT THAT ARMS RESTRICTIONS UNDER THESE CONDITIONS would not greatly diminish the dangers of catastrophic war. As long as adversaries possess catastrophic weapons, they may use them. Indeed, some fear that the speed, technical complexity, and destructiveness of these weapons may increase the danger that states will use them inadvertently or in a sudden attack. At least, that is the premise of another kind of disarmament that I call "limited arms control."

Limited arms control is intended to affect the *use* of arms directly rather than by reductions and limitations. In this category are, principally, methods of mutual military surveillance ("open skies," early warning devices, inspection posts) and international communication (like the "hot line"), which are intended to provide reassurance against, or permit mutual withdrawal from, threatening military activities, including a premeditated strategic attack or an attack launched under the misapprehension of such an attack by the enemy, hostile military maneuvers that might result in open conflict, and nuclear blows resulting from a technical accident or the unauthorized use of weapons.

I shall not discuss the merits of the many arms-control measures that have been proposed. Some of these might help to stabilize the military environment by giving the signatories greater control over military activities, especially during crises. But others might have the opposite effect; for measures that facilitate surveillance and communication may also increase the opportunities for deception and misunderstanding, and they may deprive states of the secrecy and also the time they need to make prudent decisions.

Such arms control measures largely avoid the acute problems of measurement and comparison that afflict arms reductions and limitations, but they are just as susceptible to technological obsolescence, as demonstrated, for example, by the rapidly changing significance of the 1955 proposal for "open skies" aerial surveillance, which was soon outmoded by long-range missiles and reconnaissance satellites.

Like inspection to verify arms reductions and restrictions, the various arms-control devices for military surveillance have special disadvantages in Soviet eyes, but might also conflict with American security measures which depend upon denying the adversary military information.

Perhaps the most useful function of arms-control agreements is to dramatize a common interest in stabilizing the military environment, at least to the extent of states abstaining from sudden attack and avoiding inadvertent war. But now the most significant arms-control measures are the ones that states can put into effect unilaterally, like relatively invulnerable nuclear weapons, effective command and control systems, advanced methods of surveillance, and reciprocal abstention from unnecessarily provocative deployments and maneuvers. In some cases, such unilateral measures may be conditioned upon reciprocity and thereby assume the character of tacit or informal arms-control agreements, with qualities of flexibility and discreetness which are more appropriate than solemn treaties for controlling a volatile technology.

GENERAL AND COMPLETE DISARMAMENT [GCD]

IF THE FOREGOING ANALYSIS IS CORRECT, NEITHER ARMS REDUCTIONS and limitations nor arms control can have more than a marginal effect in mitigating the greatest danger of the arms race: sudden catastrophic war. At best, they both seem to entail numerous practical difficulties for relatively small benefits. For this reason general and complete disarmament has received a degree of popular and official attention in the nuclear age that only pacifists and the Soviet Union gave it before. Since 1959 "GCD" has been the ostensible end result of

37

the principal official disarmament plan in both the United States and the Soviet Union.

GCD aims not to preserve and stabilize a military balance at a lower level of arms but to do away with the whole problem of maintaining military security through national efforts by doing away with national arms, except those needed for internal security. Thus GCD is intended to avoid all the intractable political and technical problems of trying to balance and accommodate the relative power of competing states in a formal agreement. The American proposal for GCD adds that when all states have completely disarmed an international military force must guarantee national security and enforce peace and order. I shall examine the basic case for general and complete disarmament and then deal with the utility of an international military force.

The first question to ask is; How could general and complete disarmament go into effect without surmounting the very obstacles to partial disarmament which it is supposed to avoid, since all serious proposals for complete disarmament prescribe reaching it in stages of progressive reduction, each of which would provide a mutually satisfactory ratio of military power among signatories? The familiar answer is that states who have taken the radical step of agreeing to do away with all arms will not be so finicky about the military balance in the transitional stages. Supposedly, each move toward the ultimate goal will be confidently accepted as evidence of good faith in getting rid of the military system rather than suspiciously scrutinized as a commitment of indefinite duration to a particular configuration of power.

This view flies in the face of all past evidence of state motivation and behavior where the level and structure of military power is at stake. Yet the original premise of GCD—that states would find it easier to abolish arms altogether than to restrict them—posits such a novel state of affairs that there is a certain logic in assuming that novel behavior would follow an agreement based upon it. In any case, let us assume, for the sake of argument, that GCD were to go into effect. Then, what would international relations be like? How would states deal with the conflicts of interest which traditionally have been contained, resolved, or contested by force and the threat of force? (For one must assume that disarmament cannot completely transform the international system, and therefore that, despite the possible avoidance of conflicts stimulated by the present military confrontations, some serious conflicts of will among sovereign nation-states would still exist.)

The Place of Disarmament in American Policy

First, one must recognize that GCD would not literally abolish all instruments of armed coercion in the hands of states and that, therefore, states would still pursue conflicting interests with countervailing armed power in some form. I refer not to the possibility of organized combat with clubs and stones, which in this technological age is quite fanciful, but to the capacity of states to use internal security forces and paramilitary forces beyond their borders and, even more important, to the capacity of states to exploit civilian science and technology to rearm. The relevant question, then, is not: What would international relations be like without arms? but: What would international relations be like with only these instruments of armed coercion?

The answer to this question must be quite conjectural, but where so much is at stake one should not act in anticipation of either the most favorable or the most unfavorable conditions imaginable. From this standpoint, the principal effects of general and complete disarmament upon the relative power of states would probably be (1) to enhance the protection of states from direct attack and invasion in proportion to the size of their territory and their remoteness from adversaries; (2) to reduce greatly the capacity of states to bring military power to bear quickly and decisively at distances beyond their borders; (3) to make states with a relatively backward civilian technology and war potential and with a relatively small population (probably the chief index of the size of internal security forces) more vulnerable to penetration by large, industrially advanced states who are contiguous or near to them; (4) to increase the capacity of even militarily weak states to harass, seize, or destroy foreign property, transportation and supply bases, and lines of communication within their reach; (5) to enhance the efficacy of paramilitary forces, unconventional warfare, and subversion, especially in contiguous areas; (6) to increase the importance of rearmament capacity (including the training and mobilization of manpower) and the military exploitation of civilian technology in comparison to forces-in-being as a factor determining the relative power among the major industrial states; (7) to create a continual threat of decisive changes in the relative power of these states because of innovations in military and militarily useful technology (which no inspection and enforcement system, given the great overlap between civilian and military technology, could prevent), the obsolescence of verification method and innovations in techniques of evasion, and the temptation to undertake ambiguous, clandestine, or sudden open violation of the terms of disarmament.

What would be the particular effects upon the vital interest of

39

Robert E. Osgood

states of these general changes in relative power? The following seem most likely and important: (1) The United States and Western Europe (assuming it were not divided by new animosities) would be much less vulnerable to sudden direct Soviet attack. (2) Eastern Europe would be more independent of Soviet influence but divided by a resurgence of old rivalries and animosities which might induce Soviet intervention. (3) The United States would be unable to protect relatively weak states adjacent or near to Communist China or the Soviet Union from Communist encroachment by paramilitary and submilitary means without violating the disarmament agreement by rearming to send counterinsurgent forces abroad. (4) The underdeveloped states not under Communist domination would be engaged in considerable combat among themselves which the major powers would be unable to limit or deter by timely intervention but which might, nevertheless, come to involve them in war in areas like the Middle East. (5) The United States, Britain, and Japan, as the principal insular states, would be especially vulnerable to local incursions, even by relatively weak states, against the supply, transportation, and communication facilities upon which their commerce and much of their resources depend. (6) Communist states, by the nature of their purposes and political systems, would be much better able to exploit ambiguous violations of the disarmament terms than the democratic states would be able to counter these violations either openly or covertly. (7) Communist states would be far better able than democratic states to prepare in peacetime for sudden rearmament and to use the threat of rearmament as an instrument of policy. (8) Present alliances among the nonexpansionist states would die or atrophy; new configurations of power and interests would not lead to local alliances capable of protecting security interests as effectively as in the armed world.

These radical changes of power and interest would greatly increase the frequency of crises and war among the strong as well as the weak states. The threat of rearmament — whether offensive, pre-emptive, or retaliatory — would be constant and, during disputes and crises among the major powers, intense. A rearmament race, starting from such a low level of power, would be extremely destabilizing and would probably lead to war. Any war involving the forces of the major industrial powers would touch off a rearmament race and would be even more likely than now to become unlimited, including the use of the most destructive chemical and biological weapons, although it would probably expand more slowly.

In short, general and complete disarmament would create a

much more volatile pattern of international relations and one much more likely to erupt into local conflicts and, before long, into a general war which might be little less destructive than the sudden catastrophe that haunts the armed world today. We need not examine the feasibility of reaching and maintaining such a disarmament agreement to reject it as an unsound policy objective.

But would not an international military force capable of enforcing peace and orderly change among states overcome the liabilites of general and complete disarmament? Unless we assume such a transformation of international relations that conflicts among states would be resolved by methods of peaceful settlement of comparable efficacy to those in a well-ordered state, the answer is, "No." To supplant national forces as an instrument of security and order, an international military force would have to be able to deter and counter armed attacks and to prevent and rectify violations of the disarmament agreement. It would have to be able to bring decisive force to bear in any part of the world under many different material and political conditions. It would have to be more powerful than any combination of states that could challenge it. Therefore, it would require extensive and reliable financing, bases, depots, transportation, standing armed forces, its own intelligence service and staff planning, research and development facilities, and armaments industries. And it would have to be under the control of a body that could maintain and operate it and authorize its use against the opposition of even the most powerful states. It could do none of these things without the continual collaboration of all the major technologically advanced states and most of the others.

All this is to say that an effective international military force would have to be the instrument of an effective international government. One need not speculate about whether such a government would be tyrannical or just or whether it would be ruled by leaders congenial or hostile to American interests. It is enough to recognize that it can not exist in this epoch of nation-states.

AMERICAN POLICY TOWARD DISARMAMENT

IT FOLLOWS THAT THE UNITED STATES SHOULD NOT LOOK TO DISARMAMENT to stop the arms race or abolish the balance of terror. Disarmament cannot get rid of the continual competitive innovation and proliferation of military technology which is firmly rooted in the international system and in modern civilization. It cannot eliminate the terrible power of sudden catastrophic destruction which results from the mobilization of science and technology for military ends. At best it can somewhat moderate the expense of the arms race, channel it away from some areas of troublesome technological development, mitigate the danger of inadvertent war, help retard the spread of nuclear weapons to other states, and generally help to stabilize the military equilibrium through modest arms limitation and arms control measures which reinforce unilateral, reciprocal restraints. America's chief reliance for her security, however, must rest upon successfully competing in the arms race, upon maintaining a quality and quantity of arms and armed forces that will enforce caution upon adversaries and reassure allies until political settlements or modus vivendi which make arms competition unnecessary can be achieved.

Should the United States therefore publicly disavow the far-reaching purposes that justify disarmament in the popular view and candidly explain the very limited objectives it can serve? To do so might be only to refute the widespread hopes and expectations of eventual relief from the burdens and hazards of the arms race, to present the United States in the eyes of the world as an advocate of the arms race and the balance of terror, and to leave the Soviet Union the uncontested champion of the most profound longings of mankind without any clear compensation except a kind of quixotic satisfaction in telling the naked truth.

In any case, this is, seemingly, an impossible position for any nation that aspires to leadership. Instead, it evidently seems more prudent to those with the responsibilities of government to adhere to the policy that the United States should advocate the complete abolition of arms as her ultimate objective, countering the Communist utopia of an harmonious, classless, disarmed world with her own utopia of a pluralistic world of disarmed states resolving their conflicts by methods of peaceful settlement under a universal law enforced by a benevolent international military force. Having affirmed this utopia, the United States can then, with impunity, it appears, repeatedly propose comprehensive schemes of progressive disarmament that would clearly favor her security and repeatedly reject the adversary's comprehensive schemes that would just as clearly favor his. She can play this game in the confidence that neither side will find a basis of mutual agreement, that both will argue their positions largely on technical grounds (especially those related to inspection), and that each will accuse the other of trying to undermine its security while exploiting world sentiment for peace. At the same time, it can be argued, the United States can genuinely seek agreements upon certain measures of arms limitation and control which, although of

42

common interest are also of limited significance, but which can nevertheless be triumphantly hailed as progenitors of universal peace or modestly commended as "first steps" toward the millennium. In this view disarmament is chiefly an arena of political warfare, with occasional value as a symbolic gesture toward détente and political accommodation.

The disadvantages of this familiar disarmament game, it is alleged, are that the United States may be outbid in propaganda by governments that can afford to be more irresponsible, that she may be compelled by foreign or domestic opinion to enter disadvantageous disarmament agreements, and that she may impede the achievement of useful but limited measures by diverting energy and opinion toward comprehensive schemes. Yet the evidence of the current arms race indicates that these are disadvantages that the American government can readily minimize.

A more important disadvantage is simply the danger that, as in the interwar period, popular enthusiasm for disarmament as a panacea may serve the democracies as an excuse for neglecting urgent tasks of collective military security, while the expansionist powers proceed to upset the military equilibrium and paralyze their victims with their own propaganda. The Soviets have recognized the immense power that appeals to peace and disarmament can have in the nuclear age. If they should demonstrate the feasibility of disarmament by accepting some of the more innocuous limited measures that the United States herself has proposed, they might be able to gain through the psychological repercussions of disarmament political advantages which years of military rivalry have failed to achieve.

This prospect may not be a sufficient argument for disavowing the ultimate aspirations that have become attached to disarmament. One must concede that myths may sometimes serve foreign policy better than candor. But in our public pronouncements and acts concerning disarmament let us at least distinguish more clearly between aspiration and practical utility. And if we must wage propaganda with the apocalyptic fears of the arms race, may our policymakers at least not confuse the reality of things with what they feel compelled to say for effect.

IN THE PRECEDING ESSAY, ROBERT OSGOOD ARGUED THAT "AMERICA'S *chief reliance for her security must rest upon successfully competing in the arms race . . . until political settlements or a* modus vivendi *which make arms competition unnecessary can be achieved." In the absence of such political settlements. the United States has sought throughout the Cold War for a central war policy that would tend to prevent the outbreak of nuclear war while at the same time providing the military might to win should war occur.*

Herman Kahn, in this analysis of central war policy, shows how complex and technical the problems of military strategy have become in the age of nuclear missiles. The range of problems that must be considered for successful competition in the nuclear arms race is bewildering. Even so, Mr Kahn shows clearly that the ultimate character of a central war policy depends less on technical military knowledge than on political assessments and assumptions.

The passport to Mr. Kahn's world of nuclear military strategy is accept-ance of the necessity of technical terminology: MFD (Mostly Finite Deter-rence), DI (Deterrence plus Insurance), and NCF (Not Incredible Counter-force First Strike). Kahn asserts that NCF (a policy of weapons and declara-tions which strives to make potential enemies believe that this nation is prepared to launch a nuclear attack in response to certain unspecified grave provoca-tions, not necessarily *including the use of nuclear forces against the United States), or even stronger policies, has been our central war policy since about 1950.*

Despite prevailing public misunderstanding of the facts of what current policy is, the question for policy-makers is now whether the United States should turn away from NCF, a first-strike counterforce policy, to DI or MFD — some other form of "controlled response" policy. But the answer to that military question depends, in part, on a political judgment: Will we be living in a period of international tension or a period of general détente?

Mr. Kahn shows in considerable detail how assumptions about different types of potential enemies, especially about their leaders govern our decisions concerning how to compete in the arms race. Policy now, as for many years past, depends on our assumptions about Soviet Leadership. In any attempt to look beyond the Cold War, formulation of future central war policy must depend on the assumptions we will make about the leadership of other potential enemies.

But Mr. Kahn's purpose is to examine the military prospects and to identify the persistent and fundamental inherent military problems that must be faced whatever turns the political situation may take. It is political fluctuation, in fact, which shows most clearly the persistent military problems.

Is there a central war policy suitable both to situations of détente *and tense crises? If not, can we dare to choose a policy which suffices in "normal" times but offers no hope for victory, should war come, against enemy leaders who desire world domination and are willing to take great risks? In a time of tension or crisis, such as the Cuban confrontation, is it not imperative to have a central war policy that speaks clearly and with complete conviction? Must not our posture, in words and deeds, display unmistakably that we do not believe in peace at any price and that we have armed ourselves with weapons that would enable us to limit the damage and to win if fight we must?*

Must we choose between a policy of attitude and armament which says believably that we are willing and able, if provoked, to strike with nuclear weapons, thus tending to generate tension in normal times and a policy like MFD, which many believe will help us to progress beyond the Cold War but which others believe is dangerous in a crisis when one's bluff may be called or when one's total military posture may be very carefully examined and weighed by a determined enemy?

By posing this underlying military dilemma, Mr. Kahn instructs us in the military elements of any attempt to look beyond the Cold War.

HERMAN KAHN

•

UNITED STATES CENTRAL WAR POLICY

MILITARY POLICY FOR A COUNTRY IN THE POSITION OF THE UNITED States in the mid 1960's[1] covers a wide range of subjects including: counterinsurgency operations, various types of military advisory and support activities to governments ranging from Abyssinia to Vietnam, various alliance obligations including SEATO, METO, NATO, etc., and finally the development, procurement and operation of a variety of general-purpose and central-war forces. During a period of relative detente such as seems to obtain and which promises to continue for some time, the earlier subjects on this list are still likely to get a good deal of attention. (Detente does not, of course, rule out the possibility of "wars of national liberation" or other sublimited wars; postures, doctrines, and capabilities for such operations still come in for much searching scrutiny and debate.) But when, as is the case

[1]The author was originally asked to write on "United States Military Policy" for this conference; however, on noting that Robert Osgood was to discuss "Disarmament Problems and Policy" and Myron Rush "Political Use of Strategic Power in the Cold War," he decided to focus his paper on those issues which seemed most likely to complement their papers; hence the change in title.

45

today, the Soviet military threat to Europe and the United States is perceived by nearly everyone to be virtually "invisible," the same concern is far less likely to be shown for the problems of organizing and maintaining general-purpose and central-war forces. Many people feel, and perhaps correctly, that just a facade of strategic military capability can fulfill our likely peacetime needs, and that even if we insist on providing more than a facade one need hardly worry about details. There is enough validity in this position to make it worth while for us to indicate why we feel that a paper which concentrates on relatively esoteric questions of U.S. central war strategy is nevertheless important.

Policies for the conduct of central war clearly provide both a context for and complement to all the other military policies. In a period of detente however, these relationships will not necessarily seem—or, in practice, be—very important. Nevertheless, even if it seems quite clear that a strategic facade will by itself suffice to "deter" an attack on Europe or the United States, one may still feel it necessary that we possess much more than a facade, or at least that the facade we possess be a carefully designed one. Both objectives require explicit analysis of how deterrence works and of what might be needed in various situations. Moreover, there may exist situations— and for some these seem the most important contingencies to take account of—where the system is strained to the breaking point. Even in a detente, nuclear forces are held by potentially hostile states, and they could cause enormous devastation to our allies, to Europe, and to ourselves. While it may not be either practical or desirable to assume the worst about what may eventually happen, military policy must be prepared to confront the possibility that deterrence could, through a variety of circumstances fail; such policy must therefore be concerned with the feasibility in each of these circumstances of alleviating the consequences should deterrence fail.

We intend in this paper to concentrate on how various central war policies might affect different crisis and escalation situations, and how capabilities can be chosen to achieve favorable results in different eventualities. We will also attempt to illuminate some important strategic issues by the use of scenarios, i.e., hypothetical political-military sequences of events. When there is little connection, or no easily perceived or deeply felt connection, between strategic capabilities and postures and the day-to-day requirements of foreign policy, the need for such analysis and illumination grows greater rather than diminishes: precisely because there seems to be less external motivation, it becomes all the more important that these issues be deliberately and consciously considered.

It is convenient to start with some issues of the immediate past. Let us consider two widely held positions in their *extreme* (and therefore *simplest*) forms.

The first of these—held most firmly by some Air Force officers, but which was also avowed in some sense the declaratory policy of the United States government—was a policy which emphasized the threat that we would hit the Soviet Union with a counterforce-countervalue "spasm" attack[2] if the Soviets committed any of a number of provocative acts, including particularly the invasion of Europe. In effect, if a war occurred, all the buttons available were to be pressed in the very first few minutes; the primary purpose of keeping troops in Europe was to increase the credibility of our declaration that we would push the buttons. Some attention was beginning to be paid to COIN (counterinsurgency) and internal war problems, and a doctrine and supporting postures for limited, conventional, and tactical nuclear warfare were, if unevenly, being constructed. In Asia and the Middle East, for instance, the use of nuclear weapons was usually visualized as being one-sided (only we used nuclear weapons). In Europe of course, the use would admittedly be two-sided. But since the major importance of any operations in Europe would be their part in triggering an all-out (spasm) war, the deterrence contained in such a threat was thought to extend effectively to every level of war.

The other extreme position was especially fashionable among civilian intellectuals (and some officers) in OSD and the Executive Office. It could be called the pure Finite Deterrence position—based on the belief that the only purpose of the strategic forces is to deter major attack on the United States or its forces by threatening an assured countervalue (again spasm) "second strike" capability. It was often held that the best way to do this would be to have a reasonable number of missiles (say something between 10 and 1,000) based and operated so as to be almost invulnerable to enemy attack and themselves targeted solely against Soviet industrial and population targets. If the Soviet Union struck the United States or its major forces, all of

---

[2]This jargon-laden phrase introduces three modifiers of the word attack: (1) counterforce—attempt to degrade or destroy the enemy's offensive capability; (2) countervalue—attempt to destroy or damage things which the enemy values, usually people or property; (3) spasm—implies that the first attack is total and in a certain sense a reflex rather than controlled action, i.e., a function of the central nervous system, but not of the brain.

Herman Kahn

these missiles were to be launched by a simple "go" order at counter-value targets. This attack would presumably so punish the Soviets that they would be sorry they had attacked the United States; they would note this ahead of time and not attack. The rest of United States military problems were to be handled by conventional (or nuclear) limited-war or "controlled-war"[3] forces.

This Finite Deterrence position has many things in its favor. First of all, the word finite implies that only a finite force is required (because there is only a finite target system), and thus as long as one's forces can survive a potential attack (perhaps by being mobile, hidden, or very hard) there is no need to match enemy offensive forces even if they are increased. This tends to slow down the arms race — or so at least it is hoped. Finite Deterrence seems compatible with all kinds of measures for arms control and also is compatible with the Soviet desire to prevent inspection of their country. (One cannot hide large cities and industries.) In particular Finite Deterrence is compatible with "parity," nuclear stalemates, a "no first use of nuclear weapons" doctrine, a "no first strike" doctrine, and other attempts to achieve limits and stability. And to the extent that one viewed the situation as a kind of spiraling arms race trap in which the Americans and the Soviets were involuntarily caught, this was a way to get out of it. Indeed the position is so obviously nonaggressive and defensive that if combined with the advocacy of conventional war, it seems to abolish the use of nuclear force. One might conjecture that if the spirit of Finite Deterrence had been adopted by all nations it might have led eventually to some kind of "agonistic" war[4] doctrine in which nuclear war, while still technically possible, had become literally unthinkable.

Those who advocated pure Finite Deterrence tended to ignore or de-emphasize the fact that United States strategic arms had been procured in the early 1950's not so much for the direct defense

[3]A "controlled war" doctrine is any doctrine in which an attempt is made to control the strategic forces so that the attack is never, or almost never, automatic (under the control of the "central nervous system"), but is under the control of the highest (usually civilian) authorities and conducted with care and attention to the national interest as calculated or recalculated at that moment. The current "controlled response" doctrine is a specific kind of controlled war doctrine emphasizing the "pause" strategy in Europe and a "no cities except in reprisal" central war. There is a connotation of "restraint," "bargaining," and "moderation." See Herman Kahn, *On Thermonuclear War* (Princeton, N. J.: Princeton Univ. Press, 1960), esp. pp. 174-75, 288-305, and Klaus Knorr and Thornton Read (Eds.), *Limited Strategic War* (New York: Praeger, 1962), and Herman Kahn, *On Escalation: Metaphor and Scenarios* (New York: Praeger, 1965), esp. Ch. IX.

[4]War conducted according to rules because of custom, religious injunctions, morality, feelings of fair play, or other noninstrumental reasons. Agonistic war differs from the usual limited war in that the limits are absolute and do not depend on fear of reprisal, limited objectives, etc.

of the United States as for the defense of Europe and Asia at a time when the Soviets seemed to be threatening these two areas. To the extent that Finite Deterrence was concerned with Europe and Asia, it relegated their defense to limited war forces, either nuclear or nonnuclear. However, in spite of its apparent emphasis on arms control, one of the most important objections to Finite Deterrence was that it promised to accelerate the spread of nuclear weapons. The nations of Europe — and eventually those of Asia — would no longer have an American strategic guarantee under this strategy and would be faced with becoming a battleground — either conventional or nuclear — , and entry into nuclear great power status would be easy.

The advocates of Pure Finite Deterrence did seem caught in at least one other logical inconsistency. While most of them were against active and passive defense of population as "destabilizing" because it reduced the amount of terror in the balance of terror, they did not object to reducing the number of missiles on a side (in a hypothetical arms control agreement) from say 200 to 50. In principle at least, each side could have 200 missiles with an active and passive defense just effective enough to make the balance of terror, for all practical purposes, equivalent to having 50 missiles on a side and no defense. (For reasons to be mentioned later, the two situations are not likely to be equivalent for all considerations, but in most situations the former position — 200 missiles with defense — is probably preferable to the naked 50.) Probably one of the main reasons for the failure even to notice the inconsistency was that the first position requires a relatively serious and sophisticated analysis of various ways in which the arms control agreement could break down; i.e., it is not compatible with a "war is unthinkable" philosophy. More important, the technological process of obtaining an offense-defense balance would involve the extension of defense programs to such new areas as civil defense and antiballistic missile defense, and so seemed likely to accelerate the arms race in ways the simple missile balance did not.

Since the early 1960's, the debate has been to a significant degree among three positions which might be characterized as:

1. Mostly Finite Deterrence (MFD)
2. Deterrence plus Insurance (DI)
3. Not Incredible Counterforce First Strike (NCF)[5]

[5]Actually there are at least two more positions in addition to these three which should be noted. The first, which has been discussed and recommended by Secretary McNamara, is the so-called Partial Damage Limiting (PDL) Strategy. The term "Damage Limiting" indicates that the criteria for choosing among various options is no longer how many Russians can be killed in a "second strike," but how much damage to the United States can be limited. Partial Damage Limiting is therefore similar to Deterrence

Herman Kahn

These policies may be defined briefly as follows. The MFD policy is much like Finite Deterrence except that it does not invoke a spasm response and it tries to protect people from being unnecessary bonus targets, if the enemy should choose to avoid cities and attack only United States military bases. That is, if deterrence fails, then to the extent that the Soviets do not wish to kill American citizens or destroy American property, the United States should implement measures which make it feasible for the Soviets to make such distinctions. But the MFD policy does not make any serious attempt to rule out a large number of United States hostages: 50 to 100 million people are to be left concentrated in relatively soft shelters in the major cities without serious active defense to protect them from missiles or bombs deliberately aimed at them.

Advocates of the MFD policy do not try to protect such United States hostages from potentially "malevolent" enemies out of such considerations as effect on the arms race, feasibility, cost, or "image" considerations. That is, they fear such an attempt might touch off an enemy reaction that will either negate the program or lead to a spiraling arms race, or they feel that in the modern era of thermonuclear weapons it is not technically possible to protect people, or they are not willing to see resources—often intellectual, social, or political as well as physical—diverted to this purpose, or they feel that any intense effort to protect the population will give rise to at least the appearance, and perhaps the reality, of an aggressive or warlike policy. The choice of an MFD policy is usually motivated by some combination of these four concerns.

---

plus Insurance or Not Incredible Counterforce First-Strike in emphasizing, to some degree, active and passive defense and counterforce operation. But in many cases people advocating Damage Limiting strategies simply do not discuss the foreign policy issue which is the major distinction between the DI and NCF strategies, preferring to leave the issue ambiguous. Partial Damage Limiting is like Damage Limiting except that it does not try to do very much—that is, PDL advocates argue that deterrence can fail and war can happen, and that we should therefore at least try to buy hedges and cheap insurance; but we must be almost as interested as advocates of MFD in limiting budgets, preserving the detente, and tranquilizing the arms race. However, unlike MFD, PDL does try to preserve at least a facade of extended deterrence capability so that there will be some kind of credibility to U.S. strategic guarantees and escalation adequacy, though this is normally not specifically discussed.

Another position is the so-called Arms Control through Defense (ACD) Strategy. (It might also be called Defense through Arms Control because the defense is made to work by limitations on offense.) The major argument for this is that arms control generally, and limitations on offense specifically, is more feasible and more stable if it is hedged by both sides' having a great deal of active and passive defense. In particular having such active and passive defense furnishes a hedge against the other side's cheating or Nth powers' trying to gain an advantage. While the arguments for this position are complicated (because a lot of separate problems and issues have to be looked at), this policy seems likely to get increased attention in the future.

MFD is thus a very nonaggressive policy, closely related to the Finite Deterrence policy just discussed. The major difference, in addition to programs to protect people from being collateral targets, is the previously mentioned (see note 3) doctrine or strategy of "controlled response." In this strategy there is no intention to automatically press all buttons and launch our forces at Soviet cities, but rather to use our offensive capability in a very controlled way, in exemplary attacks, say, or to reduce Soviet threats, while at the same time bargaining and threatening the Soviets with appropriate reprisals if they kill American civilians or injure American property unnecessarily. Such a controlled response doctrine can also be an important part of the other two strategies.

The MFD policy is also willing to buy some degree of active and passive defense, but the major purpose of this defense is to protect civilians from collateral or accidental damage, rather than to protect them from active attempts by the enemy to destroy them.

The DI policy is much more preoccupied than is MFD with the possibility that war can happen and with the necessity for being able to alleviate the consequences of war if it occurs. Thus it not only intends to try to survive that war, it intends to get as favorable a military and political result as is practical. It employs much more active and passive defense of the population so that even if the Soviets were to attempt to kill Americans at some point in the course of war, substantial resources (which may not be available at that point) would be required for them to do so. It also demands more and better offensive forces, both to destroy Soviet offensive forces (if appropriate or feasible) and to threaten the Soviets so that intrawar deterrence (controlled response) is more likely to work.

In the third policy, "not incredible counterforce first strike" (NCF), each term is important. The "not incredible" refers to the fact that its advocates intend to use the strategic forces as part of an explicit strategic guarantee or extended deterrence policy. Therefore, there must be sufficient credibility that the United States can be provoked into using these forces for what is a "first strike" as far as the strategic forces are concerned, but may be a second (or later) strike in the actual order of attacks (e.g., conventional invasion of NATO or Japanese territory). Presumably credibility can be measured by the actual deterrent effect on the Soviets or the Chinese, by the assurance it provides our allies, and by the assurance of our own diplomats in and out of conferences. The double negative in "not incredible" implies that even a low level of credibility will suffice for all of the above. The announced use of "counterforce" operations

51

(combined, as explained below, with intrawar deterrence and a controlled response doctrine and limited objectives) is one of the ways of increasing both the credibility and actual utility of the posture.

NCF, of course, is but one of many possible Extended Deterrence policies. In such policies one attempts to use strategic threats to deter much more than direct attacks on the United States or its major forces. In trying to estimate the credibility of such threats one must have a scenario in which to evaluate or judge credibility. Table 1 indicates the four typical scenarios which are usually considered, though there are others of interest.

TABLE 1
Scoring Situations for an Extended Deterrence "Posture"

Opponent	Scenario	Minimum U.S. Objective (if deterrence fails)
Soviet Union	S.U. Conventional attack on Europe	to help hold or force back S.U.
Soviet Union	"nuclear blackmail"	limit impact of probes, teach S.U. a lesson, and restore confidence
China	attack on Formosa (Japan?)	win the peace
China	"nuclear blackmail"	same as with S.U. plus win peace

The first column indicates the opponent that is being deterred, the second column, the action that is being deterred, and the third column, the minimum United States objective if deterrence fails. It is important to consider these minimum United States objectives because they may determine or influence the tactics to be chosen, which, in turn, may affect the consequences of United States intervention. Expectations about these consequences will in turn greatly affect credibility.

For example, if one is going to annihilate the Soviet Union in reprisal for an attack on Europe, one can, of course, expect the Soviet Union to exert a maximum effort to punish the United States and the Europeans. If, however, one has, as indicated in the table, a very limited objective such as simply holding or forcing back the Soviet Union, then one is talking about compromises and peace treaties rather than annihilation and unconditional surrender: one tends to use the forces in a controlled fashion. Thus one can hope to terminate the war with large forces still unused on both sides.

The term Nuclear Blackmail in Table 1 is in quotes to distinguish it from simple verbal threats that are not taken seriously (Khrushchev indulged in these a great deal). By "blackmail" we mean here the actual demonstration or use of nuclear weapons in an aggressive or offensive way so as actually to coerce a nation into doing something it desperately does not wish to do. To date the Soviets have not tried to do this. The Minimum United States Objectives as we have shown would then be to limit the impact of probes and, to the extent the United States was unsuccessful, to teach the Soviet Union a lesson, i.e., to punish them enough so they would not consider the precedent worth repeating. This would have to be done in a public enough fashion to restore confidence among allies and neutrals.

Vis-à-vis China the problem is much different than vis-à-vis the Soviet Union. In the next decade or two it would probably not be technically difficult to eliminate Chinese strategic forces by a United States first strike. The major difficulties would arise with the term Win the Peace. It must be realized that after a United States-Chinese war the United States would have to live in a world envioronment not very significantly unlike that before such a war: i.e., the Soviet Union would exist, probably ready to exploit anti-United States feelings; there would be still Japan and various European powers whom we must not gravely antagonize; and the other nations, particularly the underdeveloped ones, would still be reacting in various ways to the manner in which the United States conducted the war. Therefore such a war should be fought in a fashion that would not complicate inordinately United States postwar political and military problems. Probably the most important requirement is not to kill an excessive number of Chinese. Take, for example, an extreme case — the Chinese attack Japan and in retaliation we disarm the Chinese but kill 300 million civilians in the process. Even though subsequently the Chinese government were to surrender totally to the United States and sign the precise peace treaty we desired, we would probably have, in some real sense, lost that war. Our relations with the Europeans, with the Soviets, with the other underdeveloped nations (to whom we will have shown that we would have a total disregard of human life if we were ever to get involved in a war with one of them), and even relations with Japanese we were defending and our own citizens will be such that to the extent that the United States found it necessary to justify its conduct of the war (with its appalling and seemingly unnecessary one-sided slaughter), we would find ourselves in enormous moral and political difficulties.

As can be seen from Table 1, the NCF strategy attempts to continue what has been United States policy over the last decade and a half, that is, to use United States strategic forces in direct support of our foreign policy. It embodies a policy of United States strategic guarantees meant to protect the Europeans and possibly also the Japanese and others, from Soviet invasion. It attempts to deter the Soviets from using "credible atomic blackmail." It intends to provide the United States "escalation dominance" in crises, so that we do not have excessively strong incentives to back down. It also tries to contain just enough of a first-strike threat so that the Soviets cannot risk procuring extremely large, vulnerable, unalert first-strike forces. And finally, it contains enough capability so that if the Soviet Union or some other nation embarked on an aggressive and immoral adventure, perhaps involving large-scale nuclear blackmail, and if the aggressive nation also seems likely to continue its aberrant behavior to the point where it would become dangerous or impossible for the world or even the United States to try to co-exist with it, then the NCF policy would enable us to go to thermonuclear war if necessary to remove the nation's government. The prototype for this situation is, of course, Hitler (who for several years did not threaten England and France — only their allies).

Very briefly, the MFD and DI policies make very similar foreign policy use of their major central war forces (restricted to the "passive" deterrence of major attacks on the United States and its forces) but assume force postures that differ importantly from one another while the DI and NCF policies have very similar (war-fighting) postures but make very different foreign policy uses of these postures.

In all of the above policies, there would be either strong reliance on (or a willingness to exploit) a strategy of "controlled response" or some kind of controlled war tactics which furthers national policy, such as the use of "graduated" attacks for purposes of reprisal, punishing, fining, or bargaining. A typical example of this would be an attempt to extend deterrence to the intrawar period by a "no cities except in reprisal" doctrine. Another (extreme) example might be one in which the United States were to react to a forcible takeover of Berlin by destroying two or three gaseous diffusion plants in the Soviet Union. While these plants would be comparatively nonemotional targets in terms of public opinion, they are very valuable objects (some billions of dollars) of considerable long-range (100-1000 days) military significance, and thus the Soviet Union would feet great pain at losing them. The Soviets might find it credible enough that the United States would do such a thing that, even if there were no other defense of Berlin, they would still be deterred from taking over Berlin by fear of this punishment (and possible further escalation). This kind of technique has already been employed by Khrushchev, as when he announced that he had given Malinowski orders to destroy any base from which U-2 planes took off to fly over the Soviet Union. We call this controlled use of strategic weapons an exemplary or reprisal tactic. Many analysts who advocate MFD or DI strategies believe that various forms of exemplary use (going even to relatively lengthy controlled reciprocal reprisals) are sufficiently credible and deterring so that we do not need other strategic options, aside, of course, from an all-out retaliatory spasm if the United States itself is struck a major blow. Others believe that no matter how many options we need, we need some degree of capability on almost all the "rungs" of an "escalation ladder"[6] such as the example given in Figure 1.

Another reason for softening the starkness of having only a simple central war tactic—an all-out spasm war—is that, after all, deterrence can still fail. For example, as President Kennedy said,

> the history of this planet, and particularly the history of the twentieth century, is sufficient to remind us of the possibilities of an irrational attack, a miscalculation, an accidental war, or a war of escalation in which the stakes by each side gradually increase to the point of maximum danger which cannot be either foreseen or deterred.[7]

One prefers terminating such wars before total devastation has occurred. The controlled response doctrine, by giving the opponent strong incentives to restrain himself, by giving the centralized command sufficient flexibility, and by allowing for communications between the two opponents, makes the systems much less accident-prone. And, if accidental or other wars do occur, they are much less likely to be totally destructive.

Advocates of NCF usually base their position partly on the current political and strategic situation and partly on the hope that something like the current strategic relations can, at least to some degree, be preserved. They will generally emphasize that NCF is not a new policy

[6]Escalation ladders, a typical example being shown on pp. 56-57 are useful metaphors in analyzing the possible uses of violence and coercion in the next decade or two. The one shown is from Herman Kahn. *On Escalation: Metaphors and Scenarios* (New York: Praeger, 1965). Many analysts now believe that the important problems are likely to involve other rungs of the ladder than 23 (local Nuclear War—Military) and 41 and 43 (various kinds of ultra-destructive all-out wars), the ones which are usually studied.

[7]*New York Times*, July 20, 1963.

but a continuation of current policies, while the competing MFD and DI Policies actually represent a break with the military policies of the last decade. They feel that it is important to emphasize this distinction because usually the debate is cast in exactly opposite terms; indeed

Figure 1. AN ESCALATION LADDER: A Generalized (or Abstract) Scenario

—————————————————— AFTERMATHS ——————————————————

	44.	Spasm or Insensate War
CIVILIAN	43.	Some Other Kinds of Controlled General War
CENTRAL	42.	Civilian Devastation Attack
WARS	41.	Augmented Disarming Attack
	40.	Countervalue Salvo
	39.	Slow-Motion Countercity War

(CITY TARGETING THRESHOLD)

	38.	Unmodified Counterforce Attack
	37.	Counterforce-with-Avoidance Attack
MILITARY	36.	Constrained Disarming Attack
CENTRAL	35.	Constrained Force-Reduction Salvo
WARS	34.	Slow-Motion Counterforce War
	33.	Slow-Motion Counter-"Property" War
	32.	Formal Declaration of "General" War

(CENTRAL WAR THRESHOLD)

	31.	Reciprocal Reprisals
EXEMPLARY	30.	Complete Evacuation (Approximately 95 per cent)
CENTRAL	29.	Exemplary Attacks on Population
ATTACKS	28.	Exemplary Attacks Against Property
	27.	Exemplary Attack on Military
	26.	Demonstration Attack on Zone of Interior

(CENTRAL SANCTUARY THRESHOLD)

	25.	Evacuation (Approximately 70 per cent)
	24.	Unusual, Provocative, and Significant Countermeasures
BIZARRE		
CRISES	23.	Local Nuclear War—Military
	22.	Declaration of Limited Nuclear War
	21.	Local Nuclear War—Exemplary

(NO NUCLEAR USE THRESHOLD)

	20.	"Peaceful" World-Wide Embargo or Blockade
	19.	"Justifiable" Counterforce Attack
	18.	Spectacular Show or Demonstration of Force
	17.	Limited Evacuation (Approximately 20 per cent)
INTENSE	16.	Nuclear "Ultimatums"
CRISES	15.	Barely Nuclear War
	14.	Declaration of Limited Conventional War
	13.	Large Compound Escalation
	12.	Large Conventional War (or Actions)
	11.	Super-Ready Status
	10.	Provocative Breaking Off of Diplomatic Relations

United States Central War Policy

	9.	Dramatic Military Confrontations
	8.	Harassing Acts of Violence
TRADITIONAL	7.	"Legal" Harassment — Retortions
CRISES	6.	Significant Mobilization
	5.	Show of Force
	4.	Hardening of Positions — Confrontation of Wills

(Don't Rock the Boat Threshold)

SUBCRISIS	3.	Solemn and Formal Declarations
MANEUVER-	2.	Political, Economic, and Diplomatic Gestures
ING	1.	Ostensible Crisis

———————————————— Disagreement — Cold War ————————————————

many analysts have anticipated (perhaps overanticipated) the probable future, regarding MFD as *being* current United States policy and the attempt to achieve NCF as being a radical (right-wing advocated) change. In justice to the NCF advocates one must agree with them that this is not so. NCF or stronger has been the policy since about 1950 and probably will be until 1965, or possibly even later if those political, technological, and economic trends which permit the policy of the United States guarantees to Europe, and to a lesser extent to Asia, continue on their current course. (Naturally, no statement about the specifics of almost any nation's policy can be completely correct even conceptually, especially with respect to hypothetical questions. Thus the previous statement is to some degree ambiguous as well as controversial.)

In a way, NCF tries to carry into the nuclear era a traditional view of warfare: When the interests of a great state or of its major allies are being menaced, the "proper" reaction, if the other side continues its menacing actions, is to declare war and to attempt to win the war. "Win" does not mean unconditional surrender or total devastation for the enemy, but merely putting the other side into such a disadvantageous position that it becomes willing to sign a reasonably satisfactory (to the victor) peace treaty rather than continue to wage the war. In this traditional (but not American) view of war it is assumed that there will be bargaining and coercion as well as destruction and death and that the usual outcome of war will be neither the extremes of total victory or unconditional surrender but rather something between them.

A DI policy tries to deter nuclear attack on the United States (and possibly major nuclear attack on NATO) but also devotes substantial efforts to providing insurance if deterrence fails (i.e., it places less reliance than MFD does on the willingness of the enemy to observe a

57

"no city" convention and also improves the intrawar deterrent threat to make the observance more likely). If one restricts the deterrence to the continental United States and its major forces, then DI is politically much like MFD, but with more emphasis on active and passive defense of population plus a better and more flexible counterforce capability because the insurance requirement—i.e., if deterrence fails—is considered more important. If one includes deterring major nuclear attack against NATO or Japan under the DI strategic umbrella, then all the above comments do not hold completely, and the policy is somewhat more like NCF except for the contingency of a ground invasion of NATO. The DI policy presumably envisages handling conventional ground invasions conventionally, or at most with tactical nuclear weapons, while one current form of NCF, as in the strategy of the "pause,"[8] handles the ground invasion only for a time on its own terms, using the pause to bargain, exert pressure of various kinds, and give ultimatums.

To summarize the above very briefly, three major current (controlled response) Central War choices are:

Mostly Finite Deterrence (MFD).   No attempt to deny "adequate" hostages, but prevent "unnecessary" collateral damage—desired because of feasibility, cost, image, or arms control considerations.

Deterrence Plus Insurance (DI). War can happen—need better deterrence (pre-attack to prevent crisis escalation and postattack to increase likelihood of control), also need ability to survive and perhaps to win as a hedge against the failure of deterrence; however no explicit attempt to get any "offensive" foreign policy benefits from possession of these "war-fighting" forces (i.e., no first strike threats).

Not Incredible Counterforce First Strike (NCF).   The weakest of the extended deterrence strategies—attempts to continue, to some significant degree, the current system of explicit and implicit strategic guarantees throughout the decade, tries to maintain escalation dominance, also maintains some degree of preventive (just) war potential.

However, as already discussed, the three categories described are neither absolute nor objective. They depend not only on the postures of each side, but on how one thinks about these postures, on such psychological qualities as resolve, courage, determination, and caution, and on the starkness and unpleasantness of the alternatives which

---

[8]In the current strategy of the pause it is asserted that NATO would react against a conventional ground attack conventionally for a time (say two weeks to two months), using this conventional pause to bargain and threaten. However, before accepting defeat in the ground war, the United States would launch SAC at the Soviet Union if there were no other means of preventing defeat.

are being presented by the other side or by the situation. It should also be clear that we might have an MFD policy vis-à-vis the Soviet Union and an NCF vis-à-vis the Chinese People's Republic.

All of the above policies — MFD, DI, or NCF — pay considerable though varying amounts of attention to limiting the consequences of wars caused by minor incidents, accident, miscalculation, unauthorized behavior, etc. Current United States policy, one rather suspects, falls somewhere between NCF and DI. The biggest gap we have today in implementing either of these policies may be in civil defense; under current programs the strategy seems to be moving rapidly to MFD, though many will argue that there are strong reasons for attempting to slow this movement or to have it move backward in the direction of NCF or DI.

Whether or not a significant degree of DI or any NCF is feasible and desirable and for how long depends on many things. The most important variables are more likely to be political than technological, although clearly the technological variables will be very important. This is so mainly because many questions of technological feasibility or desirability in turn depend on questions of what funds and intellectual resources are available and what will be the actions and reactions of potential opponents. Within wide but reasonable limits we probably know most of the technological possibilities for the next decade or so, although there will doubtless be some startling and important surprises. Yet we can probably predict them better than the size of the military budget or the speed and efficiency of each side's countermeasure program. To see why the first is true let us note that it seems quite likely that in 1975 the United States GNP will be about a trillion dollars. (A trillion dollars per year GNP during fiscal 1975 would result from an average growth rate of about 4 per cent from the end of 1965.) However, even a trillion dollars per year GNP does not necessarily imply large military budgets.

One can easily imagine that if the current state of detente and the current tendency of the Europeans to become independent of the United States persist, there will be a weakening of NATO ties, possibly a withdrawal of most or all United States troops from Europe, and a general easing of military pressures. One could under such circumstances foresee a United States military budget of about $25 billion a year (or less than 3 per cent of the likely GNP). However, if only one-fifth or so of this budget were put into strategic central war forces, we could still maintain — at least for some years — a very respectable offense force, say 1,000 (or more) Minuteman (or better) type missiles, a few tens or hundreds of larger missiles of the Titan II class, possibly ten to thirty 15-plane wings of B-52's, and about 50 Polaris submarines. This is a very large force indeed for a peaceful world, so it is unlikely that the United States would feel underarmed.

On the other hand, if there were a reversal of current tendencies, if tensions reached a level like that of 1950 — when the North Koreans invaded South Korea and Congress stopped debating whether the defense budget should be $14, $15, or $16 billion (and whether or not we would be bankrupt at $18 billion) and authorized an increase from the previous year's $13 to $60 billion — one could imagine our going back to spending about 15 per cent or so of our GNP on military products as we did during the Korean War. This would be about $150 billion a year. And, of course, the figures of 3 per cent to 15 per cent do not mark the potential limits — the swing could go even wider. In other words, between now and 1975 we may spend on military preparations as little as a third of a trillion dollars or as much as a trillion dollars, and in 1975 we might be spending less than $25 billion a year or more than $150 billion a year. Corresponding predictions can be made for the Soviet Union and some of the European countries — and to a somewhat lesser degree for Japan (in the next few years the Japanese are likely to become the third largest industrial power in the world, surpassing West Germany). Such countries as China and India may also be important, though they are not likely to have as direct an impact, at least in military terms, unless aided by a more advanced power.

We can give some greater concreteness to all of the above and bring the discussion closer to realistic policy considerations with concrete examples. Let us start by hypothesizing two possible postures which the United States might have in the early or mid 1970's and four postures which the Soviet Union might have. For the United States the two possibilities respectively assume, among other things, a gradual (approximate) halving and doubling of the central war budgets, or a somewhat smaller range but comparable to that indicated by the 3 per cent to 15 per cent swing we have just discussed — a range well within possibilities. The six postures — two for the United States and four for the Soviets — are listed below.

U.S.-A (A Possible Early-to-Mid Seventies MFD Posture)
10 to 30 (15 plane) wings of B-52's.
4 or 5 wings of B-58's
1000 A, B, and C Minuteman missiles
100 heavy-payload ICBM's (Titan II and ?)

United States Central War Policy

50 Polaris submarines (with 800 A_1, A_2, and A_3 missiles)
A retrofitted air defense
A "symbolic" anti-ballistic missile defense
250 M fallout shelter spaces
Blast and thermal protection around SAC bases
Mobilization base for improvised and crisis protection

U.S.-B (A Possible Early-to-Mid Seventies DI or NCF Posture)
    10 to 30 (15-plane) wings of RS-52's
    4 or 5 wings of RS-58's
    2000 improved Minuteman
    100 improved heavy-payload ICBM's
    50 improved Polaris submarines
    An improved air defense
    A light cover of anti-ballistic missile defense
    120 M "dispersed" urban blast shelters (mostly 10-300 psi)
    150 M nonurban shelters (mostly 5-10 psi)
    Adequate shelter survival and support systems
    Mobilization base for improving protection and recuperation
        capability during crises

S.U.-A (A More or Less Predicted Soviet Posture If We Have
    U.S.-A)
    100 long-range bombers
    500-1000 "ordinary" ICBM's
    100 heavy-payload ICBM's
    200 missiles on submarines
    Elaborate but "ineffective" air defense
    Elaborate but "ineffective" anti-missile defense
    Modest civil defense preparations — capability for improvising
        more

S.U.-B (A Possible Reaction to U.S.-B)
    Add 1,000 missiles on submarines to S.U.-A

S.U.-C (Another Possible Reaction to U.S.-B)
    Add 1,000 ordinary ICBM's

S.U.-D (A Third — and Very Effective — Reaction to U.S.-B)
    Add 5,000 heavy-payload, well-protected ICBM's to S.U.-A

Herman Kahn

In U.S.-A we assume approximately the number of missiles currently programmed, the acquisition of a symbolic anti-ballistic missile defense, and some fixing up of the Air Defense system, but otherwise, more or less, the preservation of the current forces (including current officially proposed additions). While U.S.-A is a rather impressive-looking capability as measured by the early 1960's standards, we conjecture that during the 1970's it would just about amount to an MFD policy, at least if matched against something like S.U.-A, not to say S.U.-B, C or D.

U.S.-B attempts to preserve NCF or have a good DI into the 1970's. It is successful against S.U.-A, unsuccessful against S.U.-D, and uncertain against S.U.-B or C. We cannot discuss here how one might describe and analyze the detailed performance of the above postures under various assumptions and conditions, but we might make some preliminary remarks to illustrate quantitatively the above statements. If both are thought of as mid-1970's postures, the population of the United States would then be about 225,000,000 and the population of the Soviet Union would be about 265,000,000. With U.S.-A, even if the United States struck a first counterforce blow against S.U.-A, the Soviets might, if they retaliated "malevolently," be able to kill somewhere between 100 and 200 million people, depending on details that cannot be discussed here. Against S.U.-B or S.U.-C the casualty figure would almost certainly be the higher one. However, the U.S.-A posture is such as to allow the Soviets to avoid collateral damage if they choose to avoid striking at United States cities or population. It is, therefore, properly called an MFD posture.

We will make some misleadingly simple remarks: Assume for the moment a much oversimplified criterion of performance and say that U.S.-B, if it were used in a first strike against S.U.-A, could result, if the Soviets retaliated malevolently, in fewer than 20,000,000 dead Americans—possibly many fewer (assuming again that all the Americans are in shelters)—and some serious but probably solvable recuperation problems. If U.S.-B were used in a first strike against S.U.-B or C, there might be an additional 5,000,000 to 10,000,000 fatalities, plus a far greater threat to the possibility of recuperation. While against S.U.-D, even if the United States struck first, the Soviets could still inflict as many as 100,000,000 to 200,000,000 fatalities in their retaliating blow.

Thus one might argue that against S.U.-A the U.S.-B posture could be used to support a NCF policy with a certain degree of credibility and could certainly be used against either S.U.-A, B or C to support a DI posture. But against S.U.-D, even U.S.-B is clearly just

MFD, and it could only with difficulty support an NCF policy against S.U.-B. Furthermore, it seems fairly clear we would worsen our absolute and perhaps even our relative position by going from U.S.-A to U.S.-B if doing so caused the Soviets to go from S.U.-A to S.U.-D. We would therefore only go from U.S.-A to U.S.-B if we felt that the Soviets would react with S.U.-B or C or less.

All of these statements and numerical illustrations are subject to all kinds of caveats and elaborations, some of which will be discussed later. It should be noticed, however, that while the postures are chosen by assumption rather than by analysis or prediction, they are reasonable illustrations of possibilities and combinations that at least some people take seriously.

SOME CONCEPTUALLY USEFUL SCENARIOS

WE WILL TRY TO ILLUSTRATE SOME IMPORTANT TACTICAL AND STRATE-gic points by the use of what we call "outbreak" scenarios. We will divide our scenarios into three classes:

1. Alpha: assumes enemies in the "worst case," usually malevolent and competent. In the Alpha-1 version we will assume the very worst "worst case" — a Soviet Union whose only objective is totally to destroy the United States and all of its people and institutions.

2. Beta: assumes that Soviet decision-makers are motivated by considerations of the Soviet Union's national interests and desire for world domination and that they are willing to take great but not overwhelming risks to achieve the latter.

3. Gamma: assumes that Soviet decision-makers, while tough and aggressive, are mainly motivated by prudence and considerations of their national interest when it comes to the use of central war forces.

As might be imagined, Alpha scenarios all involve preplanned, malevolent, and secret Soviet attempts to annihilate the United States by a surprise attack out of the blue. These Alpha scenarios are implausible, but they are theoretically important because they represent one kind of maximal hypothetical threat. In almost all Alpha scenarios, no program which is currently being considered by the United States could protect the most vulnerable 50 per cent of the American population from being killed immediately, and under all but the most expensive programs ($50 to $100 billion annum), the major portion of the economy would be destroyed so that even the immediate survivors would have a bleak if not hopeless future. Indeed, under most programs almost everybody is immediately killed. Luckily these Alpha scenarios seem so extreme that one is

Herman Kahn

tempted to disregard the possibility of their occurring (i.e., we do not consider "worst" cases seriously).

The next type of scenarios, the Beta scenarios, are somewhat less extreme and represent a class of problems which, in fact, the United States might face. In Beta scenarios the Soviets are not so much interested in destroying the United States as in furthering their own national or ideological interests—often a very different objective. In some of the Beta scenarios, active and passive defense programs would perform rather badly as insurance for survival. In others, such programs would perform very well.

Finally, we will consider a Gamma group of scenarios in which crises erupt into thermonuclear war. We believe that Gamma scenarios should be given a high priority in the design and evaluation of alternative central-war strategies.

ALPHA-1: AN EXTREME SCENARIO

1. United States maintains an "adequate" retaliatory force.

2. Soviets procure great numbers of large-yield, soft, concentrated (perhaps hidden), unalert missiles.[9]

3. They set, perhaps years ahead of time, a D-day, H-hour, M-minute, S-second.

4. They launch an optimized salvo at the two or three hundred largest United States cities, most of which they destroy.

5. They also launch a supplementary area attack at United States rural regions, causing immense, perhaps total, damage.

6. However, the portion of the force allocated to destroy SAC is unable to do its job, and SAC launches an all-out retaliatory blow at Soviet society.

7. Their country is then destroyed by this United States retaliatory blow. Their success in killing United States civilians does not affect this result.

8. They say, "We're sorry we launched the attack."

While the above Alpha scenario is clearly not a likely situation, neither is it just a straw man to be knocked over and forgotten. It is intended to establish the point that our protection today depends, to some extent, on the Soviets' having some combination of caution, restraint, apathy, or incompetence. In the future it may depend on

[9]Such missiles require only one crew (rather than the five required for twenty-four-hour, seven-day-a-week operation) and are much cheaper to base, operate, and maintain. One might expect a factor or two or three in savings in each five years of costs, thus allowing the Soviets to buy two or three times as many missiles for the budget than normal operating procedures would allow.

other nations' (e.g., China) having some combination of these qualities. Thus we must live with the fact that there are forms of the Alpha
scenario, some of them more plausible than Alpha-1, which could
occur. The problem is that it is so difficult to handle Alpha scenarios
in almost any of their forms, even the most reasonable ones, that it is
national policy today, and likely to continue to be national policy, to
depend upon line 8, i.e., that the Soviets (or other potential attackers)
would *not* be willing to accept the possibility, of reliatory damage and
would be deterred. It is also, currently, part of national (NCF) policy
to have sufficient offensive nuclear force so that the Soviets are
unlikely to procure only or even many large-yield, soft, concentrated
(perhaps hidden), unalert missiles, partly because these are "provocative" and partly because they need to invest their money elsewhere.
The same need to reduce vulnerability that led us to small Minuteman, small Polaris, and relatively small Titan II's (compared to
what one could have) are more likely than not to lead the Soviets
to do much the same. They too must worry about our striking
them in some intense crisis (such as the Gamma-1 scenario to be
described), and they too must worry about having insurance and
being able to stand firm. In addition, using secrecy as a primary
defense is not practical. No great nation can depend, by means of
security procedures, on the other sides' (1) not having a secret agent,
(2) not getting a purloined or stolen document, (3) not having a
special reconnaissance technique (e.g., U-2 or Samos), and so on.
Secrecy is simply too unstable a method of protection to be relied on
as a mainstay[10] by a great nation if it can pursue some other technique; therefore, it is almost certain that in the long run the Soviets
will go in for hardening, dispersal, and perhaps mobility — all of which
entail great expense and tend to reduce the efficient size of the
missiles.

In addition, by comparison with their interest in smaller, or
European wars, the Soviets have not shown great interest in central
war. One way to explain much of the Soviet strategic posture is to
argue that they have focused most strategic attention on Europe and

[10]Secrecy may also be undesirable as a supplement because it tends to accelerate
the opponents' efforts (and also the arms race). For example, the current United States
missile superiority is largely the result of Soviet Union secrecy which in turn resulted in
overestimation of the Soviet rate of procurement of missiles. Originally, the major
Soviet interest in secrecy was more related to privacy than secrecy, but the Soviets have
since picked up the probably mistaken notion that it is one of their great national assets.
In fact, the Soviet's almost pathological desire for secrecy is probably incompatible in
both the short and long run with their national interests, and it is probably doing all
concerned a service to point this out on all possible occasions.

also, to some extent, have suffered a lag in military doctrine and thus been more or less intending to refight a World War II type of war with modern equipment. Hence, in the early 1960's, hundreds of Soviet IRBM's faced Europe, while only tens of Soviet ICBM's faced the United States. While there are indications that the Soviet military establishment is changing, there is no great reason for believing this change will be dramatic, thorough, or necessarily even very effective, and there is some reason for believing that the Soviets will continue to be plagued by various service and civilian doctrinal lags. While the United States cannot rely completely on possible Soviet ineptitude or apathy toward central war for a defense, it should be prepared to exploit such weaknesses if they persist.

Let us go on to the Beta scenarios, which are somewhat more reasonable and thus more to be worried about.

BETA-1: A LESS EXTREME SCENARIO

1. United States maintains retaliatory force it considers adequate.
2. Soviets procure, secretly or openly, a counterforce capability.
3. At some point, they launch an optimized attack at United States population and SAC.
4. Attack goes well, but their population is hit by a residual SAC force which has survived the Soviet Union attack.
5. However, their society survives this attack, while United States society never recovers from the war.

BETA-2

1. United States maintains a retaliatory force it considers adequate.
2. Soviets procure, secretly or openly, a counterforce capability.
3. At some point, they launch an optimized attack at United States population and SAC.
4. Attack against United States SAC goes badly and they are "annihilated" by United States retaliatory forces.
5. Both societies are destroyed or grievously damaged by war.
6. The fact that United States society is destroyed does not recompense the Soviets for the destruction of their own society. Even though in some sense the Soviets have "won" the war, the Communist Party does not have the strength and the resources to control the world or even the remnant of their own society, and they are sorry they started the war.

United States Central War Policy

1. United States maintains retaliatory force it considers adequate.

2. Soviets procure, secretly or openly, a counterforce capability.

3. At some point, they launch a "counterforce with avoidance"[11] attack and send a blackmail ultimatum.

4. We reply "counterforce with avoidance" and start bargaining.

5. There is a pause or abatement of hostilities and a period of negotiation.

6. The war is terminated without ever having a large countervalue attack.

7. The terms of the termination reflect the military situation.

The above three Beta scenarios all start with the same first two or three steps, and then branch out. From the point of view of survival, the first scenario is the hardest to deal with, but it is presumably also the least likely. Its probability is low partly because it would be difficult for the Soviets to procure such a large counterforce capability secretly; and, if they procured such a force openly, we would not be likely to permit it to become large enough, relative to our own force, for it to be able to disarm our retaliatory force in a major way. But equally important, even if they think (possibly wrongly) that they can disarm us, they are not likely to be willing to rely on that belief to the extent of launching a major part of the first wave at the United States population, thus guaranteeing, or making likely, a United States countervalue spasm response. They would lose little or nothing by waiting to see how effective their counterforce is. In other words, they would be too concerned by the possibility of a Beta-2 version of the scenario to use Beta-1; therefore they would most likely pick the Beta-3 version, which they might judge would maximize the United States incentive to have a controlled response and which would enable them to respond flexibly to what actually happens on their first strike, Beta-3 is not only far and away a safer scenario for them to attempt than Beta-1, it may even lead to a more desirable result than Beta-1 (from both the Soviet Unions' and United States' point of view). The Beta-3 scenario is, of course, exactly what the controlled response doctrine (in either its MFD, DI, NCF, or other forms) is designed to deal with.

---

[11]This is an attack in which, whenever the military penalty is small, the attacker chooses options which minimize collateral damage to civilians and property. As opposed to an "augmented counterforce attack," in which, whenever possible, "bonus" damage to civilians and property is sought, a "counterforce with avoidance" attack on the United States might cause 1 to 10 million United States dead, while an augmented counterforce attack of roughly the same size and same "military results" might cause 20 to 100 million dead.

Herman Kahn

Let us now assume a Beta-3 scenario. In this case, if we have an MFD policy, and the Soviets succeed in their counterforce operation, about all the United States can do is surrender. While this is not the sort of remark that goes down well, it is realistic. After all, the Germans and the Japanese were probably just about as tough as the Americans, and when military events went badly for them and their forces were destroyed—and their populations were hostages to our forces, which then had the ability to wreak unlimited amounts of harm—they surrendered, even though it was "against their religion." It is reasonably clear that we are likely to do the same. If we do not, the MFD program for survival is not likely to work, and the Soviets would presumably simply annihilate the population of the United States.

In the case where they try the Beta-3 scenario and the attack goes badly or not as well as they expected, and we have an MFD policy, about all we can aspire to is to call the war off, perhaps after wreaking some punishment on the Soviets. If our people are vulnerable to later waves of the Soviet attack, we cannot presumably compel any major degree of surrender from the Soviets. All we can do is punish the Soviets, to some degree, for what they have done (presumably accepting retaliatory punishment in return) and then call the war off. This is a major weakness of the MFD policy.

IF we have either a DI program, which would include active and passive defense for the population, or an NCF program (with even more active and passive defense), then presumably we are prepared, to some degree, to wage the war and hope that in addition to surviving, either we can win or gain much more advantageous terms than we would with an MFD policy.

Let us now look at the third set of scenarios which we will call the Gamma scenarios.

GAMMA-1: A STANDARD CRISIS SCENARIO

1. Crisis in East Germany or Berlin.
2. High level of internal violence.
3. Intervention by "NATOnians."
4. Soviet Union "ultimatum."
5. Limited evacuations.
6. United States or NATO reply.
7. Soviet Union ground attack, other major violence, or nuclear demonstration of force.
8. Exchange of messages.
9. A cessation or abatement in hostilities.

10. "Armistice" is violated.
11. More evacuations.
12. Soviet Union advances.
13. United States ultimatum.
14. Soviet Union sends new ultimatum along with "counterforce with avoidance" strike.
15. United States announcement of open cities, NATO announcement of "open Europe" west of Rhine, selective creation of other open areas in Germany.
16. United States also sends ultimatum along with its "counterforce with avoidance" strike.
17. . . . .

Almost everybody who tries to write a plausible scenario about the start of World War III tends to focus attention on the German problem, either on Berlin or the East German-West German border. Therefore, we will illustrate the Gamma-1 crisis scenario by assuming some kind of crisis in East Germany or in Berlin, or both, which reaches a high level of violence but is still internal. This level of violence eventually causes, possibly against West Germany's official objections, intervention by German citizens and/or the military. A reasonably high level engagement then occurs between the East Germans and the West Germans, possibly with Soviet troops involved. At this point the Soviets send an ultimatum that the West Germans must withdraw. One can assume that the crisis will have reached such an intensity that in many cities around the world some people will start to evacuate. There will be some sort of reply to the Soviet ultimatum which will express feelings of sympathy for the East Germans, but which very likely will largely accede to the Soviet request not to intervene. However, it may not be possible because of "technical problems," or official or unofficial sabotage, or defiance, or unauthorized behavior, actually to disengage the West Germans from the East Germans. At this point, the Soviets could make a punitive ground attack or initiate other major violence, such as an exemplary or demonstration use of nuclear weapons.

For the purpose of our scenario, assume a Soviet ground attack which is moderately successful. There would be another exchange of messages; one could easily imagine at this point a pause or even a formal truce. Given the current balance of terror and current attitudes toward thermonuclear war, it is almost overwhelmingly probable that things will be settled at this point (if they have not been settled earlier). But let us assume that for some reason they are not settled.

Herman Kahn

There would then be more evacuations, continued Soviet advances, presumably eventually a United States or NATO ultimatum.

We are now at the point where the war actually starts. There can be many, many versions. We consider two: In the first, a Gamma-1 version, there is a Soviet Union "counterforce with avoidance" strike. In the second, a Gamma-2, there is a United States "counterforce with avoidance' strike. Let us discuss each in turn.

If the public statements by various administrative officials are reasonably correct, the Soviets really do not have anything like an overwhelming superiority. In fact, they very likely have a rather pronounced inferiority. Let us assume, however, that they strike hard enough to take out the most important United States strategic retaliatory forces. Once they have done this, it should be clear to the United States that it can no longer "easily" win the war. In other words, after the Soviet strike, while the United States may still have some degree of superiority, it is nowhere near as superior as it was before the strike. In some sense, what has happened is that the Soviets have called our "bluff," and have risked an all-out or spasm response by us. If we do respond with a devastation attack, it may well be the end of the Soviet Union, but they in turn would fire their withheld forces at United States countervalue targets. Depending on what they have and the state of our active and passive defense, this response could inflict anywhere from ten to 100 million United States casualties and set us back economically for from a few years to as much as a century.

Assume that we wish to avert this last eventuality. We in turn attack the Soviets very carefully, avoiding all of their major population and industrial centers. Depending now on the details of the military events, there would then be some asymmetrical threats available to each side. While the asymmetries might tend on balance to favor the United States, destructive capacities are not likely to be so asymmetrical as to enable us to have our way completely. One would guess that a relatively likely occurrence would be an armistice and some kind of a settlement. The risk that each country is now running has by this time far outweighed the local issues in Germany and Berlin.

Another possibility is continuing military operations with one side getting decisive superiority. A third possibility is continued military operations which finally erupt into all-out countervalue attacks. If in the above scenarios we have entered the war with preparations suitable to an MFD policy (or less), then our civilians and major cities will have been hostages to whatever residual Soviet forces existed at any time, since our urban population would, at best, be in relatively soft shelters, unevacuated, and with no active defense. If we had adopted (or continued) either the DI or the NCF policies, then, of course, as Soviet forces decrease in capability, more and more United States cities and populations are rather rapidly removed from the position of being Soviet hostages.

Let us now consider the Gamma-2 version in which the war is initiated by a United States "counterforce with avoidance" strike. We strike the Soviets quite carefully, simultaneously sending messages of what we want and describing in detail to the Soviets (if we have not already done this ahead of time) what will happen to the Soviet Union if they fire a spasm response or launch any large countervalue attack. At this point, we have probably degraded the Soviet Union to the point where, even if we have only an MFD policy, they could not kill much more than 10 or 20 per cent of the United States population, and they may not even be able to do as much as that. This is particularly likely if it turns out that various kinds of Soviet weaknesses conjectured about by some United States strategists actually do exist. At this point, we have, in a sense, called the Soviet "bluff." We did strike and accepted the risk of their spasm. Let us assume the Soviets withhold their spasm, either because they cannot fire it, or because they are fearful of the United States counterreply. About all the Soviets can then do is negotiate. Now the asymmetry in threats could be so large (particularly if we had a DI or NCF posture) that it is quite likely that the United States would get most of its minimum demands.

It should also be clear by referring to Figure 2 on various thermonuclear targeting options, that there are various Gamma versions of the standard crisis scenario which can arise. In fact, any of the strategic attack options that are listed in Figure 2 could initiate the

Figure 2. VARIOUS THERMONUCLEAR TARGETING OPTIONS

1.	Countervalue devastation	Classical
2.	Mixed counterforce-countervalue	
3.	Augmented counterforce	
4.	Unmodified counterforce	Current Doctrine
5.	Counterforce with avoidance	
6.	Constrained disarming	Avant Garde
7.	Countervalue salvo	
8.	Slow motion countervalue	
9.	Slow motion counterforce	
10.	Force reduction salvo	
11.	Exemplary or reprisal	
12.	Show of force or demonstration	

13. Special instrumental
14. Anonymous or covert
15. Environmental counterforce
16. Environmental countervalue   } Also-To-Be-Considered
17. Antirecuperation
18. Blackmail-enhancing
19. Weak link   } Never-To-Be-Forgotten

hostilities, or almost any pattern of events suggested by the escalation ladder shown on pp. 56-57 might take place.

IMPORTANCE OF PREPARATIONS FOR CRISIS IMPROVISATIONS AND MOBILIZATIONS

THE GAMMA SCENARIOS ILLUSTRATE ONE IMPORTANT TYPE OF CRISIS situation. There are other kinds of crises which are also worth considering. There are, of course, many important reasons for studying the relationships between crises and central war policies. Most obviously, a crisis can lead to a small or a large war. The ways that a war can start have an important bearing on whether we can avoid having one or, failing avoidance, wage and survive it. More important, the fact that a crisis could lead to war has an important effect on the behavior of the various participants.

There has been a curious dichotomy in American military planning in recent years. On the one hand, we find that almost all the attention has been concentrated on the deterring or waging of central or general wars that might start out of the blue, either as a result of a surprise attack on the United States or because of accident or miscalculation. On the other hand, polls[12] reveal that most research analysts believe that any thermonuclear war, whether it is caused deliberately or inadvertently, is likely to be preceded by a very tense crisis. These analysts believe it unlikely that any country today would start an all-out general war unless a very intense crisis made the situation so desperate that the country regarded war as less undesirable than any alternatives. The decision-makers are more likely to be motivated by the conviction that the peaceful alternatives are bleak than by a conviction that they will win easily and cheaply. Such desperation is likely to occur only in a very intense crisis. Similarly, during an intense crisis, possibilities for inadvertent war increase, possibly to the danger point. By contrast, in a non-crisis period, the preliminary safety precautions and the unwillingness to take any precipitate action that might have irreversible effects are likely to

---

[12]Such as those conducted by Paul Johnstone at WSEG and Andrew Marshall, Olaf Helmer, and Thomas Schelling at RAND.

prevent a war, even in the case of an incident that otherwise, that is, in the absence of such safety precautions and "conservative" attitudes, might cause war.

Nevertheless, very little effort and attention has been paid by United States military planners to the deterring and waging of wars arising out of crisis situations and to the range of other military and political actions these crises might necessitate.[13] Probably one important reason for this is that an intense crisis is intrinsically unpleasant and somewhat bizarre, and many believe there is something sinister about planning to cope with such a contingency. Others fear that special preparations for or during a crisis may increase the probability of war. In some cases people wish to bind the hands of the Executive Office by giving it no choices except holocaust or surrender, hoping, paradoxically, to avoid both. The notion is that if a decision-maker is given too large and flexible a capability to "use' a crisis, the danger of either runaway escalation or piecemeal surrender is increased. The contrary may be more true. In any case, it would be indefensible to try to tie the President's hands without giving him a choice in the matter. Yet this idea has not been thoroughly debated within the government.

Many officials react to the suggestion that they consider crisis improvisation and mobilization programs by saying that it is dangerous to take such action. This could be correct if one were in an inferior military situation, but as long as our strategic forces are sufficiently strong to deter attack on the United States, then this objection is sharply diminished in importance, though some small residue still remains. Actually in a sufficiently tense crisis, other events are likely to overshadow mobilizations. The other common objection, that improvised protection or other mobilization will create tension and perhaps accelerate the arms race, is almost undoubtedly correct. This is one reason that the President, although the decision is his, should not initiate such programs—either as deliberate policy or as an unavoidable by-product of measures done for other reasons—except after due thought and care. It will do well to remember, however, that probably the main reason for World War II was the unwillingness of the British government to increase tension and accelerate the arms race; and such a situation could arise again.

While it is clear that actuating a mobilization program will accelerate the arms race, it is less clear that actuating a crisis-improvisation

---

[13]This is particularly odd since the strategy of the "pause" and other aspects of controlled response particularly require such discussion and consideration. See, however, A. J. Wiener and H. Kahn, *Crises and Arms Control* (Harmon-on-Hudson, N. Y.: Hudson Institute, October 9, 1962, HI-180-RR).

program will do so. There are at least three mechanisms by which such an action could accelerate the arms race:

1. An undoubted legacy of the crisis—an increase in tension (unless the crisis is terminated by a mutually satisfactory settlement)— is likely to lead to a higher level of military preparation and greater efforts generally.

2. The thought of war would have been made real to many, many people. They will then take it much more seriously.

3. There may be a hardening of attitudes and positions as a result of 1 and 2 and other effects of the crisis.

Of course, things could go the other way. For example, the sobering and frightening aspects of improvised protection may make a government weaker or more "flexible." That happened to both the British and the French governments after their success in May 1938, in forcing Hitler to back down from putting pressure on Czechoslovakia.

In any case, I would like to emphasize that little has been done about dealing with the problem which many analysts think of as the most important of all: the intense crisis situation in which it is important to stand firm or even deliberately to risk or threaten strategic war. Less intense crises characterized more by a deterioration in international relations than an immediate, high risk of war can also be decisive, for in such crises it may be critically important to improve rapidly the effective strength of the nation—i.e., to mobilize. One should also consider the kinds of wars which might arise out of situations occurring subsequent to such actions, i.e., in which either improvised crisis preparations or mobilization have already taken place. There has been even less serious consideration of spending money on preparations to facilitate our capability in any of the above circumstances.

A recent report[14] shows that a number of possible civil defense tactics can be employed to increase our survival and recovery capability during crisis periods. In a general way, a range of alternative programs is described in Figure 3.

The most effective kind of improvised action to be taken in anticipation of a possible thermonuclear war is evacuation of civilians to places of shelter (which may have been hastily built during the evacuation) in rural areas. Other actions, while important, rarely have such a dramatic effect on the vulnerability of people.

[14]W. M. Brown, *Strategic and Tactical Aspects of Civil Defense with Special Emphasis on Crisis Situations* (Harmon-on-Hudson, N. Y.: Hudson Institute, January 1963, HI-160-RR), A Report to the Office of Civil Defense.

United States Central War Policy

Improvised Programs, which are of great urgency, differ from Mobilization Programs in that they have little or no interest in legacy value and are based on a willing acceptance of great economic costs (interruption of normal activities, crash program to decrease vulnerability, etc.) to obtain some immediate capability. In order to achieve speed, one is anxious to cut red tape and normal procedures even at the sacrifice of "efficiency" (in the sense of protection per dollar) and fraud protection. A Mobilization Program, on the other hand, is con-

Figure 3. A RANGE OF CRISIS TACTICS

	Estimated Time Available
I. Crisis programs	
A. Improvised action	0-6 months
1. Desperate	1 hour-7 days
2. Crash	2 days-2 weeks
3. Emergency	1 week-6 months
B. Mobilization action	3 months-2 years
1. Wartime	3 months-1 year
2. Peacetime	6 months-2 years
II. Accelerated programs	1 year-4 years
III. Normal programs	3 years-7 years

cerned with questions of cost and efficiency and of the needs of competing programs, especially for military activities. It signifies an intention to prepare for the possibilities of a long cold war or hot war siege. It is prudential in the sense that it tries to prepare for the future, even at the risk of some increase in tension, by adopting protective measures appropriate to the degree of international tension.

The ability to institute a Mobilization Program after a crisis has begun, or an Improvisation Program at the height of a crisis, could have important effects other than that of providing protection. The actual development of events during crises would be affected, in many cases favorably. Perhaps even more important, the crises themselves may be deterred if we have a visible pre-crisis improvisation or mobilization base, that is, an obvious capacity to put highly accelerated programs into being in the event of a crisis. The legacy value of such programs may also be very important as a deterrent. For example, Western mobilizations and alliance-tightening resulting from the Korean War had permanent effects large enough to have constituted a setback for the Communists even if they had succeeded in conquering South Korea. The Communists seem to have been more careful ever since about provoking Western mobilizations.

75

The effectiveness of crisis mobilization programs can be considerably increased by prior planning, which can reduce the long lead times that some phases of the required actions might otherwise require. Detailed planning itself is the most obvious phase of the work that should be done in advance, because, relative to other phases of the work, it is both somewhat time-consuming and very inexpensive. Research and, to a lesser degree, development also share these characteristics and are prime candidates for being done well in advance. Next in priority would come some kinds of stockpiling, special training and education for various cadres, and some exercising of emergency procedures in expensive ways. More extensive preparations could also be made that would cost a small percentage of the defense budget but could save time and money if a need to improvise arose.

We have been discussing details of military policies that, in normal times, have little impact on international relations. While moving from an NCF to an MFD policy would, abstractly, greatly decrease our ability to deter a Soviet attack on Europe by a credible threat of nuclear retaliation, there is little reason to think that even such a greatly decreased deterrent would not be adequate, at least as long as "normal times" continue. When incentives are low, a low probability of retaliation, or a low level of retaliation, is sufficient. But acute crises and wars are not normal times. Stakes become very high, the credibility and strength of response are put in question, and the "unacceptability" of damage becomes a matter for weighing rather than assumption. Such circumstances may occur, and when they do the details of military policies can have major consequences.

JUST AS HERMAN KAHN'S ESSAY SHOWED HOW POLITICAL JUDGMENTS *intrude in formulations of central war policy, so this essay by Laurence W. Martin shows how military considerations underlie and influence the political problems of the Western alliance.*

Are new patterns becoming discernible among and between the Western bloc and the Communist bloc, patterns and combinations quite unlike those of the Cold War? Mr. Martin sets out to answer this question by examining the changing nature of the Western alliance. This task requires, however, consideration of a prior question: "Whether nuclear technology and alliances are fundamentally compatible?" The unilateral action of the United States in the Cuban crisis indicates one answer. The controversies over control of nuclear decisions that have arisen within the Western alliance since the almost immediate relaxation of Communist pressure after Cuba, indicate another. How to arrange the disposition and control of nuclear weapons has become "the touchstone of all well-being in the alliance."

From the military viewpoint, the test is whether the disposition of weapons gives all of the allies adequate protection. But a political test intrudes and dominates: Is the source of the protection compatible with national self-respect? The simplest military solution — United States control of the disposition of nuclear weapons for all of NATO — is politically unsuitable. Conversely, politically acceptable proposals have grave military drawbacks. In the light of this tension of military and political aspects, Mr. Martin considers in detail why proposals for joint nuclear forces have not succeeded.

Are joint nuclear forces little more than schemes to give Europeans "as much of the appearance and as little of the substance of a nuclear role as will persuade them to comply with American strategic doctrine"? Why can we not arrange for the creation of a truly European *deterrent? If the present loose European political structure cannot serve as the foundation of a nuclear force, why not seek to accomplish a politically united Europe, "a single European partner," "an equal associate for America"? Would a united Europe be a difficult and "recalcitrant partner"? Is there any reason to believe that the United States intends to reduce itself to a position of equal partnership? Is there an alternative to the United States' retaining its role as "the Grand Deterrer"?*

The tension inherent in American foreign policy described by Charles Burton Marshall in the introductory essay finds an echo here. Looking beyond the Cold War, the long-run aim is to nurture a pluralistic, co-operative, and orderly world; but the short-run task persists: to organize and lead the global resistance to the spread of Communism. Can both be achieved in a consistent course of policy toward our Western allies?

LAURENCE W. MARTIN

•

THE WESTERN BLOC

THROUGHOUT THE PRESIDENCY OF JOHN F. KENNEDY, MEMBERS OF HIS
Administration encouraged a widespread belief that some Europeans
were gratuitously precipitating a crisis in the North Atlantic Treaty
Organization and the Western bloc of which NATO is the chief
military expression. Alarmed proclamations of crisis have been such a
persistent feature of NATO that it is surprising more observers have
not perceived that what passes for crisis is the normal state of an
alliance as it adjusts its configuration to changing circumstances.
Many are perhaps deluded, by the frequent self-congratulatory declarations that NATO represents an unprecedented measure of peace-
time military coordination, into forgetting that it remains essentially a
classic alliance subject to constant reassessment of the advantages it
offers each sovereign member.

The illusion that the Atlantic alliance represents something considerably more than cooperation to further national purposes, which
are still distinct and frequently divergent, encourages an attitude of
moral indignation toward dissatisfied members, whose complaints
must surely be trivial and mischievous measured by the merits of the
alliance. This attitude, in turn, fosters the belief that some clearcut
formula must be discoverable that would dissolve dissent and bring
about a final cure for NATO's maladies.

In reality the problems of the alliance are neither so serious nor
so readily soluble as the weavers of designs and ideologues of Atlanti-
cism suggest. Certainly there are pressing problems and a sense of
disarray. But it is unlikely in the extreme that we are on the verge of
such a collapse or reversal of alliances that a military assault will
become a remotely attractive option for the Soviet Union. On the
other hand it is hardly reasonable to hope that we shall very speedily
hit upon a formula to take full account of the far-reaching changes in
our situation implied by the resurgence of Europe, the rifts in the

Sino-Soviet bloc, and proliferation of destructive power. We shall probably discover that the road immediately ahead is marked by *ad hoc* and barely workable makeshifts rather than any comprehensive and clear-cut new deal. In the long run we may have to discern new patterns for relations both among and between blocs to embrace the curious combination of pluralism and interdependence that seems to be emerging. Such patterns, however, are unlikely to be created by over-hasty attempts by the phrase-makers of Atlantic Community to shore up the structures and attitudes inherited from the immediate post-war years.

CURRENT PROBLEMS

THE DOMINATING PREOCCUPATION OF THOSE CONCERNED WITH THE present health of the alliance can be summed up as the need to redefine if not necessarily reshape the relations of Western Europe and America to take account of changes both in their own circumstances and in the challenges they face. This is complicated by the fact that, while Europe has come up spectacularly in the economic world since 1949, it has not made comparable progress toward strategic self-sufficiency. While the United States has suffered a relative decline economically, its military situation is more complex. On the one hand its military pre-eminence in physical terms is greater than ever. But on the other, it is not easy to decide whether this pre-eminence is still translatable into terms that will serve the interests of its allies. The old question, latent since Russia first acquired a nuclear armory, as to whether nuclear technology and alliances are fundamentally compatible is posed with increasing urgency. Curiously, both American and European answers suggest that, at bottom, they are not compatible if we insist on completely logical solutions. For, while the preferred American answer is to escape the dilemma by substituting what would amount to an American nuclear protectorate for alliance, some Europeans incline toward transcending the nuclear alliance in a different way, substituting national nuclear independence. Fear that each of these solutions is unattainable and would in any case weaken Atlantic solidarity to the point of offering Russia great opportunities for mischief has inspired a fervent search for some intermediate answer.

This military debate reflects a wider reassessment of the proper relation between Europe and America. Several developments have brought such questions to the fore in recent years. Most striking of these has been the second coming of General de Gaulle to give explicit and vehement expression to the view that the rise of Western Europe

79

to economic prosperity and political self-confidence makes it essential to recast the balance of the alliance. Britain's capitulation in its efforts to stay aloof from the European Economic Community and her subsequent rejection by De Gaulle for being the alien tool of the United States demonstrated that the Gaullist challenge could not be ignored. The Cuban crisis and its aftermath gave point to doubts as to whether American policies still served the best interests of Europe. To some extent American conduct offered confirmation that the United States would stand firm despite its vulnerability to nuclear attack. But it was noted in Europe that Cuba, an issue close to the American home, illustrated both the extra-European interests of the United States and its willingness to go it alone with minimal consultation. Moreover American victory in the immediate confrontation with the Soviet Union was generally linked to conditions of local tactical superiority that had disturbing implications when transferred to Europe.

The contrasting aftermath of the crisis, an almost ostentatious Soviet-American rapprochement culminating in a test-ban treaty that many regarded as essentially a bilateral and certainly an anti-French deal, coupled with talk of more pacts to come, served further to arouse European fears that their interests might not always be safe-guarded. Quite apart from the smell of reversal of alliances that some detect in these events and in contemporaneous Sino-Soviet divergencies, mutual overtures between the Americans and the Russians cannot but present NATO with all the problems that relaxation of tension always poses for an alliance. At the same time, French efforts to strike separate bargains alternately with Germany and with Russia thicken the atmosphere of realignment and compel attention to the merits and vices of a self-contained European alternative to NATO.

THE STRATEGIC RELATIONSHIP

FOR MANY OBSERVERS THE DISPOSITION OF NUCLEAR WEAPONS IS THE touchstone of all well-being in the alliance. The nuclear problem is twofold. The management of nuclear weapons—still predominantly in American hands—so as to deter direct aggression or indirect threats to the vital interests of the various European nations is what determines whether an American guarantee is adequate protection. This is a question of capacity and reliability. A second and not wholly subsidiary question is whether this protection is extended in a form compatible with the self-respect of nations now enjoying an increased sense of their own importance.

The Western Bloc

The outlines of the strategical debate are fairly well known. American threats to retaliate with a nuclear attack on Russia in the event of an otherwise irresistible Soviet assault on Western Europe lose in credibility as the United States itself becomes vulnerable. Many before De Gaulle pointed out that suicidal threats are impressive, if ever, only from entities with a strong sense of self or one-ness. The response of American military leaders under Secretary of Defense Robert McNamara has been to prepare a flexible strategy, with a scheme for counterforce bargaining by nuclear weapons short of massive annihilation and with a build-up of conventional forces capable of meeting sizeable attacks without any nuclear measures at all. This strategic doctrine, however, has raised as many doubts as it has allayed in European minds, which fear that the necessary flexibility may be secured at their expense. These fears range from simple misgivings that the very search for such a policy confirms the infirmity of American purpose to more refined anxiety that targets for counterforce action may be in Western Europe, arriving at a situation in which tolerable use of nuclear weapons will be defined as use upon targets not in the territory of the two nuclear super-powers.[1] Ironically, the doctrine of controlled and selective response creates a new motive for the Europeans to have nuclear forces of their own; that is, in order to thwart uses that may seem limited to the super-powers but are catastrophic for Europe.

Similar misgivings surround the plan for increased conventional forces. Preparing a conventional defense, many Europeans think, means preparing to fight a destructive campaign on their soil. This, if it has to come, though doubtless better than thermonuclear war in Europe, is still not as attractive an alternative as it is for Americans. Moreover there are fears that conventional preparedness increases the risk of war by reducing credibility of the massive deterrent. That is why Britain, in particular, tried to retain a first-strike capacity and why both Britain and Germany have continued to emphasize the early use of tactical nuclear weapons. That is to say that, paradoxically, many Europeans believe in depending on tactical nuclear weapons as a deterrent because they think their use as a defense would be intolerable. Finally, conventional forces call for expenditures, especially in manpower, that are politically difficult to sustain. There is undoubtedly an interaction between European unwillingness to pay the price of certain strategies and their refusal to admit the validity of the doctrine in question.

[1] For this fear see W. F. K. Thompson, *Daily Telegraph*, May 7, 1963.

Laurence W. Martin

Such considerations and a sense of Europe's renewed industrial competence have refreshed the enthusiasm of some who believe in national deterrents. De Gaulle's resolution in this regard is well known, but the British Conservatives, too, after an interlude in which their nuclear efforts were subtly downgraded to "an independent contribution to the Western deterrent" later reverted to asserting the need for assurance against ultimate abandonment by America.[2] Neither did the new Labour Government make any such drastic breach with its predecessors' nuclear policy as its earlier protestations might have suggested. These national programs persist when American leaders regard the European nuclear forces as militarily ineffective and, more than ineffective, dangerous as an accident-prone interference with the control of response that alone can preserve the credibility of deterrence. Paradoxically, many Europeans are encouraged to ignore these warnings by a widely diffused if not always conscious confidence that no major military challenges are likely to arise in Europe, given the uncertainties the Soviet Union must face and the wide range of non-military courses open to it. By not falling in with American suggestions, by not producing larger conventional forces, and by not relinquishing independent control of nuclear weapons, many Europeans feel they can multiply these uncertainties and compel American support. This view rests on the belief that American demands represent a preference and not a *sine qua non:* that Europe is too important to abandon even if optimum American conditions are not met. Russo-American rapprochement reinforces this readiness to reject American advice, for if the *détente* raises fears of a bilateral deal, it also brings an atmosphere of relaxation in which increased military efforts or really tiresome reappraisals of strategic concepts are unlikely to be made.[3]

MILITARY SOLUTIONS

A VARIETY OF SOLUTIONS HAVE BEEN PROPOSED FOR THESE DILEMMAS. None is wholly satisfactory, for the dilemmas arise from truly divergent national circumstances. The solution that would perhaps be simplest from the American point of view, complete surrender of Western nuclear efforts to the control of the United States, is as unlikely to be adopted as it would be unlikely to prove enduring. In

[2]See, for example, Alec Douglas-Home's speech in the Commons, November 12, 1963, setting the tone for his election campaign.

[3]Looking within, as well as between, nations, one is struck by the extent to which complex strategic conclusions are colored by the basic hunch of the author as to whether major war is a remote contingency or an ever-present possibility.

addition to the strategic case for independent European capacity already alluded to, a number of other considerations keep European interest in nuclear weapons alive. So long as each exists, the French and British programs feed on each other, neither nation being likely to concede the sole European nuclear role to the other. Nor are Western European countries likely to surrender the prestige that participation in nuclear matters confers, the leverage upon the United States, the access to negotiation on nuclear questions, or the possible commercial advantages of keeping up with an important branch of modern technology.[4]

The other "pure" solution, the proliferation of national nuclear forces, is also unsatisfactory and improbable for reasons now widely understood. Such policies are not open to a majority of the allies for technical reasons, and the capacity of even the major members to sustain large nuclear efforts is widely questioned. The dangers of such a solution, were it available, may have been exaggerated. A direct correlation between a rise in the number of nuclear centers and an increased danger of catastrophe cannot be conclusively demonstrated. But in any case the likelihood of proliferation in Europe is less than it superficially seems to be. There are few signs that any new members of the coalition are contemplating such a departure. The most vexed question is the case of Germany. Here the legal, technical, political, diplomatic, and geographical obstacles the Germans would face are formidable. The prospect of German access to strategic nuclear weapons, however, even in indirect forms, undoubtedly does arouse fears both in the West and, quite genuinely, in Eastern Europe. Moreover, a pronounced move toward reliance on local deterrents, available only to some, could not fail to sharpen disruptive questions of status within the alliance. Present German interest appears to be directed more to securing assurance as to the general nuclear strategy of the alliance than to setting out on the road to nuclear sovereignty. Nevertheless, the long-term prospects must remain in doubt and, if the Chinese example is emulated by many other nations, German restraint will be severely tested.

Much attention has been devoted to the possibility of collectivizing nuclear enterprises. Crudely put, the task here, from the American vantage point, can be regarded as giving Europeans as much of

[4]See, for instance, the rather vehement refusal of Viscount Hailsham to abandon "all the advanced and sophisticated technologies," quoted by Governor Rockefeller in his February 9, 1963, press conference, and the thought-provoking assertion by Douglas-Home in Ottawa in May, 1963, that "We have decided that Britain must be equipped to be present in the councils of war and peace—and to be there by right. And this means nuclear power."

Laurence W. Martin

the appearance and as little of the substance of a nuclear role as will persuade them to comply with American strategic doctrine. It is impossible to predict what arrangements, if any, would fulfill such an essentially psychological purpose. So long as Europeans proceed on a rational basis, however, they need assurance that nuclear weapons will be available for their defense when necessary, that the Soviet Union is impressed by this, and that if they have to be used the weapons will be employed in ways least harmful to European interests. This means taking care of targets dangerous to Europe—the MRBM sites for example—in a "clean" fashion and avoiding any unnecessary nuclear fire—from friend or foe—on Western Europe. Ideally Europeans also need safeguards against American action in any other part of the world—particularly nuclear action—that might expose them to attack when they do not themselves believe their vital interests are at stake.

Neither Americans nor Europeans are likely to achieve a full measure of their demands. So long as they remain separate political entities it can never be wholly satisfying to leave even a portion of vital decisions in other hands. Efforts to approximate a solution have ranged from sharing information on existing policy, to consulting on the design, deployment, and contingency planning of nuclear forces, and, finally, to a share in deciding when to employ such weapons. Somewhere along this continuum appears the question of whether it is necessary for others than the United States to own or have complete custody of the actual nuclear weapons.

Schemes for collective nuclear activity are varied and complex. Various arrangements have been made in recent years for informing the other NATO nations of American nuclear strategy, apparently without greatly assuaging the feeling that these are essentially matters that the United States keeps to itself.[5] Ever since proposals made by General Norstad in 1959, ideas of an operational nuclear role for NATO itself have been in the air. The Nassau meeting between President Kennedy and Harold Macmillan in 1963 produced ambitious if vague schemes of this sort. By far the most ambitious of these was the trouble-fated plan for a multilateral seaborne force based on the principle of mixed-manning.

The distinctive features of this scheme were common ownership by the contributing nations and the homogenization of national elements in the crews to make it impossible for any participating nation to make individual use of the force. Advocates of this force

[5]On this and many of these matters see the useful account, *Problems and Trends in Atlantic Partnership* (Washington: Committee on Foreign Relations Staff Study, 1963).

hoped it would be a dramatic symbol of unity that would offer Germany participation on equal terms and also make it possible for smaller allies to take part by subscription of money and men.

The proposal for an MLF did not receive a rousing welcome in Europe or, indeed, in many American circles. To many it seemed a needless expense and a dangerous concession to Germany. Upon their accession to office in the autumn of 1964 the Labour Government suggested, as an alternative, an Atlantic Nuclear Force which might combine elements of the national forces of the existing nuclear powers under a joint command to which a multilateral element might also be added to accommodate the Germans if they insisted. This proposal, it was argued, economized by making use of existing forces and was slightly less contrary to the apparent principles of French policy. If the MLF, however, had irritated many as an undue concession to Germany, the ANF was regarded by the Germans as yet another indication of their inferior status.

After two or three years of discussion of joint nuclear enterprises, a number of important questions remained almost as obscure as ever. So long as the system for command and control remains obscure it is impossible to decide whether such plans are likely to satisfy European desires. The Europeans presumably secure a veto over use of a joint force, but arrangements so far suggested would give them neither a positive power to employ or threaten to employ the force nor any control over the use made by America of its remaining preponderant national forces. Would such a force ultimately resign Britain and France to abandonment of their national deterrents? If not, will a joint force persuade Germany permanently to accept what will remain a secondary status so long as national forces continue to seem important to other European nations? From the American point of view also there are other questions unanswered. Would such joint efforts lead to a relaxation in European support of other military activities? Past experience certainly makes it seem probable that a successful launching of the MLF would, by creating a sense of achievement, of greater security, and of having done something for the Americans, encourage Europeans to relax rather than redouble their efforts.

One important, obscure, and little discussed question concerns the exchange of information and consultation involved in schemes for joint forces or for other elaborations of the NATO planning mechanism. It is never made clear exactly what information would be shared or on what subjects consultation would take place. Few know, indeed, who is privy to what information in the United States itself on arcane strategic questions. Agencies of American government, let alone foreign allies, have been known to go unconsulted. The question is important because, given the nature of nuclear war, it is influence on the road to confrontations with the enemy and on their subsequent management that counts rather than actual operations. Yet, exactly because this is the heart of security in the nuclear age, it is a big step for the United States to begin to impair its autonomy in this regard. Allies do not always see eye to eye in such confrontations; European governments have been far from confident of the wisdom of American tactics in Korea, in Cuba, or in Viet Nam. It is consequently remarkable how little attention is given to how far joint forces or the admission of allies to the American planning process would increase their ability to affect and possibly obstruct American management of crises, perhaps the most important aspect of modern military affairs.

As a limited expedient for the solution of the Germans' peculiar problem and as a possible additional vehicle for cooperation and consultation, a joint force probably holds enough promise to justify its continued exploration. The vehemence of some of the architects of the MLF, however, indicates the need to ensure that such limited expedients do not come to be regarded as blueprints for the future of the West. It is certainly possible to discern the assumption in some expositions of the MLF that such a continuation of the NATO venture, a tighter binding of the existing grouping, building common institutions in a quasi-federal mold, is the only proper future pattern of relations among the Western nations. Possibly this may prove true, but it is by no means certain yet that the patterns and groupings available for particular military purposes are those best suited for the long-term political future. Unless this is fully recognized, hastily erected structures could become obstacles to bolder and more novel ventures.

Even from a strictly military point of view the pursuit of elaborate schemes should not entail rejection of more limited forms of cooperation. General de Gaulle has not ruled out the possibility of coordinating his nuclear force with those of his allies, if they will only acknowledge his right to have it. He has frequently recognized the dominance of American nuclear power and its vital importance to Europe. In the very press conference in which he delivered the *coup de grace* to Britain's application to the EEC, the General confessed that "naturally American nuclear arms remain the essential guarantee of world peace." Admittedly many of the General's actions seem to be directed toward destroying cooperation. But it must be recognized that never since his accession have American policies shown much sign of anxiety for cooperation either, except on a basis of complete hostility to adjustments in the direction preferred by De Gaulle.

There have been some signs since the accession of President Johnson of a less doctrinaire approach. The best hope may therefore be for something modest in the nature of an MLF to accommodate the Germans, with British and French national forces in association; something not unlike the ANF but with more independence, formally if not in practice, for the national contingents. If this leaves Germany still somewhat less than equal, it would be no more than a recognition that Germany, as many Germans themselves perceive, suffers historical, political, and geographical disabilities that do, in fact, make her less than equal in such matters.

A EUROPEAN DEFENSE COMMUNITY

ONE VARIANT OF THE COLLECTIVE FORCE CONCEPT DESERVES SPECIAL attention for it is again symptomatic of a view going beyond the military realm. This is the belief held in many quarters that a united Europe might take over the responsibility of a nuclear power in ways acceptable to America. A joint European venture, coordinated with the United States, could, it is said, minimize proliferation of separate centers of nuclear decision—it might reduce the number—and could be on a scale commensurate with American ideas of credibility.

The most effective single American encouragement to this notion was McGeorge Bundy's speech at Copenhagen in September, 1962, when he said "we ourselves cannot usurp from the new Europe the responsibility for deciding in its own way the level of effort and of investment which it wishes to make in these great matters."[6] Some who endorse this attitude do so from the belief that a unified Europe not only can, but must, by nature, dispose of all the instruments of power. This notion has been voiced by Pierre Messmer, by such a non-Gaullist as Jean Monnet, and one of the most detailed expositions came from Edward Heath when in the full flood of negotiations for British entry to the EEC:

> We quite accept that the European political union, if it is to be effective will have a common concern for defense problems and that a European point of view will emerge ... of course, as the European Community develops, the balance within the Atlantic Alliance is going to change. In the course of time there will be two great groups in the West: North America and Europe. The growth of the Euro-

[6]Speech before the Atlantic Treaty Association, September 27, 1962.

pean point of view in the defense field will not, we believe, be long in making itself felt.[7]

There is little doubt that Europe could create a considerable nuclear force in time. Full British cooperation would of course greatly facilitate this. France, however, would not necessarily welcome loss of its nuclear primacy in EEC, and there is also no sign that Britain would dare make a contribution without retaining the American ties that justify French fears of her being a mere American agent. Despite these problems, and despite the difficulties of deployment that European demography presents, a European force is not technically absurd.

What makes the discussion academic is, of course, the fact that no Europe exists or is likely soon to exist to create, far less operate, a European deterrent. The existing "Six," and still more the Six with Britain and her followers added, are unlikely to have more than a rudimentary political organization in the near future, and the whole problem of the alliance is the incompatability of loose political structures and nuclear policy. It is certainly conceivable that a nuclear force could be the center around which community might be built. But it seems unlikely. Past experience suggests nuclear matters are more divisive than solidifying and, as in the alliance as a whole, federal structures demand explicitness in areas sometimes best spared too minute a scrutiny.

THE TWO PILLARS

WHAT IS OF MORE FUNDAMENTAL INTEREST IS THE VISION OF A FUTURE structure for the Western bloc that underlies the advocacy of a Europe, united, including Britain, and acting as a diplomatic, economic, and military unit at the highest level. Many have been attracted by the idea of America acquiring a single European partner, thereby basing the alliance on what has been called the two pillars. Such a dualism, indeed, usually seems to be what is meant by the slogan of "partnership," and many of the advocates of Atlantic Community complete with institutions believe it can come about only by the approximation of Europe and America as equals.[8]

[7]Speech before the Council of Western European Union, April 10, 1962.

[8]See, for example, Andre Philip, "to have a dialogue there must first be two and not an anarchic crowd," "Socialism, Neutralism, Pacifism," *Atlantic Community Quarterly*, [March, 1963], p. 71. The official communique of a Johnson-Erhard meeting in Texas declared: "The President and the Chancellor agreed that the central requirements in the policy of the West must be to increase the strength and effectiveness of the emerging Atlantic partnership. They reaffirmed their conviction that an increasingly unified Europe is vital to this effort" (*The New York Times*, December 30, 1963, p. C8).

The Western Bloc

This prospect suits those in America whose view of Europe, consciously or not, is a projection of American experience so that their solutions for problems of cooperation in the free world partake of the nature of state-building with an ultimately federal mold for the whole Atlantic area. Others believe that only equals can whole-heartedly cooperate and that a united Europe offers the sole prospect of an equal associate for America. The solution to the problem of American predominance must be the end of predominance, though perhaps not all advocates of the two pillars phrase it this way themselves. Creation of Greater Europe also has the definitiveness and tidiness that appeals to many Americans in their approach to political questions, to the aspect of American foreign policy that thinks of diplomacy in terms of establishing and running "operations" rather than manipulating autonomous entities. In this sense, pushing Britain into EEC would have removed the complication of dealing with an important unit that did not fit the preconceived scheme. Nor can it be forgotten that, for some, the vision of a united Europe revived prospects of ultimate disengagement from trans-Atlantic problems that originally underlay NATO and the Marshall Plan.

The merits of the two pillars design for the Western bloc depend in large part on the nature of the pillars and their probable mutual relations. Recent events have made it clear that, for the time being, the design fails—as in the strategic field—because there is little prospect of the European pillar being erected. The problems the Six face, with their existing degree of cooperation, make the prospect of a Europe capable of acting with a cohesion comparable to the United States seem even more remote than when the ideologies of Atlantic Community first seized on it.

This leaves open, however, the question of whether it would be wise for the United States to continue to put pressure on Europe to unite with a view to ultimately producing a political partner. Events have made it difficult not to notice that Greater Europe might prove a recalcitrant partner. Concern about one aspect of this is expressed in the frequent exhortations that Europe be "outward looking," by which rather loose phrase it is meant that she should be a liberal trader and a reasonable negotiating partner willing to shoulder burdens of the alliance and tailor its policies to the broader concept of free world. A cynic might more briefly define outward looking as ready to fall in with the Grand Designs of Washington.

It is now obvious such complaisance is not to be taken for granted. Most now agree that, whatever his idiosyncracies, General de Gaulle's self-assertiveness represents a pervasive streak in European opinion. To this way of thinking, "interdependence" is an abhorrent idea. A cautious Canadian observer comments "it is strange how few Americans have recognized the deep-seated anti-American aspects of the European movement, the urge to be independent of American aid and American policy...."[9] One source of this blindness seems to have been the impression that the EEC was chiefly about free trade, whereas it is really concerned with economic growth, community building, social planning, and self-respect. The question therefore becomes whether a European political community, capable of equal partnership, can be created at a level of self-willed deviation from American guidance compatible with the degree of coordination regarded as essential by the United States. This being far from certain, it is not impossible that a loosely knit Europe might be more serviceable than a coherent but recalcitrant unity.

One theory behind partnership is that only equals can cooperate freely. But it can be argued with equal force that there are real differences of interest between Europe and the United States — some economic, some arising from the tasks of community building, some from competition for primacy in dealing with the single adversary, yet others from inevitable divergencies of strategic view that geography imposes — and that these would be compounded by synthesis into a single center of responsibility disposing of the resources to attempt an independent course. The argument that only equals can cooperate can thus be countered with the thesis that divergent interests become irresistible when the parties concerned have pretensions to self-sufficiency.

Two other considerations suggest the wisdom of a cautious second look at the prospect of uniting the Europe of Brussels. One is the likely political complexion of such an entity, which should be significant for its future outward behavior if half the charges of needless chauvinism levelled against General de Gaulle are justified. Admiration for the achievements of the EEC cannot obscure the doubtful political future of such components as France, Italy, and Germany. Indeed the moderating virtues of Britain form one of the arguments of those intent on forcing an entry for her. Whether Britain could justify these hopes in a system constructed on continental lines seems doubtful. Assuming she could, might this not result in a balance tending to inertia? Thus Europe might fulfill hopes for a dynamic, cooperative partner; it could also become either an uncooperative, dynamic power or a neutered if not a neutralist force.

[9]John Holmes, "Implications of the European Economic Community," *Atlantic Community Quarterly*, March, 1963, p. 31.

The Western Bloc

All this leaves unexplored the many misgivings that have been expressed about the effect of uniting Western Europe on the chances of moving closer to Eastern Europe, on the place of such odd elements as the neutrals, and on the particular problem of German unification. The latter may be a hopeless cause but it might well be more readily transcended in a loose than in a formalized European framework. In any case, the policy favored in some circles of making Germany America's chosen ally, even perhaps on nuclear matters, needs careful examination. Pushing Germany to the fore in Western policy—a process many Germans instinctively shrink from—seems very unlikely to encourage Eastern Europe in its disengagement from Russia and its increasing *de facto* intimacy with the West in general and West Germany in particular. The gradual elaboration of these interrelations until they also embrace the two Germanies and Berlin seems as close to a solution of the German question as can now be foreseen. A sense of movement in this direction might indeed provide West Germans with enough satisfaction to reduce such drive for nuclear weapons as they may possess, and it would seem unwise to let military schemes prematurely obstruct those possibilities without the most thorough consideration.

THE ROLE OF THE UNITED STATES

MANY OF THESE DOUBTS ABOUT THE AVAILABILITY AND DESIRABILITY OF the European partner are now widely entertained. Much less often is it realized that the American end of the axis is also lacking. The existence of a great American center of power and decision is not of course in doubt. But it is equally clear that the United States has no real intention of trammelling its formal independence or reducing itself to an Atlantic partner. All the more remote then are elaborate schemes for Atlantic federalism on other than the most rarified symbolic level.

The question arises therefore as to whether it is wise even to encourage the development of such symbolism as the proponents of Atlantic Community have done. America is an Atlantic power only in an inclusive and certainly not an exclusive sense. The United States has a global role peculiar to herself, in which she has no conceivable equal partner and in which her only true opposite number is the Soviet Union.

Regardless of all the nuclear possibilities discussed previously, the

Laurence W. Martin

United States remains the Grand Deterrer. Whatever progress the Europeans may make in the next few years, the possibility of American nuclear action, however watered by doubt, will pose by far the most weighty uncertainties faced by Soviet strategists in Europe.[10] In addition, America's power is engaged in many areas of the world where few Europeans, if any, are still concerned. The United States cannot submit its actions in these areas to European consent without encouraging a lowest common denominator of resistance to Communist initiative that would gradually permeate all diplomacy as well as the directly military confrontation.

In the long term, the United States is trying to nurture a pluralistic, cooperative, and orderly world. In the short term it is organizing a global resistance to communism which is, in its present form, incompatible with such a world. As the great deterrer, as a Pacific power, indeed as the only truly world power now existing in the democratic camp, the United States cannot accept an essentially local Europe as an equal partner. Indeed, does encouraging the coagulation of Europe render in itself an unqualified service to the ultimate goal of a pluralistic world? The anxieties aroused by the emergence of this unit in African, Asian, and Latin American breasts are already well recognized. The reluctance of many European leaders to share the American vision of a future order is increasingly obvious. It must also be asked whether it is wise to encourage the remaining European nations that profess a concern for global affairs to submerge their identity in a more parochial community; to insist, for instance, on extinguishing a distinct British voice in the alliance. Would it be more valuable to preserve an associate, however junior, with a world-wide presence to share in the public accounting for such operations as military aid to India or the policing of S.E. Asia, and to act as an informed critic on matters so removed from the concerns of Brussels?

AMERICAN LEADERSHIP

ONE IS DRIVEN TO CONCLUDE THAT NEITHER OF THE TWIN "PILLARS" IS available and, more controversially, that such an edifice would be of doubtful value to the West. America must therefore resign itself to an untidier coalition than is perhaps congenial to the American political

[10]Thus one can probably take seriously—all the more for its tart phrasing—the General's remark in his July 30, 1963, press conference "en cas de guerre générale la France, avec les moyens qu'elle a, serait aux côtés des Etats-Unis, et je crois reciproquement."

92

genius. For the political and technical reasons sketched in this paper, the United States cannot resolve the tensions occasioned by its primacy in the alliance by conjuring up Europe in an effort to shed its predominance. On the contrary, America must remain the dominant member of the Western grouping in the foreseeable future, retaining a lion's share of decisive power, symbolized by its independent retention of overwhelming nuclear force.

This is not to say that a number of changes might not usefully be made in the alliance. The impossibility of taking Europe as a full partner in global policy naturally does not mean that the fullest possible diplomatic and military coordination is not desirable everywhere. Some substantial gestures are necessary to the widely diffused belief that a turning point has arrived. In this regard some projects for a joint force and the various proposals made for reform of the NATO staff structure may yet prove worthwhile.

The future health of the alliance, however, is likely to depend more on the quality of American leadership than on adjustments of machinery. The inevitable primacy of the United States certainly does not mean that American schemes will readily be accepted and followed. On the contrary, a realistic grasp of leadership means resignation to interminable frustration and the final abandonment of the belief that somewhere there exists a way to transcend the perpetual wrestle with problems never susceptible of complete solution. The right to cut the knots of allied indecision in the last resort can only be gracefully retained, if at all, by virtue of inexhaustible patience with associates, deference for their views, and tenderness for their interests. Given the present nature and distribution of nuclear power, the American President as commander-in-chief has the ultimate capacity to destroy both East and West. What America's allies need above all in such a situation is confidence that they can share in moulding and defining the framework of strategic ideas within which he takes his fateful decisions.

Analogies with the deference of the superior to the inferior in the Commonwealth that resulted in the free entry of the Dominions into two world wars are tempting but perhaps farfetched. One feature of British experience is relevant however. The now much derided "special relationship" was no complete illusion, as any familiarity with the intimacy and mutual confidence of British and American officials, compared to their continental opposites, will confirm. In essence, by cooperation, the British purchased a close hearing whenever they felt obliged to dig in their toes on a truly vital interest. The skill the British showed in cultivating this relationship is often acknowledged. Curiously, Americans have been slow to recognize it as a considerable achievement on their part, too.

By its nature, the special relationship cannot be extended to others without dilution. But the adjective and the noun are not completely inseparable. If "specialness' is not very extendable, the substance of the relation may be more elastic. It should not be impossible to develop among the leading allies something of the same sense of being less than foreign to each other, the confidence that their major interests are consistently and sympathetically taken into account, not from time to time, but as a natural part of the daily workings of American government. Some, it is true, would reject such intimacy, but it is not easy to believe we have exhausted the possibilities in this direction.

The future seems unlikely to vindicate either those who expect rapid progress toward the ever tighter binding of the existing grouping within institutional frames or those who seize on the current loosening of ties in both East and West to predict a return to a classic balance of power characterized by simple alliances and pacts of guarantee. Rather we may expect a prolonged period of mixed expedients and a continued groping for pragmatic arrangements to serve the many compatible, but by no means yet identical, interests and preferences of the Western nations.

As THE PRECEDING AUTHORS HAVE ARGUED, IF THERE EVER IS AN *opportunity to formulate United States policy beyond the Cold War, the nature of that formulation will be governed—as it is now—very much by our understanding of and assumptions about the Communist nations, their leadership, their intentions, and their aspirations.*

In this essay, Philip E. Mosely examines the characteristics of the Communist Bloc and the course of the great political and social changes since the Stalin era, seeking to detect signs of an approaching new era significantly different from the situation of bipolarity that has characterized the Cold War.

Mr. Mosely traces the nature of bipolarity, as in the Cuban missile crisis of October, 1962, and asks whether that bipolarity will end. Does the world-wide goal of Communism allow "any permanent and continuous relaxation of international tension"? If not, what is the prospect that the Soviet Union will change its goal? There are, to be sure, many discernible changes in Soviet society, but are there changes so basic as to permit the West to alter its "consistent and costly policy of vigilance and effort"?

How are we to understand the Soviet talk of peaceful co-existence when the Soviet leaders themselves explain it, "patiently and repetitiously," as a period "in which the conflict between opposing systems will be pressed by the Communists, in power and out, as vigorously as they dare, short of becoming involved in a nuclear war"? Mr. Mosely urges that we keep in mind this Soviet view of co-existence as we posit our assumptions about the policies and intentions of the Communist powers.

And we must also remind ourselves that the Communist leaders are, at the same time, making assumptions about us. The conflict between the Soviet Union and China, perhaps the greatest unplanned consequence of nuclear bipolarity, hinges almost entirely on "their differing appraisals of the strength and determination of the United States...." And thus we must face again the question of our military stance, and whether it tends to encourage or discourage developments that might lead to nuclear war, such as the escalation of local conflicts into nuclear exchanges.

Mr. Mosely urges us to welcome peaceful competition and develop policies which will enable us to compete successfully under the conditions of "co-existence, Soviet style." The era he foresees beyond the Cold War will not be a total replacement of Cold War animosities but a kind of modification: "The central prospect, thus, is for a decade of intensified, wide-ranging, and versatile forms of competitive co-existence."

By Philip E. Mosely

•

THE COMMUNIST BLOC IN THE 1960's

FOR SOME FIFTEEN YEARS AFTER WORLD WAR II THE KREMLIN EXERTED a relentless pressure to nail down its expanded sphere of control while from time to time moving forward or probing into real or supposed power vacuums. This pressure, which met with the countervailing American determination to resist the Soviet thrust, made bipolarity the inevitable and central axis of world politics. With the weakening or collapse of other power centers and the development of long-range nuclear power, only the Soviet Union and the United States were strong enough to operate as truly independent centers of ultimate decision. All other states were obliged to adjust their aspirations and trim their actions more or less directly, and more or less voluntarily, to patterns set by the two greatest powers.

In the Soviet-dominated countries of East Central Europe this meant that full-blown Stalinist regimes, between 1947 and 1955, were ruthlessly substituted for the transitional forms of "people's democracy." For all practical effect, Soviet purposes displaced any assertion of the national interest by the satellites, even any "national-Communist" divergence from Moscow's demands and norms. Numerous other states elsewhere, feeling their survival, their national identity, or their interests menaced more or less directly by Soviet ambitions, clustered self-protectively around the opposing pole, that of American power. Finally, for still other nations, the choice of an "uncommitted" status was in turn made both attractive and possible, for geographical and ideological reasons, through the existence of an uneasy balance of bipolar power.

Once bipolarity had been carried to its logical conclusion through the development of Soviet nuclear missile power, dramatically displayed in 1957 and subsequent years, this new situation opened the way, by an ironical or dialectical twist of history, to a weakening of the bipolar stabilization of power. In the mid-1960's both America and

The Communist Bloc in the 1960's

the Soviet Union are confronted with unforeseen and awkward challenges to their positions of leadership within their respective blocs. American policy-makers are groping for new ways of adjusting their perspective and planning to these developments. Meanwhile, the similar problems of adjustment that have confronted the Kremlin have in many ways been more difficult for it to cope with. For one thing, Moscow must, for doctrinal and practical reasons, regard monolithic unity of ideology and politics as the normal and only workable basis of a world-wide Communist policy. Merely because Soviet leaders, since around 1951, have been using the term "commonwealth of socialist peoples" as a euphemistic way of describing the bloc does not mean that they really understand or accept the implications of having to manage a "commonwealth" of independent nations.

The deadlocking of bipolar nuclear power, which received an awesome demonstration in the Cuban missile crisis of October, 1962, has coincided with the growth of internal resources available for independent decision-making by individual governments within the opposing blocs. Again the effects of the process of de-polarization are different in the two camps. Ever since 1947, American policy has worked purposefully to build up a more or less united Western Europe, and for this the United States has made many sacrifices. Thanks in part to that policy, the renewed vigor and ambition of free Europe now make it possible for its various nations not only to stand increasingly on their own feet but also to tread on American toes! For Soviet policy-makers, on the other hand, the political independence and the ideological rivalry proclaimed by Communist China, as well as the increasing flexibility and diversity that Moscow has had to tolerate in its satellites, have been unplanned, unforeseen, and unwelcome. In the meantime the Soviet system, as it has been released in stages and in growing and uneven measure from the most glacial pressures of Stalinism, has been undergoing a variety of important social and intellectual changes from within.

I

BASICALLY, POST-STALIN AND POST-KHRUSHCHEV RUSSIA HAS BEEN experiencing a revolution managed from above and designed to meet a "revolution of rising expectations" from below, with the aim of re-establishing a consensus of purposes and mutual confidence between the rulers and the ruled in the hope of thereby replacing the blunderbuss discipline of crude fear by voluntary and intelligent cooperation. This is not Russia's first experiment in relaxing the pressures of absolutism. In the similar experiments of Elizabeth II, Alexander I, and Alexander II, the two interacting partners who were mainly involved were not the "broad" undifferentiated masses and the throne, but the ruler and the nobility, later the educated groups. Today, similarly, the interacting factors are primarily the leaders and those numerous intermediate and "active" (or activist) strata of society through whom the Kremlin manages the system of rule. And as in those earlier periods of guided change, the "rising expectations" that seek satisfaction are as much psychological, or spiritual and intellectual, as material. In no past instance has the end product of any one of Russia's managed revolutions turned out according to the preconceived plan. Yet, historically, each Russian thaw has released a reservoir of talents and aspirations that had accumulated in the preceding period of "freeze." All we can say with some certainty about the increasingly fluid situation of today is that a similar release of energies, material and intellectual, is visibly getting underway once again in Russia.

There is no need to recount in detail the more obvious manifestations and directions of the process of release, or its equally evident limitations. The use, and the using up, literally, of millions of lives in forced labor camps has been brought to an end. Nevertheless, the Kremlin, under Brezhnev, as under Khrushchev and Stalin, still holds in its hands many means of controlling the lives, the places of residence, the educational advancement, the professional careers, and the thinking of its subjects. The administration of justice has likewise been markedly improved, and the definition and punishment of crimes defined by the regime as "political" have been greatly narrowed. Yet the old means of indiscriminate repression are available to the leaders should they decide to put them to work again. The leadership has appealed to the middle ranks of the system to speak up against administrative inefficiency, arbitrariness, and corruption, and, after an initial period of hesitation, the response has now become a more vigorous if still wary one.

The range of incentives available to encourage and reward efficient work has been considerably enlarged through providing much larger supplies of food, clothing, housing, and consumer durable goods. Yet the regime's controls over the allocation of skills, manpower, equipment, and investment funds are still powerful today. "Consumer sovereignty" is not just around the corner, and the leaders are able to assign large and growing resources to defense, foreign policy, and economic growth.

Two major problems of economic management continue to baffle the Kremlin. One is how to render the process of industrial decision-making more flexible, more rapid, and more rational than it now is and still keep the levers of control firmly in its own hands. The frequent reorganizations that have been imposed since 1957 on the Siamese-twin systems of economic administration and planning show how far the Kremlin still is from "squaring the circle." Khrushchev has been denounced by his heirs for his "reorganization mania," and still new forms of management are being introduced into the top-heavy Soviet system. The other problem, which Stalin suppressed rather than solved, is how to bring collectivized agriculture up to a par with industry in efficiency and productivity. In part, this is a problem of Soviet agriculture's traditionally "low place on the totem pole" in competing for large-scale investment funds. In part it is mainly one more facet of the old problem of providing adequate material incentives and stimulating voluntary cooperation from below so as eventually to persuade the rank-and-file of collective-farm peasants to labor as hard for the collective as they would work for themselves. Under Brezhnev and Kosygin the Kremlin has promised, for the umpteenth time, to raise both investment levels and incentives in agriculture.

Less tangible and more difficult to grasp and appraise are the changes that have been occurring in Soviet intellectual life. In this sphere some part has been played by increased contacts with the West. Yet by far the more basic changes are being generated from within Soviet society. Both the first and the second stages of de-Stalinization, launched in 1956 and 1961, have had important repercussions on the Party's role in relation to scientific, literary, and artistic life. The decision to reopen communications with the West was itself one by-product of de-Stalinization. In this the regime was motivated, in the beginning, by the need for strengthening Soviet research in the natural sciences and technology, and this purpose has been well served by the new policy. The regime was also eager to display to the outside world Soviet achievements in sports and the performing arts, which offer a maximum of gains in prestige abroad with a minimum of ideologically dangerous exposure of Soviet intellectuals to the West. But once certain prestige-earning groups had received a limited license for contacts with their counterparts abroad, many others could also present, and have presented, strong claims to enjoy a similar privilege.

As a consequence of the new scientific and cultural exchanges with Western countries, a modest range of mutually interesting and helpful contacts has been established. Some thirty to forty thousand Soviet scientists, engineers, officials, writers, and artists have gained a limited acquaintance with the West. They have had opportunities to take home with them a knowledge which goes beyond and differs from the generally grim picture painted by routine Soviet propaganda. The effects of such experiences are necessarily diffuse and indirect. Since Soviet intellectuals selected for travel abroad are well indoctrinated, trusted, and patriotic, the main direct effect is probably to stimulate in them a heightened aspiration to do even better work in their various callings and perhaps to arouse in them a clearer awareness of the domestic impediments to better performance. Although the published reports of returned travelers almost always confirm the line of official propaganda about the superiority of the Soviet way of life, many of them, each important in some aspect of intellectual life doubtless have taken back a somewhat fuller and less simplified view of other countries and their ways of life. Since Khrushchev's removal the program of exchanges has continued at about the same or a slightly higher level, with somewhat closer supervision of Western visitors to the Soviet Union.

II

THE ASPIRATIONS THAT HAVE BEEN RELEASED WITHIN THE SOVIET UNION by the process and promise of de-Stalinization are far more important to the tone and creative level of intellectual life than the partially opened "window to the West." The on-again-off-again attitude of the Party leaders toward de-Stalinizing tendencies among the writers illustrates once again the great importance Russians have traditionally attached to the role of creative literature in shaping life. It also illustrates vividly the unresolved conflict between the doctrines preached by the Party and the demands presented by real life. Both Party doctrine and a strong Russian tradition regard the function of literature as that of setting a model for people, especially for each new and malleable generation, to live by—not as a leisure-time amusement, a surrogate *voyeur*-ism, or a branch of applied psychoanalysis.

The turbulence of this inner conflict can be measured by the ups and downs of the Kremlin's attitude to Evtushenko, even though this magnetic young poet is not the most significant or most influential representative of the new trends. Evtushenko aroused strong dismay and resentment in the Kremlin when he allowed his autobiographical essay to be published in Paris without first submitting it to any of the customary political "controls." Just a few weeks before that act of defiance, his bitter poem, "Stalin's Heirs," which denounced both Stalin and the numerous camouflaged Stalinists of today, had received the highest Party accolade, publication in *Pravda*. The question of whether or not to publish this poem, it was later stated officially, had been debated for several months, and the final decision to print it was made directly by Khrushchev. Evtushenko's dual role as "poet Laureate" of de-Stalinization and hero of the younger generation explains Khrushchev's violent reaction to the writer's unexpected departure from the norms of Communist discipline. Yet it is a mistake to regard the conflict over Evtushenko as an incident of the Cold War. Evtushenko, we must remember, is above all a Soviet patriot. He is proud of the Soviet Union, and he wants to be even prouder of it by persuading the leaders and the people to remove the blemishes he sees around him in Soviet life. He is a vehement supporter of Soviet foreign policy. He also (in all this he is only one of many) wants to be "sincere" and to "speak the truth to the Party." But can the Party tolerate the assertion of other truths, private or moral truths, that differ from "the truth" as defined by the Party for its own purposes? That question has remained unanswered in the recurrent spells of thaw and freeze. It was left unanswered in the Second Congress of Russian Writers, held in March, 1965.

Force and fear, pressed too far and too long as in Stalin's time, seal off men's minds and hearts and turn them into isolated and lifeless human atoms. Under conditions of terror, "activists" of all kinds and ranks survive and prosper through learning by rote the self-protective ritual of doctrine and slogans, but most people retreat into the silence of conformity and apathy. Khrushchev and his successors are alike in wanting to end this silence and break down the rigidities of bureaucratic unanimity. At the same time they want the scientists, writers, and artists to end up saying voluntarily exactly what the Party orders them to say. This dilemma, a tragic one, has been a continuing burden of Soviet life. Stalin, once he had full power in his hands, imposed one solution to this challenge. Today even those who worked most closely with Stalin sense that his methods eventually became counterproductive and would again become counterproductive in the increasingly complex Soviet society of today.

Many observers speak of a "Khrushchev compromise" between initiative and obedience. But is "compromise" an accurate term? A compromise is a working arrangement between two forces, neither of which can destroy the other. What Khrushchev and his successors seem in reality to be seeking in the intellectual, literary, and related fields is not a compromise, for the regime retains the ultimate if now seldom used power of destruction, but a working definition of the range of permitted and completely loyal thinking, investigation, and creativity. This is the parallel, in the field of thought, to the "all-people's state," which will, Khrushchev said, consign to oblivion the coercive functions of the Stalinist "dictatorship of the proletariat" while perfecting and perpetuating the primacy of the Party.

These complex processes of change raise one further question, one that is of central importance to the rest of the world. Will the increased demands of Soviet people for "sincerity'—sincerity being defined by individual people according to some general, human, ethical standards which are not necessarily those of the Party—as much as for a better material life diminish the ability of the Kremlin to apply its steadily growing material and military resources toward achieving the world-wide goals set by Communist doctrine? Despite the strenuous efforts of the regime to manage its domestic policies and its international purposes in separate compartments, there is an inevitable, if indirect, communication between them. When Brezhnev, for example, tells his people that the military might of the Soviet state is now so great that it can deter the "imperialists" from venturing into a new war, all Soviet people are deeply pleased to hear this reassurance. But some of them go on to ask, rather logically, whether it is now necessary any longer to accept the hardships, rigid discipline, and sterile monotony of life in a garrison-state. If Soviet literature, art, and music are in fact "the greatest" ever known, why should Soviet people not read, see, and hear the works of all other nations so as to appreciate this superiority for themselves? If the future institutions and practices of the "all-people's state" are one day to be the freest ever enjoyed by man, why should not Soviet people examine the workings of other systems for themselves? These are questions that the Khrushchevian compromise does not choose to answer.

III

To carry to their logical extreme the implications of the Khrushchevian reforms—and Russians, a nation of chess players, are often very logical and sometimes extreme—would mean either abandoning the Party's monopolistic right to rule every aspect of Soviet life, or else transforming the Party drastically from within, so that Party, people, and state would eventually be synonymous. The latter course is the goal at which Khrushchev hinted rather plainly in his Party Program of 1961, and for which he was bitterly attacked by Mao Tse-tung. Despite these hints, Khrushchev and his successors have and can have no intention of destroying or even weakening the monolithic Party-state. And to survive, the Party-state must safeguard and enforce, perhaps within somewhat relaxed limits, its claim to possess the sole correct interpretation of past and future, the sole correct "scientific" knowledge of the end-goals of human evolution, and the sole correct strategy to achieve that millennium.

Any political system contains within it the justification of its own legitimacy — its claim to exact obedience from its subjects — whether it be theocracy, divine-right monarchy, representative democracy, Fascism, or military dictatorship. A Communist regime is an "ideocracy." Its right to rule and to expand its realm is established, in its own eyes, by the possession of the "sole correct" ideology, which it alone is entitled to "apply creatively" to new conditions and problems. The Soviet leadership claims, of course, that the Communist ideology has been or will be accepted so fully by nearly all Soviet people that they will carry out spontaneously, in the stage of the "all-people's state," the duties that many or most of them had to be compelled to perform in the preparatory stage, that of the "dictatorship of the proletariat." In this way the new Soviet leadership continues, in theory, to "square the circle" between Party ideocracy and intellectual freedom. In practice, of course, reality is likely to stop short of the ideal. Yet Khrushchev's first or later successors may discover that the Party can afford to grant a far greater measure of autonomy, far more intellectual leeway ("freedom" is not the word), to various semi-autonomous spheres of Soviet life without endangering the unity and survival of the Party; in doing so the Party may actually enhance its ability to lead rather than drive the people of the Soviet Union to new achievements and new power.

The goals of the Soviet ideocracy that concern the rest of the world most directly are those of foreign policy. Will there be a continuing relaxation of tensions within Soviet society, and will that softening of purpose and refinement of controls at home be reflected in a parallel relaxation of Soviet ambitions and policies toward the outside world? Will the "co-existence of different economic and political systems," which Khrushchev and Brezhnev have advocated so warmly, grow into that heretical "co-existence of ideologies," which they abhor and reject?

In rejecting "ideological co-existence" Khrushchev's successors are actually defending their own political power and the survival of the Soviet system. Hence there is no reason to be surprised at that strong instinct of political self-preservation. On the other hand, their insistence on drawing a sharp distinction between the two levels of co-existence — political and ideological — makes it clear that political co-existence is still only a tactic, or, more hopefully, a short-run or medium-range strategy, not a permanent or, to them, a welcome goal. Khrushchev constantly made plain his expectation that "co-existence" will come to an end when all obstacles have been removed to the establishment of Communist rule around the world, in other words, when communism, in its Soviet variant, has triumphed everywhere. The same theme has been sounded, in less strident tones, by Khrushchev's successors.

It is not easy for a nondialectician to understand the subtle distinction the Kremlin draws between "economic and political systems" and "ideologies." After all, for Marxist or non-Marxist analysts alike, each way of life has its own ideology, its own values, explicit or unstated, and without that inner content it would be a "nonsystem." Still, we need not ask Khrushchev or Brezhnev to prove their claims as exponents of dialectics any more than we need accept their assumptions or their conclusions. In practice, we must take them at their word when they explain, patiently and repetitiously, that a period of "co-existence" is one in which the conflict between opposing systems will be pressed by the Communists, in power and out, as vigorously as they dare, short of becoming involved in a nuclear war.

Granted the harsh fact of the Kremlin's view of world affairs, will Soviet policy actually follow this line forever? Neither "history" nor foresight give an answer. For all we now know, there may be growing within the upper ranks of the Soviet system a realization that the Kremlin's insistence on the proclaimed goals of its policy makes any permanent and continuous relaxation of international tension impossible. Or perhaps the Kremlin is counting on two other major factors of Soviet popular psychology to uphold it in the pursuit of the world-wide goals of communism, despite the general disappearance of the emotional fervor of first-generation Bolshevism.

One of these factors is the deep penetration of Marxist-Leninist assumptions into Soviet ways of thinking. After forty-eight years of rule the dictatorship has pressed its ideas and notions deep into Soviet minds. Every visitor to the Soviet Union feels at first hand the impact of Soviet dogmatism. Soviet "democracy" is "real" because "the people" rules and "owns" the factories. Western "democracy" is merely a "camouflaged bourgeois dictatorship." Wars arise only from "capitalism," and communism can be only "peaceful" because there is no private ownership, no profit-seeking, no urge to subject and exploit other peoples. And so forth and so on.

This deep-reaching penetration of Soviet grooves of thought by a simplified and fact-repellent Marxism has been re-enforced by a second factor, the great upsurge of national pride and even chauvinism. After being reminded over and over, most recently by Hitler's invasion, of the many occasions on which Russia was defeated in war, Soviet people now believe for the first time in Russia's history that their country is one of the two greatest powers, and they are told constantly that it will soon surpass the only other great power, America. It should be remembered likewise that the establishment of a Communist regime in Cuba, whatever its defects and risks, has renewed flagging Soviet confidence in the "inevitable" triumph of communism. Similarly, the throwing of the mantle of Soviet nuclear protection over a small island in the Caribbean has convinced Soviet people of the reality of the Kremlin's claimed ability to project its power and influence to any and all parts of the globe. It is difficult for Americans, who carry reluctantly the responsibilities and risks of greatest-power status, to appreciate the emotions of national pride and expansionist chauvinism that sweep through those "activist" strata on which the Soviet leadership relies to carry out its ambitions. But emotions are as real in politics as missiles.

What is the outlook? Will the Kremlin's temporary and expedient policy of "co-existence" grow into something more stable, more enduring? Will the pursuit of expansionist ambitions by less risky political and economic means become a comfortable habit? Will goals of well-being at home come to appear to the Soviet leaders less dangerous and more rewarding than political gains abroad, as they do to rank-and-file Soviet people?

These are the central questions of war and peace, and no clear-cut answer can be given to them. One thing is plain. Soviet society is changing, even though slowly, from within, and the fulfilment of its domestic aspirations would benefit greatly from a relatively peaceful and secure prospect in world politics. On the other hand, the Kremlin has not given reliable evidence of any changes in its basic thinking and purposes that would permit the West to run the risk of either dropping behind in the power struggle or abandoning a consistent and costly policy of both vigilance and constructive political effort.

IV

THE DEVELOPMENT OF NUCLEAR MISSILE BIPOLARITY HAS HAD ONE GREAT and unplanned consequence for the Soviet position in the world: the separation and conflict between the policies of the Chinese Communists and the Soviet leadership. If Soviet decisions were actually based on the claimed Marxist-Leninist ability to predict events "scientifically," Russia's China experts would by now be in a very serious plight.

Philip E. Mosely

Among its several faulty assumptions, the Kremlin surely believed that China would for a very long time remain dependent on the Soviet nuclear deterrent to neutralize an American threat to contain or resist its ambitions and that China's leaders would adjust their policies willingly or reluctantly, to that basic fact. Moscow also saw how heavily Peking was relying on Soviet and other bloc deliveries to equip its armed forces and build new industries. It must have believed that, while there would be frictions and conflicts, these could be compromised in secret Party conclaves so as to uphold the impressive outward image of a united, infallible, and irresistible Communist movement.

All these expectations have been scattered to the wind. Peking and Moscow now vie in heaping the most damaging and public accusations on each other. "Revisionists," "dogmatists," "bourgeois degenerates," "cowards," and "war-mongers" are among the mildest epithets. Without going into the psychopathology of Communist controversies or tracing the long path that has led the two great Communist powers into this disarray, we must note that the dispute hinges on a single basic question which has two facets: their differing appraisals of the strength and determination of the United States, and their sharp disagreement over the prospect of local conflict escalating to nuclear war.

Peking stubbornly insists that the Kremlin's estimates exaggerate American strength and therefore overstate the risk that a direct confrontation may lead to nuclear war. By implication Mao has been demanding, ever since 1958, that the Soviet Union offer its full nuclear backing for a policy of forcing a showdown against American policy in Asia. Moscow has clearly been reluctant, for very sound reasons, to allow Peking to play the ultimate card of nuclear war, either by waving the big stick of Soviet nuclear missile power or, since 1959, by carrying out its promise to help Communist China build a modest deterrent of its own. The American escalation, since February, 1965, of the civil war in South Viet Nam to an air war against North Viet Nam has confronted Moscow and Peking with a direct challenge and with an almost insoluble dilemma.

The dispute, we must understand clearly, has not been waged over obscure questions of ideology or theory. Very concrete and serious decisions have been under discussion. As the Soviet reply of July 14, 1963, said in one somewhat cryptic passage, the Chinese "comrades" have been demanding that Moscow join with them to oppose the "imperialists" "spearpoint to spearpoint," in other words, to open new and multiple fronts of active and militant struggle. In urging this, the Moscow letter goes on, Peking seeks to bring on a nuclear war for national and even racialist purposes of its own, "which have nothing in common with proletarian internationalism."

Does the public explosion of the conflict mean that a clear decision one way or the other has now been reached by Peking? Will it at some point decide to devote its main efforts to rebuilding its own backward economy, even without substantial aid from the Soviet Union? Or will it, on the contrary, be tempted by its dangerously one-sided interpretation of world politics into intensifying or widening the areas of conflict in Asia, making the expulsion of American influence and power its central purpose with the ultimate aim of building a "Greater-Communist China" sphere of power in Asia to the exclusion of both Soviet and American influence?

The omens are serious but inconclusive. Perhaps Mao Tse-tung feels that his ambitions have been dangerously unveiled by his controversy with Moscow and must be postponed for a time. Perhaps China's need for Soviet oil, military equipment, and industrial machinery limits its ability to wage local wars of subversion and incursion. Perhaps the Kremlin's clear warning to Peking not to rely on Soviet nuclear backing has given its leaders pause.

Or perhaps not. Maybe China's leaders are unwilling to devote twenty or thirty years to patiently building a strong economy at home before reaching out for new political and territorial gains. Perhaps China's industrial recovery from the nadir of 1960-61 has already reached a level that would allow Peking, if necessary, to forgo all trade with the Soviet Union and the European satellites for a time. And maybe Mao believes that the United States could actually be deterred, even without specific Soviet threats, from using its nuclear forces directly against mainland China, just as it has refrained from overthrowing the Castro regime. One thing seems clear. If the Peking leadership decides to offset its domestic failures by political-cum-military expansion, the direction it will choose will be South East Asia, and its actions will be an outright challenge to America's political position in Asia. The U.S. challenge to North Viet Nam leaves open to Peking a wide range of possible responses. Its determination to respond is clear; the choice of means is not.

V

ONE FURTHER CONSEQUENCE OF NUCLEAR BIPOLARITY HAS BEEN TO diminish the strategic importance of the European satellites in Soviet military planning. Still, no outright change is presently possible in the postwar partition of Europe between East and West except at the risk of nuclear war. Stalin regarded the satellites as a base from which to ward off a possible Western attack and from which to mount a future advance to the Atlantic; therefore he insisted on absolute conformity by the various Communist-run regimes to every detail of the Soviet system. This rigid conformity has now become strategically obsolete and politically costly. From the launching of de-Stalinization in Russia on, the satellite parties have received a modest measure of leeway in modifying their domestic systems and policies. They have used this to broaden somewhat their economic and cultural ties with the West and in varying degrees to adjust the burdens of Communist rule and ambitions to the differing situation within each country.

Khrushchev's third "reconciliation," in 1962 and 1963, with Tito and his independent brand of communism has for the first time had a visible influence on the evolution of the neighboring satellite regimes. In addition, Moscow's attacks on the "dogmatists" and "warmongers" in Peking make it awkward for for the Kremlin to support "dogmatists" in Prague or Pankow. At the same time, the Kremlin's desire to enlist other Communist regimes and parties on its side in the conflict with the Chinese heretics and rivals offers some modest bargaining strength to the satellite leaders, if or as they choose to use it.

The United States cannot hope, realistically, to see the Communist regimes in the satellites overthrown from within, nor do the various peoples most directly concerned want them overthrown from without if that could be done only at the price of nuclear war. On the other hand, the peoples of East Central Europe want to see their situation made a little more bearable from within by regaining some measure of economic and cultural autonomy. For the United States the reasonable policy to follow is, without expecting any political intimacy, to use every opportunity to strengthen both national and Western economic and cultural influences within nations that chafe at their enforced separation from Western Europe and also to re-enforce the bargaining power their Communist governments have acquired in their dealings with the Soviet Union. Needless to say, such a policy of limited cooperation and encouragement is in direct conflict with the all-or-nothing impulse that moved the United States Congress in 1962 to deprive Yugoslavia and Poland of their most-favored-nation status in trade with the United States, an arrangement which had been negotiated by them with Washington as only one part of a carefully balanced settlement.

De-Stalinization, bipolarity, "co-existence" even of the dog-eared Soviet type, and the Moscow-Peking conflict offer the European satellite regimes a modest chance to enlarge their freedom of choices somewhat within a Soviet grouping that is less subject to control by Moscow and less uniform in outlook. The degree to which any regime makes use, or tries to make use, of these opportunities depends largely on its relations with its own people. In Poland, Gomulka has been determinedly shifting the balance toward tighter Party controls, especially over intellectual and religious life and over the younger generation. In Hungary, on the other hand, people feel that the balance between Communist demands and their own desires is more satisfactory than it was in the years preceding the national uprising of 1956. Rumania has been feeling its way toward livelier economic and cultural relations with the West. In Czechoslovakia, a partial adaptation to the Soviet pattern of de-Stalinization has at long last been getting under way. Only East Germany, faced with a hopeless contrast to West Berlin and the Federal Republic, clings abjectly to Stalinism in its full panoply. Obviously, American and Western policy in a period of co-existence should adjust its actions flexibly to the differing situations in the satellites rather than indulging in emotional outbursts of pique and prejudice.

VI

MANY OR MOST AMERICANS MAY NOT LIKE THE PRESENT AND PROSPEC-tive conditions of "peaceful co-existence" Soviet-style, but there are powerful factors at work to make this the central prospect for the rest of the 1960's. After investing excessive political expectations in the American semi-monopoly of atomic power for a decade or so, more and more Americans have come to realize that, despite its tremendous costs and vast risks, nuclear missile power is probably good for only one thing: to deter the use of similar power by the Soviet Union. Therefore, viewed in the large, the present decade is one in which a highly competitive "peaceful co-existence" will be pursued under the ever-present shadow of a possible nuclear war.

Despite various predictions of "survival" and "recuperation" after a nuclear holocaust, such a catastrophe would surely leave behind a very different America (and Russia) and a greatly changed situation in world politics. Hence, if "co-existence" means competition on the Kremlin's terms, that is, by all means short of nuclear war, Americans should accept this prospect and press on with the competition. If we admire competition as much as we believe, we should not draw back from it. And since we believe we can outcompete all other nations in the ways of peace and construction, we should not fear the challenge of a more or less "peaceful" competition.

Philip E. Mosely

The main difficulty is that the Kremlin's definition of coexistence leaves the door wide open to all kinds of "wars of liberation," with the Communists, like ourselves, free to define who is "liberating" whom, and from what. Still, as the Kremlin presently views the prospect ahead, there is one not unimportant safeguard: The Soviet leaders understand, if we read correctly their vehement exchanges with Peking, that local wars can and may lead quickly to a nuclear confrontation and thus to a nuclear war. The same risk places serious but undefined constraints on the U.S. use of force.

In effect the Kremlin implies that a local war in which Soviet, Chinese Communist, or American forces are directly involved would not remain a limited war for very long. Likewise, Soviet spokesmen specifically reject the "game theory" of limited wars, under which supposedly one or another great power, having lost the first round of a conflict, would gracefully retire from the contest rather than raise the risks to the next level of violence and ultimately to the stage of nuclear exchange. From this rationally cautious view Peking dissents strongly, perhaps as a consequence of its misreading of the unique and unrepeatable course of the Korean War. However, the Soviet doctrine of avoiding large-scale local wars still leaves a wide field for small-scale wars of subversion, supported and encouraged by Moscow's promise of all-out backing, or by Peking's. Still, as was shown in Greece between 1946 and 1949, the question of whether a neighboring Communist regime will or will not come to the aid of domestic insurgent forces often plays a decisive part in determining the outcome of wars of subversion.

Actually the only major areas that are now directly subjected to subversion across a Communist border are Laos and South Viet Nam. More generally, however, all countries of South East Asia are vulnerable in varying degree to this kind of indirect attack. Elsewhere along the periphery of the Communist grouping ("bloc" is now a misnomer) the situation is more stable than it was a few years ago. Because the fall of South Viet Nam would open the rest of South East Asia to Communist take-over, the United States has made a major commitment of men, resources, and prestige to defend it, including large-scale aerial attacks on North Viet Nam.

If the U.S. effort in Viet Nam should fail, still greater efforts and sacrifices would have to be made, probably in several nearby countries, to offset the damage such a defeat would inflict on America's influence in the rest of South East Asia, indeed, throughout Asia. If local factors are decisive, as they often are in subversive warfare, the role of an outside power is an especially difficult and uncertain one. In this respect the ability of the Communists to recruit, train, and discipline, for political as well as military warfare, substantial bodies of local adherents and even fanatics remains an exceedingly important asset. It can be offset, how completely no one can say yet, by the more indirect processes of offering assistance to new nations in training their future military, administrative, and intellectual leaders, in order to help them define and freely pursue the national interests of their own peoples.

The Kremlin believes that, if the danger of nuclear war can be reduced or contained, the decisive arena of competitive co-existence over the next decade or two will be in the newly independent and developing nations. The values of freedom, it asserts, mean nothing to these new nations, compared with the imperatives of economic growth. The claimed outpacing of capitalist systems by the Soviet economy will, it says, lead them willingly to choose the Communist pattern both at home and in world affairs. To back its political bets, the Soviet Union has made substantial investments of economic development credits and assistance in a number of key countries in Asia and Africa as one way of demonstrating the advantages of choosing the Soviet way. With the addition of Cuba to Communist ranks, the Kremlin has embarked on a similar demonstration, a costly one, in the Americas. These economic attractions, re-enforced by the growing military might and political influence of the Soviet Union, will, Soviet ideologists predict, bring about a rapid and decisive swing by the new or newly independent countries to "Socialism" Soviet-style, sometimes by peaceful means, sometimes by revolutionary violence.

The glowing Soviet picture of an "inevitable" march or slide of the developing countries to Moscow-type "Socialism" is strongly rejected by Peking. Moscow, it says, is pouring its resources down a rathole when it builds up "bourgeois" regimes which, in a showdown, will turn out to be anti-Communist. Instead of playing up to non-Communist leaders, Moscow should, Peking says, be preparing future party cadres in each country for the inevitably violent seizure of power. Meanwhile it should share its substance, not among "traitorous" nationalists, but with the deserving poor among its Communist brethren.

Moscow's policy is certainly the stronger, more subtle, and more dangerous one from the point of view of Western democratic hopes and fears. What it should mean to shapers of Western policy is that the United States and its allies, far from cutting back their development efforts, must strive to render more effective their programs for fostering economic growth and integrating the new countries into the world market and the society of nations. In these fields the advantages of the democratic world are formidable.

Another way in which the democracies can utilize their growing assets more effectively is through continuing to back the integration of Western Europe, which has the potential of becoming one of the greatest powers in the economic and cultural fields and perhaps eventually in the arena of strategy. The Soviet leadership has constantly displayed a deepset and genuine anxiety over the prospect of having to face a unified Western Europe. While this is not sufficient reason for the West to favor European integration, it must also not be forgotten that the relative weight of the Soviet Union in world politics would be considerably lessened if it should be faced on the West by an integrated Europe, cooperating closely or loosely with the United States and Canada, and on the East by a fanatically hostile China. While Soviet threats have regularly been more effective than American encouragement in making the goal of an integrated Europe seem both attractive and indispensable to a great many informed Europeans, the Kremlin may be engaged in a last-minute campaign of blandishments to make European unity appear both unnecessary and hardly worth all the trouble it entails. For this very reason the movement toward greater unity of action in Europe should be pressed on its own merits so that the West can be in a stronger position, regardless of any Soviet reversals in policy, to assert its values and its goals in a changing world.

If the Soviet Union should decide at some stage to cooperate in a lasting relaxation of tension, the fields of United Nations action and arms control would offer many possibilities for limited cooperation. And as the new nations become more familiar with the many modest but real advantages to them of a strengthened United Nations, they may be more successful than the West has been in persuading the Kremlin to join in building up the great unutilized potential of the United Nations as a stabilizing factor in an era of prolonged coexistence. An effective United Nations is even more indispensable to the great majority of middle-rank and small powers than it is to the major states.

VII

THE COMMUNIST COUNTRIES AND THEIR LEADERS LOOK AHEAD TO THE end of the 1960's with great hopes of new gains at home and on the world scene. After more than three decades of upheaval, violent reconstruction, and invasion, both the Soviet people and the Communist leadership expect a steady upward curve in material achievements, strategic power, and world-wide influence. The Kremlin goes beyond that simple projection of present trends to proclaim that within another full decade the entire world will be moving irreversibly toward communism.

The Soviet arsenal of political, economic, and cultural means of attraction will, it is true, be growing steadily in size and perhaps in effectiveness. And while the open conflict between Soviet and Chinese Communist methods and purposes is deeply disturbing to the Kremlin, the clash of policy is likely to lead to a direct confrontation between Communist China and American policy in Asia rather than between Moscow and Peking. The race for strategic preponderance will also go on, and neither major power can lightheartedly risk falling behind in it. Finally, the Kremlin's boast that its doctrines and its political methods offer the only workable formula by which the developing nations can achieve their ambitions is likely to be put to the test in a number of countries before the decade is over.

Within an increasingly complex pattern of "competitive co-existence" the main opposing forces are also likely from time to time to discover that they have some parallel though not identical interests. They may see that their contest for influence among developing countries needs to be tempered by a tacit avoidance of armed confrontation. They may decide that their contributions and sacrifices should be made to serve the rational and real requirements of the self-advancement of the developing countries, rather than being shaped to the narrow political purposes of great powers. Moscow and Washington may find that they have a tacit but shared interest in restraining Communist China from dangerous adventures.

As bipolarity comes to be modified by the growth of other power centers, Soviet policy-makers may decide that it is also useful to their interests to strengthen orderly international procedures and particularly to expand the conflict-muffling functions of the United Nations. Now that both major nuclear powers see that the menace of bipolar nuclear missile power has become too destructive and too undiscriminating an instrument for the sensible achievement of any limited political purposes, they may some day join in seeking ways to lessen the burden of risks and fears and to bring under control the enormous costs that are imposed by the arms race. Finally, both sides acknowledge a shared interest in avoiding mutual nuclear annihilation. Such a declaratory recognition, however important in itself, is quite insufficient to remove the continuing and real dangers of nuclear holocaust. Yet this admission is perhaps a necessary first step toward bringing nuclear terror under control.

The central prospect, thus, is for a decade or more of intensified, wide-ranging, and versatile forms of competitive co-existence. In this contest the Communist powers, even when divided, wield important and growing assets. The advantages on the side of the democracies are also very great and are growing. A Communist, by definition, must believe in a single "inevitable" outcome of the struggle. People of democratic beliefs, on the other hand, are convinced that, within certain broad and flexible limits set by material and historical factors, both individuals and nations have the ability to move forward purposefully toward goals they themselves freely define and choose. Just because they reject the Marxist-Leninist and other doctrines of "inevitability," the democracies, old and new, must exert their full range of talents, ingenuity, and determination, in this new period of competitive co-existence, in order to win for their own and other peoples a broader and more secure future for progress and freedom.

The Communist Bloc in the 1960's

PHILIP MOSELY HAS ARGUED THAT THE DISPUTE BETWEEN MOSCOW AND *Peking stems almost entirely from "their differing appraisals of the strength and determination of the United States." In this essay by Tang Tsou, we have an historical and theoretical explanation of just how the Chinese Communist leaders reach their appraisals of the United States, the Soviet Union, and the world situation in general. We see the world from their viewpoint and we see how their appraisals affect the prospects of peaceful co-existence between the Western nations and the Communists.*

Mr. Tsou argues that in order to understand the behavior of the leaders of the Chinese Communist Party (CCP) we must try to see the world as they see it, not as we see it or as Soviet leaders would like us to see it. We must acquaint ourselves, above all, with the relevant facts of the history of the Chinese Communists' rise to power. Their own words reveal that they understand the present world situation and their hopes for world revolution in terms of their own successful revolutionary strategy—surrounding the cities with the countryside.

Understanding the world view and strategy of the Chinese is complicated by the Soviet propaganda effort to depict the CCP leaders as "maniacs bent on promoting world revolution through nuclear war." Moscow depicts itself, of course, as striving to restrain the Chinese "madmen," in hopes that Western leaders will make concessions to strengthen Moscow's hand in its dispute with China. Mr. Tsou argues that "this reading of the Soviet motive is of doubtful validity: The Sino-Soviet dispute is not the primary motive for the Soviet search for a détente with the West. On the contrary, the Soviet search for a détente was itself the basic cause for the Sino-Soviet dispute."

Recent official Peking statements denying the inevitability of nuclear war have led some observers to conclude that the Chinese position has softened and that they now support peaceful co-existence. Mr. Tsou examines the meaning of these denials of the inevitability of nuclear war and shows that for Peking such statements have a special meaning, grounded in the basic theories that guided Mao Tse-tung's joint struggle against the Japanese invaders and the Kuomintang (KMT).

By a brief recounting of the CCP's revolutionary strategy ("united front" with the KMT against the Japanese, and "encircling the cities with the countryside" to defeat the KMT), Mr. Tsou shows its point-by-point correspondence with present-day Chinese international policy and strategy. Mr. Tsou then applies this analysis as a means of answering the major questions: What is Peking's position on the great question of war and peace? What is their policy regarding peaceful co-existence with the United States? What is the real issue in the Sino-Soviet dispute? Is there any way that will serve the interests of the West for the United States to intervene in the Sino-Soviet dispute? Can the United States formulate an effective counterstrategy to oppose the strategy of the Chinese in Southeast Asia and other underdeveloped areas in Asia, Africa, and Latin America, the "countryside" of the world?

And, finally, if we try to look beyond the Cold War, what hope is there "that some form of peaceful co-existence as we understand it in the West may eventually become the basis of relations between the United States and Communist China, and between the Communists and the West"?

TANG TSOU

•

PEKING AND PEACEFUL COEXISTENCE[1]

ON DECEMBER 30, 1963, IN AN INTERVIEW ON THE FRENCH GOVERN-ment-owned television network, Chou En-lai expressed his belief that "a world war opposing the Communist camp against the imperialist camp is not inevitable."[2] But he went on to say that the risk of war remained because of the U.S. policy of "war and aggression." On the question of Sino-American relations, he declared that China sought a solution to differences with the United States; "in the first place a solution to the question of the retreat of American armed forces from Taiwan and the Taiwan Strait by peaceful means without recourse to force or threat of force." Some Western observers and news media immediately seized upon these remarks as an indication that Communist China was changing her position on the fateful question of the inevitability of war.

Actually, Chou merely reaffirmed the long-standing position of the Peking regime, and reiterated the views embodied in the 1957 Moscow Declaration of Communist Parties and the 1960 Statement — documents on which the Communist Party of China has established its line of "no retreat" and bases its counterattacks on the Communist Party of the Soviet Union (CPSU) in the dispute over ideology and

[1]This is a revised version of "Mao Tse-tung and Peaceful Coexistence," which appeared in *ORBIS* (Spring, 1964), a quarterly journal of world affairs published by the Foreign Policy Research Institute of the University of Pennsylvania.
[2]New York Times, December 31, 1963, p. 1.

revolutionary strategy. While Chou's tour of Africa and Europe was a significant diplomatic foray, his remarks on the inevitability of war signify no change in the doctrinal position of the Chinese Communist Party (CCP). The superficial impression to the contrary merely reflects the widespread ignorance in the West about Communist China — in particular, the Chinese position on the question of war and peace.

This ignorance and misunderstanding have been deepened by the Soviet propaganda drive which seeks to depict Communist Chinese leaders as madmen or maniacs bent on promoting world revolution through nuclear war. Whatever the motive behind this propaganda drive, it has had the effect of creating a Western image of a Soviet Union striving desperately to restrain the Chinese from precipitating a nuclear war. It has created the feeling that perhaps the United States should inject itself into the Sino-Soviet dispute on the side of the Soviet Union, or make concessions to the Soviet leaders merely because these concessions would strengthen their hand against the Chinese.

This reading of the Soviet motive is of doubtful validity: The Sino-Soviet dispute is not the primary motive for the Soviet search for a *détente* with the West. On the contrary, the Soviet search for a *détente* was itself the basic cause of the Sino-Soviet dispute. If the Soviet Union had not sought a *détente* with the West in opposition to China's view on revolutionary strategy and at the expense of China's interests, the dispute would not have arisen, or at least it would not have been intensified to such an extent. The Soviet Union seeks and has been seeking a *détente* because Moscow has already pushed its sphere of influence as far as it can by the use of force or threat of force. If this was not obvious to everyone in the mid-1950's, there can be no doubt on this point today. Furthermore, the Soviet Union had scored great gains in the period of cooperation with the United States during the Second World War. It is now possible, psychologically and politically, for the Kremlin to make a few minor concessions to the United States in order to obtain a *détente*. By means of the *détente*, the Soviet Union apparently hopes to consolidate its shaky control over Eastern Europe, preferably through a formal Western recognition of the status quo there; to resolve its many difficult economic problems through the reallocation of resources, expansion of trade with the West and the negotiation of loans from the West; to weaken the Western alliance; and finally to create a better political atmosphere for the strengthening of communist parties in the NATO countries. This

Tang Tsou

search for a *détente* led to the Sino-Soviet dispute. Seeking to make the best of a presumably unwelcome development, Khrushchev managed to turn the dispute into an asset in his dealings with the West.

The United States rightly welcomes a *détente* with the Soviet Union provided that this development does not endanger American interests. From the point of view of the West, the Soviet policy of *détente* and peaceful coexistence is to be preferred to Chinese militancy. Soviet hesitancy to support the rebels in Algeria and South Vietnam was preferable to the more aggressive policy of the Chinese. Soviet pressure on Berlin has been successfully resisted, but the guerrilla warfare waged by the Viet Cong confronts the United States with serious and perhaps insurmountable problems. Yet, for all his talk about peaceful coexistence, Khrushchev surreptitiously placed missiles with nuclear capabilities in Cuba, not for the avowed purpose of defending Cuba against an imminent American invasion, but for the principal aim of overcoming quickly and inexpensively a worldwide strategic inferiority—in order, as Castro said, to "reinforce the Socialist camp the world over."[3] Mao Tse-tung, for all his verbal militancy, showed extreme caution in the Quemoy crisis of 1958, avoiding the use of his air force to bomb the island, taking care that his artillery fire and torpedo boats would not hit U.S. ships, and then declaring a unilateral cease-fire on alternate days.

The Soviet Union, a nuclear superpower which has not hesitated to back up its diplomatic moves in the past with the threat to use nuclear weapons, poses a grave and ever present threat to the security of the United States. This threat would become even more grave and immediate if Washington, under the pressure of a major confrontation with the Kremlin—e.g., a crisis comparable to the Cuban missile showdown—should weaken in its resolution to employ whatever weapons and degree of force are necessary to meet the Soviet challenge. By contrast, the threat posed by Communist China takes the form of a series of minor local military actions and subversive activities which, over a fairly long period of time, might undermine America's position in the underdeveloped areas. Peking is adapting Mao's revolutionary strategy of encircling the cities from the countryside to her struggle against "American imperialism." She is trying to encircle the developed countries with the underdeveloped areas. Peking's

[3] *Ibid.,* December 12, 1962, p. 1. For a detailed anlysis which supports by view, see Arnold L. Horelick, "The Cuban Missile Crisis: An Analysis of Soviet Calculations and Behavior." *World Politics,* April, 1964, pp. 363-389. See also Albert and Roberta Wohlstetter, *Controlling the Risks in Cuba* (London: The Institute for Strategic Studies, 1965).

threat is serious because, up to the present period, the United States has not been able to work out a successful political-military counter-strategy, as the events in South Vietnam forcefully remind us every day. But Peking's strategy does not call for the use of nuclear weapons to promote revolution. It envisages a long series of protracted local military conflicts. The protracted nature of Peking's program gives the United States time to work out a counterstrategy, if we are resourceful enough.

II

THE FIRST PREREQUISITE FOR WORKING OUT THIS COUNTERSTRATEGY is to understand Peking's military-political strategy, including her doctrines of peaceful coexistence and the inevitability of war. In our attempt to understand Peking, we should not rely unduly upon Soviet interpretations. Let us recall that during the Pacific War, U.S. officials and newspapermen developed the thesis that the Chinese communists were "agrarian reformers," sincere democrats, and the like. In so doing, they were trying to understand Chinese communism in Ameri-can terms. They were also influenced by Stalin's remark that the Chinese communists were "margarine communists."[4] At that time, Stalin was sincere in advocating the establishment of a coalition government in China. In order to give the United States a good reason to support the formation of a coalition government, the Soviet leaders insincerely voiced the view that the Chinese communists were not dedicated communists. Khrushchev may very well have been sincere in his search for a *détente* with the West. But he distorted Peking's views on war and peace so as to discredit the Chinese in the eyes of the nonaligned countries and to convince the United States that it should make concessions to him.

In order to make an objective analysis of Peking's views on war and peace, one must first of all understand Mao's views in his own terms. This is no easy task. For unlike political theorists in the West, Mao has not published any systematic writing on the questions of peaceful coexistence and the inevitability of war. But as part of the debate with Moscow, Peking published a series of statements which provide a glimpse of Mao's views. Furthermore, Peking has published many of Mao's writings, from the period between 1926 and 1949, which discuss the question of war and peace with the Nationalist

---

[4]Herbert Feis, *The China Tangle* (Princeton: Princeton University Press, 1953), p. 140. For an analysis of the American image of Chinese communism, see Tang Tsou, *America's Failure in China* (Chicago: University of Chicago Press, 1963), Chapter VI.

Party. If one reads the recent statements from Peking in the light of Mao's earlier writings, and examines the latter in the light of the current political-military situation confronting Communist China, one can reach an understanding of Mao's view of these questions. Although not a truly original thinker, Mao is a careful and meticulous writer whose works deserve thorough analysis. Moreover, his views on the revolutionary strategy of the world communist movement have been shaped largely by his experience in the Chinese revolution. No one can claim to understand Mao's thought on international relations unless he has a firm grasp of Chinese history from 1919 to 1949.

What are Mao's views on the questions of the inevitability of war and peaceful coexistence? How do they differ from and agree with the views of Khrushchev and his successors? What is the source of the Sino-Soviet dispute? The basic and the original source of the Sino-Soviet conflict is a dispute over revolutionary strategy for the world communist movement. Naturally, this dispute involves both questions of ideology and national interests. But the world revolutionary strategy proposed by Peking is less influenced by China's national interest than by its revolutionary experience. It is, as a matter of fact, a direct projection to the international arena of Mao's political-military strategy in the struggle with Generalissimo Chiang in the Chinese revolution.[5] In the present debate over the questions of peaceful coexistence and the inevitability of war, the Chinese arguments follow closely Mao's analysis of strategy and tactics in the period between 1937 and 1945, when an anti-Japanese united front existed between the Chinese Communist Party and the Nationalist Party. Mao's policy was to uphold the united front, or in other words, "peaceful coexistence" with Chiang, as a shield behind which he pushed forward his program of armed struggle against the Kuomintang.

By 1937 Mao had developed a strategy of surrounding the cities with the countryside, because the Kuomintang's hold on the cities was firm and incontestable while its control over the countryside was weak and vulnerable. It is a new version of this strategy which Mao proposes to use to defeat the United States. Mao realizes that the power of the West in the developed areas cannot be challenged successfully for the time being, but he believes its position in the underdeveloped areas is weak and vulnerable. His strategy calls for the world communist movement to concentrate its energy and resources on the under-

[5]Tang Tsou and Morton H. Halperin, "Mao Tse-tung's Revolutionary Strategy and Peking's International Behavior," *American Political Science Review*, March, 1965, pp. 80-99.

Peking and Peaceful Coexistence

developed areas of Asia, Africa, and Latin America in order to promote national liberation movements and revolutionary civil wars. Soviet leaders have had little experience and aptitude for this sort of warfare. Their attention is centered on Eastern and Western Europe and the United States. They attach less importance to the underdeveloped areas as an arena of struggle.

This controversy over priorities and the relative importance of the various parts of the world has taken the form of a debate over "the main contradictions of our time," and where these contradictions are concentrated. Soviet leaders charge that the CCP has put forward a "new theory." They assert:

> According to this new theory the main contradiction of our time is . . . contradiction not between socialism and imperialism, but between the national liberation movement and imperialism. The decisive force in the struggle against imperialism . . . is not the world system of socialism, not the struggle of the international working class, but again the national liberation movement.[6]

In rebuttal, the Chinese argue that

> Of course the contradiction between the socialist and capitalist camps is undoubtedly very sharp, but Marxist-Leninists must not regard the contradictions in the world as consisting solely and simply of the contradiction between the two camps. . . . The fundamental contradictions in the contemporary world are the contradictions between the socialist camp and the imperialist camp, the contradiction between the proletariat and the bourgeoisie in the capitalist countries [so far so good from the Soviet point of view, but the Chinese add these other things], the contradictions between the oppressed nations imperialism, and the contradictions among the imperialist countries and among the monopoly capitalist groups.

Moreover, the Chinese add (and this is the significant point):

> . . . the various types of contradictions in the contemporary world *concentrated* in the vast areas of Asia, Africa, and Latin America; these are the most *vulnerable* areas under imperialist rule and the storm centers of world revolution dealing direct blows at imperialism. . . . In a sense, therefore, the whole cause of the international proletarian revolution *hinges* on the outcome of the revolutionary struggles of the people of these areas, who constitute the overwhelming majority of the world's population. . . . Today the national liberation revolutions in Asia, Africa, and Latin America are the *most important forces* dealing imperialism direct blows.[7]

[6]*Peking Review,* October 25, 1963, p. 10.
[7]*Ibid.,* June 21, 1963, pp. 7, 9. (Italics added.)

Tang Tsou

This theory of the concentration of contradictions in the underdeveloped areas echoes Stalin's explanation of the success of the October Revolution. According to Stalin, although Russia was not a highly developed industrial society, all the contradictions in the era of imperialism found concentrated expression in Russia. Russia was the weakest link of imperialism.

That Peking's global strategy is a direct projection of Mao's strategy developed in the Chinese civil war — of surrounding the cities from the countryside — was officially revealed to us, at first, in an indirect way. At the Second Plenum of the Seven Central Committee of the Communist Party of Indonesia held between December 23 and December 26, 1963, Chairman D. N. Aidit declared:

> On a world scale, Asia, Africa, and Latin America are the village of the world, while Europe and North American are the town of the world. If the world revolution is to be victorious, there is no other way than for the world proletariat to give prominence to the revolutions in Asia, Africa, and Latin America, that is to say, the revolutions in the village of the world. In order to win the world revolution, the world proletariat must "go to these three continents."[8]

Interestingly enough, the idea expressed in these sentences was not mentioned in the page-long summary of this speech printed in the *Jen-min jih-pao* on December 31.[9] But the March 27, 1964, issue of the *Peking Review* carried excerpts of the resolution by the plenum approving Aidit's report. After affirming that the contradiction between the oppressed nations and imperialism is "the major one" and after repudiating the idea that "'Europe is the centre' [of the world revolutionary storm], as maintained by certain persons," the resolution declares:

> The plenum attaches great importance to the conclusion of the political report that from a world-wide viewpoint, Asia, Africa, and Latin America represent the *countryside* of the world, while Europe and North America are its *cities*; that in order to win the victory of world revolution, the world proletariat must assign an important place to revolutions in Asia, Africa and Latin America, that is to say, to the revolutions in the *countryside* of the world.[10]

It is generally agreed that the Indonesian Communist Party had been moving ever closer to the Chinese position in the Sino-Soviet dispute. The fact that extracts of this resolution were reproduced in the *Peking Review* indicates that these statements reflect the views of the CCP, or received its approval.

[8]D. N. Aidit. *Set Afire the* Banteng *Spirit! Ever Forward, No Retreat!* (Peking: Foreign Language Press, 1964), p. 87.
[9]*Jen-min jih-pao,* December 31, 1963, p. 5
[10]*Ibid.,* March 27, 1964, p. 17 (emphasis added).

Peking and Peaceful Coexistence

Peking, of course, also sees the prospect that the arena of struggle will shift from the underdeveloped areas to the developed areas, just as the arena of struggle shifted from the countryside to the cities in the final phase of the Chinese revolution. An article by the editorial departments of the *People's Daily* and the *Red Flag,* commenting on the open letter of the Central Committee of the CPSU, declared:

> The center of world contradictions, of world political struggles, is not fixed but shifts with changes in the international struggles and the revolutionary situation. We believe that, with the development of the contradiction and struggle between the proletariat and the bourgeoisie in Western Europe and North America, the momentous day of battle will arrive in these homes of capitalism and heartlands of imperialism. When that day comes, Western Europe and North America will undoubtedly become the center of world political struggles, of world contradictions.

This statement can best be understood in the light of Peking's belief that by waging national liberation wars and revolutionary civil wars in the underdeveloped areas, the revolutionary peoples are actually helping the proletariat in their struggle against the bourgeoisie.

If there remained any doubt over the substance of Peking's global strategy, it was dispelled by an article written by Lin Piao, a Vice-Chairman of the Central Committee, a Vice-Premier, and the Minister of National Defense, to commemorate the 20th anniversary of the surrender of Japan. This most revealing and most important doctrinal pronouncement on global political-military strategy since the establishment of the regime was published at a time when the rapid build-up of American forces in South Vietnam and their increasingly active participation in the war had caused the Viet Cong's 1965 monsoon offensive to lose its momentum, and had begun to arrest the further deterioration of an already dangerous military situation and when American planes had been bombing military targets in North Vietnam for over half a year. At this time also, Khrushchev's successors showed little willingness to adopt Peking's views on global strategy, and the Sino-Soviet split appeared irreparable, at least in the near future. These circumstances called for a public and authoritative exposition of Peking's global strategy which would justify its insistence on the continuation of the war in Vietnam, further challenge the Soviet views, and hold out the hope of ultimate victory. The result was Lin Piao's article.

Lin Piao emphasized that "Comrade Mao Tse-tung's theory of the establishment of rural revolutionary base areas and the encirclement of the cities from the countryside is of outstanding and *universal* practical importance for the present revolutionary struggles of all the oppressed nations and peoples, and particularly for the revolutionary struggles of the oppressed nations and peoples in Asia, Africa, and Latin America against imperialism and its lackeys," and that "the basic political and economic conditions in many of these countries have *many similarities* to those that prevailed in old China."[11] In these individual countries, "the countryside, and the countryside alone, can provide the revolutionary bases from which the revolutionaries can go forward to final victory." "Taking the entire globe, if North America and Western Europe can be called 'the cities of the world,' then Asia, Africa and Latin America constitute 'the rural areas of the world.'" "In a sense, the contemporary world revolution also presents a picture of the encirclement of the cities by the rural areas. In the final analysis, the whole cause of world revolution hinges on the revolutionary struggles of the Asian, African, and Latin American peoples who make up the overwhelming majority of the world's population."[12] At present, the vast area of Asia, Africa, and Latin America is "the main battlefield of the fierce struggle between the people of the world on the one hand and U. S. imperialism and its lackeys on the other." The revolutionary storms in this area have become "the most important forces pounding U. S. imperialism." The contradiction between the revolutionary peoples of Asia, Africa, and Latin America and the imperialists headed by the United States is "the principal contradiction in the contemporary world."[13] Because of the inadequacy of its resources the United States is vulnerable to the struggles waged by different peoples which reinforce each other and merge into a world-wide tide. "The more successful the development of people's war in a given region, the larger the number of U. S. imperialist forces that can be pinned down and depleted there. When the U. S. aggressors are hard-pressed in one place, they have no alternative but to loosen their grip on others." The peoples of Asia, Africa, Latin America, and other regions can destroy the colossus of the United States "piece by piece, some striking at its head and others at its feet." Nuclear weapons cannot save the United States because they cannot be used lightly and because "in the final analysis, the outcome of a war will be decided by the sustained fighting of the ground forces, by fighting at close quarters on battlefields, by the political consciousness of the men, by their courage and spirit of sacrifice."[13]

[11]*Peking Review*, September 3, 1965, p. 24 (Italics added). Excerpts of this important article are reprinted in *The New York Times*, September 4, 1965, p. 2.

[12]*Peking Review*, September 3, 1965, p. 25.

[13]*Ibid.*, pp. 25-26.

Peking and Peaceful Coexistence

Peking obviously attributes great theoretical significance to Mao's global strategy. In an editorial celebrating the sixteenth anniversary of the founding of the People's Republic of China, the *Jen-min jih-pao* employed a new formulation on Mao's contribution to Marxism-Leninism. It claimed for Mao not only the credit of "integrating the universal truths of Marxism-Leninism with the concrete practice of China's revolution," as the CCP had been doing for many years, but also the distinction of "integrating the universal truths of Marxism-Leninism with the concrete practice of world revolution."[14]

Since Peking's global strategy is to encircle the developed areas with the underdeveloped areas, she accords a higher priority in her foreign policy to the support for these movements than to improvement of relations with the West. An analysis of the international situation in 1961 as printed in *The Bulletin of Activities* of the People's Liberation Army reads:

> Toward national liberation movements in colonial and semi-colonial countries, there are two different attitudes. One makes the improvement of relations with the West a primary concern and does not support or gives small amount of support to the national liberation movements. The other makes support for national liberation movements a primary concern. It permits some proper dealings with the Western countries but considers this a secondary question. Our country adopts the latter attitude, firmly supporting the national liberation movements and opposing colonialism and imperialism. We may have dealings with Western countries but do not bargain away our support for national liberation movements.[15]

Peking's policy is actively to cultivate close relationships with countries in Asia, Africa, and Latin America, but not the Western countries, particularly the United States. In 1961, Africa was considered to be the center of the anticolonial struggle. "When the time is ripe, a revolutionary upsurge will engulf the African continent."[16] In September, 1965, Lin Piao declared that the war in Vietnam "is now the focus of the people of the world against U. S. aggression," and that "Vietnam is the most convincing example of a victim of aggression defeating U. S. imperialism by a peoples' war."[17] Even the ques-

---

[14]*Ibid.*, October 1, 1965, p. 10.

[15]*Kung-tso t'ung-hsün (The Bulletin of Activities)* No. 17 (April 25, 1961), p. 22 *The Bulletin of Activities* is a journal, designed for the reading of the cadres of the People's Liberation Army at the regimental level and above. Twenty-nine issues covering the period from Jan. 1 to Aug. 26, 1961, were released by the U.S. Department of State in 1963. Hereafter cited as *The Bulletin of Activities*.

[16]*Ibid.*, p. 23.

[17]*Peking Review*, September 3, 1965, pp. 27, 29.

tion of Taiwan is viewed in the broad context of the world-wide struggle against the United States in which "one incautious move will cause the loss of the game."[18] If Communist China, "a newly emerging socialist country," should yield to the United States and allow imperialist forces to occupy her territory, Taiwan, "her international prestige will drop ten thousand feet."[19] By refusing to compromise on the issue of Taiwan and by keeping Sino-American relations in a stalemate, "we can keep the anti-imperialist banner, freely support the national liberation struggle in the colonial and semi-colonial countries, preserve our ability to attract political support, and stimulate our morale."[20]

The military-political strategy which Mao developed during the Chinese civil war and the Sino-Japanese War can be readily applied to the national liberation wars and revolutionary civil wars. The strategy of fighting guerrilla and mobile warfare with popular support does not depend for its success on modern weapons or vast financial resources, which the Communist Chinese lack. It depends rather on an ability to turn the nationalism of the colonial or anti-colonial countries, and the nationalism of the newly-independent countries, against the Western powers. It relies on exploiting the political instability, economic chaos and social turmoil in these countries, manipulating the grievances of the oppressed classes, mobilizing the masses for political-military actions, organizing them into structured groups, offering them political leadership, and guiding them with a "correct" political-military strategy. This expertise which the Chinese acquired in twenty years of struggle can be passed along through the training of new cadres. Marshal Yeh Chien-ying declared:

> No other nation in the world has more experience [in fighting a war] than we. . . . The nations which have not yet been liberated also want to overthrow imperialism and feudalism . . . and to wage armed struggle. They very much need our experience. Therefore, we should sum up our experience to hand it down to posterity and to present it to our friends.[21]

The Chinese strongly emphasize that national liberation wars and revolutionary civil wars are just wars. These wars are unavoidable. It is the duty of communist parties to give them all necessary support. Peking therefore upholds the doctrine of the inevitability of war

[18]*Ibid.*, p. 20.
[19]*Ibid.*, p. 25.
[20]*Ibid.*, p. 24.
[21]*Ibid.*, no. 12 (March 10, 1961), p. 4.

insofar as this is applied to these two kinds of war. "Revolutions are not possible without wars of national liberation or revolutionary civil war. To say otherwise is opposed to revolutionary wars and to revolution."[22] The Chinese Communist leaders are highly self-conscious of their revolutionary mission. The late Marshal Lo Jung-huan told the cadres in the Political Academy in October, 1960: "At present, revisionism is spreading. The world revolution relies on the thought of Mao Tse-tung. . . . [The thought of Mao Tse-tung] belongs not only to China but also has its international implications."[23]

III

UNTIL JANUARY, 1961, KHRUSHCHEV'S THESIS WAS, TO USE BURIN'S succinct summary, that "the absence of war will not slow down the world revolutionary process, that in the future revolution will be possible without war."[24] He probably believed that a world communist victory could and would be achieved through nonmilitary forms of struggle. Khrushchev certainly feared that armed struggle, including revolutionary civil wars and national liberation wars, would escalate into a nuclear war. In the spring of 1960, official Soviet statements contained a few hints suggesting that it would be undesirable for revolutionary struggles to be carried on so vigorously as to lead to a danger of world war.[25] Under attack by the Chinese, however, Soviet leaders conceded a point. In January 1961, Khrushchev declared that national liberation wars are unavoidable. He said: "Liberation wars will continue as long as imperialism exists; wars of this kind are revolutionary wars. Such wars are not only justified, they are inevitable, for the colonialists do not freely bestow independence on peoples."[26]

This concession did not halt the polemics. To carry out its global strategy, Peking must energetically support national liberation wars and revolutionary civil wars — despite the danger that these wars could escalate into a major confrontation or local war between the two camps, and even into a world war. Although they accept the inevitabil-

[22]*Peking Review,* June 21, 1963, p. 13.

[23]*The Bulletin of Activities,* No. 8 (February 2, 1961), pp. 16-17.

[24]Frederic S. Burin, "The Communist Doctrine of the Inevitability of War," *American Political Science Review,* June, 1963, p. 352.

[25]Harry Gelman, "Russia, China, and the Underdeveloped Areas," *Annals of the American Academy of Political and Social Science,* September, 1963, p. 132.

[26]G. F. Hudson, *et al., The Sino-Soviet Dispute* (New York: Praeger, 1961), pp. 211-213.

ity of national liberation wars, Soviet leaders are more cautious than the Chinese in supporting them. In the ideological debate, Khrushchev's formulation on the avoidability of local wars seemed to be one means by which he sought to escape from the dilemma between his desire to support national liberation wars and his fear of a military confrontation with the West. Khrushchev stated that "local wars in our time are very dangerous," and "we will work hard . . . to put out the sparks that may set off the flames of war."[27] Khrushchev's formulations suggested that he was willing to support national liberation wars only so long as these wars would not lead to a local war between the two camps. Khrushchev's reluctance to support revolutionary civil wars and national liberation wars was shown in Algeria, the Congo, and even Vietnam.

The Chinese believe that Moscow's formula on the avoidability of local war is essentially "an attempt to oppose revolution in the name of safeguarding peace."[28] They use the following argument against the Soviet position:

> In recent years, certain persons have been spreading the argument that a single spark from a war of national liberation or from a revolutionary people's war will lead to a world conflagration destroying the whole of mankind. . . . Contrary to what these persons say, the wars of national liberation and the revolutionary people's wars that have occurred since World War II have not led to world war. . . . The victory of these revolutionary wars has directly weakened the forces of imperialism and greatly strengthened the forces which prevent the imperialists from launching a world war and which defend world peace.[29]

Peking's revolutionary strategy of encircling the developed countries with the underdeveloped areas does not call for a world war or a nuclear war between the United States and the Soviet Union. Far from proclaiming the inevitability of war between the two camps, the Chinese communists have consistently discounted the danger of a world war.[30] As far back as 1946, when there was talk of a war between the Soviet Union and the United States, Mao minimized this possibility. He indicated his belief to Anna Louise Strong that "the U.S. and the Soviet Union are separated by a vast zone which includes many capitalist, colonial and semi-colonial countries in Europe, Asia and Africa. . . . Before the U.S. reactionaries have subjugated these

---

[27]Quoted in a Chinese statement, *Peking Review*, October 25, 1963, p. 9.
[28]*Ibid.*
[29]*Ibid.*, June 21, 1963, p. 14.
[30]Burin, *loc. cit.*, p. 348; *Peking Review*, November 2, 1963, pp. 9-10.

countries, an attack on the Soviet Union is out of the question."[31] By this remark, Mao meant that the immediate political-military struggle between the two camps would not take the form of a war between the United States and the Soviet Union but rather a struggle to control the intermediate zones. This appraisal of U.S. intentions reflected his own concept of global strategy against the United States. Peking uses the formula of the avoidability of world war to justify the strategy of pushing national liberation wars and revolutionary civil wars in the underdeveloped areas. Again, they are projecting their past experience to the present. They reason as follows: In spite of the fear of "certain people" over the outbreak of a third world war, the Chinese communists fought and defeated the Nationalists in the period from 1946 to 1949. There is no reason why revolutionary wars in other underdeveloped areas against imperialists and their lackeys cannot be won even though there is again talk of a world war. To bolster the argument for militancy, Peking stresses the theme that by struggling against the imperialists, the working classes and the forces of peace can prevent the imperialists from launching a world war.

IV

BUT MAO'S WRITINGS SHOW A VERY COMPLICATED MIND: WHAT IS SAID IS not always exactly what is meant. In spite of the professed belief in the possibility of avoiding a world war, there is an awareness of the fact that intensified struggle may increase the danger of a world war. Thus the argument is that

> while pointing to the possibility of preventing a new world war, we must also call attention to the possibility that imperialism may unleash a world war. Only by pointing to both possibilities, pursuing correct policies and preparing for both eventualities can we effectively mobilize the masses to wage struggle in defense of world peace. Only thus will the socialist countries and peoples and other peace-loving countries and people not be caught unawares and utterly unprepared should imperialism force a world war on the people.[32]

In calling attention to this possibility, Mao was undoubtedly influenced by his experience with the April 12, 1927, coup staged by

[31]Mao Tse-tung, *Selected Works* (Peking: Foreign Languages Press, 1961), p. 196. Yu Chao-li asserted: "The real and direct contradictions of the world since the war are not contradictions between the Soviet Union and the U.S. The Soviet Union and the U.S. can and are actually coexisting peacefully. The imperialist reactionary cliques are only using the rumor that war may break out at any moment as a smokescreen to hide their schemes to control the world and apply pressure on their own people." *Red Flag*, March 30, 1960.

[32]*Peking Review*, November 23, 1963, p. 10.

Chiang, which caught the Chinese Communists totally unprepared. He must also have remembered that his careful preparations for the outbreak of large-scale civil war in the 1940's helped him to win the civil war when it finally erupted in 1946. In the present instance, however, Mao's statement was designed to prepare the Communists psychologically for any eventuality and to demonstrate to the imperialists his dauntless courage, rather than as contingency planning for a world war of which there are no visible signs.

Having admitted the possibility of a nuclear world war, Peking is concerned that the fear of a nuclear holocaust may lead to capitulation, or at least inhibit revolutionary actions in the underdeveloped areas. They apparently believe that they can dispel this fear by proclaiming the survival and triumph of the socialist system after the nuclear catastrophe. They also feel that by loudly proclaiming this view, they will also make it less likely that the United States will launch a nuclear war. It is in this context that Mao spoke about half of mankind dying in a nuclear war, and the other half remaining to build socialism on the ruins of a world destroyed by a war launched by the imperialists.

> If the imperialists dare to launch nuclear war and plunge mankind into such an unprecedented disaster, what should the international proletariat do? It is perfectly clear that there are two alternatives, either to resist imperialism firmly and bury it, or to be afraid of sacrifice and to capitulate. But some people believe that if nuclear war breaks out all mankind will perish. In reality, such talk amounts to saying there is no alternative to capitulation in the face of imperialist nuclear blackmail. Directing himself to this pessimistic and capitulationist talk, Comrade Mao Tse-tung pointed out that mankind will definitely not be destroyed even if the imperialists insist on a nuclear war with the possible sacrifice of hundreds of millions of people and impose it on mankind. The future of mankind will nevertheless be a bright one.[33]

In other words, Mao went much further than Herman Kahn in thinking the unthinkable. He made the unthinkable thinkable by picturing the unthinkable as a bright future for socialism.

For all the talk about building a bright future on the ruins of a nuclear war, Peking does not think of nuclear weapons as offensive

---

[33]*Ibid.*, July 26, 1963, p. 27. In November, 1957 at the Moscow meeting of Communist Parties, Mao said: "The question has to be considered for the worst. The Political Bureau of our Party has held several sessions to discuss this question.... If the worst came to the worst and half of mankind died, the other half would remain while imperialism would be razed to the ground and the whole world would become socialist; in a number of years there would be 2,700 million people again and definitely more." *Ibid.*, September 6, 1963, p. 10.

weapons. Peking has gone on record in opposition to a first strike: "A socialist country absolutely must not be the first to use nuclear weapons, nor should it in any circumstances play with them or engage in nuclear blackmail and nuclear gambling."[34] This last assertion was obviously an allusion to the Cuban affair. Nuclear weapons cannot be used to support people's revolutionary struggles or national liberation wars. Nor should a socialist country use them first against an imperialist country which wages a conventional war of aggression.[35] China wants to manufacture nuclear weapons as "the means of resisting U.S. nuclear blackmail."[36] These positions remain unchanged after Peking successfully detonated an atomic device on October 16, 1964.[37]

V

WHAT, THEN, OF THE OTHER SIDE OF THE COIN, THAT IS, PEACEFUL coexistence? To reconstruct Peking's views, we must again look at Mao's revolutionary strategy, particularly during the period between 1937 and 1946. Mao's strategy throughout the whole period of the Chinese revolution was to encircle the city with the countryside. This strategy unfolded in three different phases during which the relations between the Kuomintang (KMT) and the CCP underwent important changes. During the first phase, the CCP fought an all-out civil war with the KMT. When the CCP faced the possibility of total defeat, it sought peaceful coexistence with the KMT by proposing to form an anti-Japanese united front with the Nationalists.

During the second phase, from 1937 to 1945, a united front (read for the term "united front," "peaceful coexistence") existed between the KMT and the CCP. During this period of united front or peaceful coexistence with the KMT, the Chinese Communists also sought to form a broad united front *against* the KMT. Under the protection of the policy of maintaining a united front with the KMT, the Communists rapidly pushed forward their strategy of encircling the city with the countryside by expanding their control in the rural areas behind the Japanese lines. They fought many limited local military engagements against KMT forces while maintaining the policy of united front and negotiating with the KMT. This strategy was based on several judgments made by Mao. First, so long as the Sino-Japanese War continued, the united front (i.e., peaceful coexis-

---

[34]*Ibid.*, November 23, 1963, p. 12.

[35]*Ibid.*, p. 13.

[36]*Ibid.*, September 6, 1963, p. 9.

[37]*Ibid.*, October 16, 1964, pp. ii-iii; October 23, 1964, p. 6; October 30, 1964, pp. 6-7.

tence) could be maintained, and there would not be an all-out civil war. In other words, the Sino-Japanese war not only resulted in a stalemate between China and Japan but also created a stalemate between the KMT and the CCP. This political-military stalemate formed the basis of the united front or peaceful coexistence between the two parties. Second, united front meant not only unity with the KMT but also struggle against it. Struggle against the KMT was, Mao argued, one way to maintain the united front: the KMT could be deterred from breaking the united front by the growing strength of the CCP and by the use of this strength in waging a limited struggle against the KMT. Third, the main form of the struggle against the KMT during this period should be peaceful political struggle in the sense that the CCP should not take any action which would lead to the outbreak of a general war, and that the CCP should strive to maintain the united front. But peaceful political struggle did not preclude armed struggle on a limited scale. Fourth, if an all-out civil conflict should occur, the Chinese Communists could win a protracted war. Peking's present policy of peaceful coexistence bears a close resemblance to Mao's tactics of the united front during this period.

During the third phase from 1946 to 1949, the CCP won a revolutionary civil war against the KMT.

Mao's experience with the united front with the KMT has clearly influenced Peking's doctrine of peaceful coexistence as well as other questions in her debate with Moscow. It should be emphasized that, while Peking's statements on peaceful coexistence are made more frequently in discussing Peking's relations with the nonaligned countries than in discussing Sino-American relations, Peking does not completely reject the possibility of peaceful coexistence with the West, or even with the United States. But she does not envisage peaceful coexistence as a lasting state of affairs—just as Mao did not conceive of the united front with the KMT as anything more than a useful short-term policy. In this, Peking's position is not so different from Khrushchev's as is commonly supposed. For Khrushchev has declared his intention to bury the capitalist system, and there cannot be peaceful coexistence between the corpse and those who bury it. The dispute arose with regard to the method of burying the West. In his pronouncements, Khrushchev emphasizes peaceful competition and economic progress, but in his actions he is not above making such military moves as placing missiles in Cuba, designed to improve the Soviet position in the balance of military power.

Peking emphasizes armed struggle in the underdeveloped areas to encircle the United States, but she is very cautious about taking any military action which might precipitate a direct confrontation with the United States. Despite her caution, Peking does not want peaceful coexistence to hinder in any way the development of revolutionary struggles in Asia, Africa, and Latin America. Thus, she repeatedly has proclaimed that there cannot be peaceful coexistence between oppressed nations and oppressor nations, and that the condition for the success achieved by the national liberation movements after World War II was not peaceful coexistence between the two camps—as the Soviets maintain—but revolutionary struggle on the part of the oppressed peoples. After January 1961, when Khrushchev conceded that national liberation wars are inevitable, the Soviet and Chinese positions drew closer to each other. Moscow specifically denies Peking's charge that peaceful coexistence, according to Khrushchev's formula, applies to the relations between oppressed nations and oppressor nations. Khrushchev's successors have apparently approved the view expressed by P. N. Demichev at a ceremony marking the 95th anniversary of the birth of Lenin, that "the policy of peaceful coexistence does not preclude but presupposes a rebuff to aggression and support for people fighting against alien domination." [38] But Peking has challenged the Soviet prescription that the general line of the political program of the communist movement should be peaceful coexistence. For Peking fears that this formulation would inhibit revolutionary struggles. Peaceful coexistence with the West should not rule out armed struggles in the underdeveloped areas, which constitute a form of struggle against the United States, just as the united front with the KMT did not rule out local military clashes in the countryside.

In Peking's view, peaceful coexistence not only does not preclude conflict but it can be maintained only by waging struggle against the imperialists, just as the united front with the KMT not only did not preclude conflict, but could be maintained only by waging struggle. In this struggle, Peking's policy is

> to unite all the forces that can be united in order to form a broad united front against U.S. imperialism and its lackeys.... It is possible for the socialist countries to *compel* one imperialist country or another to establish some sort of peaceful coexistence with them by relying on their own growing strength, the expansion of the revolutionary forces of the peoples, the united front with the nationalist countries and the struggle of all the peace-loving people, and by utilizing the internal contradiction of imperialism. [39]

[38] *New York Times,* April 23, 1965, p. 1.
[39] *Ibid.,* December 20, 1963, p. 10. (Italics added.)

In maintaining peaceful coexistence with the imperialist countries, it is necessary to enter into negotiations with them. "But it is absolutely impermissible to pin hopes for world peace on negotiations, spread illusions about them and thereby paralyze the fighting will of the peoples, as Khrushchev has done."[40] Sometimes it is necessary for the socialist countries to reach compromises with the imperialists. But "necessary compromises between the socialist countries and the imperialist countries do not require the oppressed peoples and nations to follow suit and compromise with imperialism and its lackeys."[41]

At times, Peking's statements on her relations with the United States have gone beyond this closely reasoned and carefully worded doctrine of peaceful coexistence in their militancy. The analysis of international affairs in *The Bulletin of Activities* describes Peking's relationship with the United States as one of stalemate or coexistence through stalemate as distinguished from peaceful coexistence.[42] A series of events in the fall of 1964 and the winter of 1965 led to a drastic change in Peking's public position on peaceful coexistence with the United States. With the downfall of Khrushchev on October 14, 1964, Peking won the first round in the Sino-Soviet dispute. But the convocation in early March, 1965, by Khrushchev's successors of the "consultative" meeting of the representatives of nineteen Communist Parties confirmed Peking's fear that "Khrushchevism without Khrushchev" prevailed in the Soviet Union.[43] Meanwhile, the intensification and escalation of the war in Viet Nam had plunged Sino-American relations to its lowest point of all time. After the Johnson administration continued to bomb military targets in the southern part of North Viet Nam, Chou En-lai declared on March 29, 1965, that

> peaceful coexistence with the United States imperialism is absolutely impossible. Does one oppose United States imperialism or not? Does one oppose it in earnest or by pretense? This is the main criterion for distinguishing between the Marxist-Leninists and the modern revisionists, it is also a basic question in the struggle against revisionism.[44]

[40] *Ibid.,* September 22, 1963, p. 15.
[41] *Ibid.,* June 21, 1963, p. 15.
[42] *The Bulletin of Activities,* No. 17 (April 25, 1961), p. 20.
[43] *Peking Review,* November 27, 1964, p. 9; March 26, 1965, p. 13.
[44] *Ibid.,* April 2, 1965

Peking and Peaceful Coexistence

With this statement, Peking rejected peaceful coexistence as a useful principle to guide Sino-American relations.

This outright rejection of the principle of peaceful coexistence can be interpreted as a move to provide the ideological basis for urging the North Viet Nam government and the Viet Cong to persist in the struggle in South Viet Nam and to achieve final victory in a protracted and *all-out* war. By taking an extreme position, Peking may also have hoped to force the Soviet Union to adopt a more militant policy toward the United States. At this moment, however, the theoretical and practical implications of this outright rejection are far from clear.

Whether Peking will adhere to the position laid down in Chou's statement of March 29, or revert to her carefully formulated doctrine of peaceful coexistence remains to be seen.[45] In either case, Peking's actions will continue to be governed by the political-military strategy which underlay the original doctrine of peaceful coexistence. Peking will seek to win over gradually the underdeveloped areas and then carry the struggle to the developed areas by promoting conflict between the proletariat and monopoly capital. To implement Mao's strategy it is not necessary to rely on a world war or a nuclear war. But it is imperative, from Mao's viewpoint, that the imperialists be deterred from launching a nuclear war. It is imperative that the communists not be paralyzed by the fear of nuclear war and thus fail to support national liberation wars and revolutionary civil wars.

VI

IF THIS ANALYSIS OF PEKING'S STRATEGY IS CORRECT, THEN PEKING POSES a threat to the United States in that she advocates the promotion of world revolution not through nuclear war or through the precipitation of a nuclear war between the United States and the Soviet Union, but rather through a global strategy which exploits what she believes to be the most vulnerable chink in America's global armor. In South Viet Nam, Washington has failed so far to devise a political-military program which can defeat the armed struggle waged by the Viet Cong, who have adopted Mao's political and military strategy. If the

---

[45] On April 27, 1965, Peking again warned that there could be no question of peaceful coexistence with the United States. *New York Times,* April 28, 1965, p. 14.

United States and South Viet Nam can win the war against the Viet
Cong, they will have demonstrated to Peking that her strategy can be
countered. Repeated success in coping with her strategy will induce
second thoughts in Peking—if not in the mind of Mao, then in the
minds of other Chinese leaders. Mao's strategic concepts, a vital part
of Mao's thought and prestige, will in time be eroded. This is a more
desirable, though more difficult, way of intervening in the Sino-Soviet
dispute than to make concessions to the Soviet Union in the expectation that these concessions might strengthen her hand against Peking.
If the Chinese are forced to abandon or to modify Mao's strategic
doctrine, some form of peaceful coexistence as we understand it in
the West may eventually become the basis of relations between the
United States and Communist China, and between the Communists
and the West.

Laurence Martin, in his essay on the Western alliance, spoke of *a certain underlying uncertainty in strategic formulations: "One is struck by the extent to which complex strategic conclusions are colored by the basic hunch of the author as to whether major war is a remote contingency or an ever-present possibility." For the United States, the "hunch" about the remoteness or closeness of major war has depended, for two decades now, on our evaluations of Soviet behavior and intentions. Myron Rush, in this essay on the Soviet leadership's manipulation of international tension, shows how deeply careful observation and analysis can penetrate the seemingly random fluctuations of Soviet policy, how far we can progress in substituting understanding for "hunches."*

The engineering of international tension may, of course, be a very old technique of international politics, but it takes on a new significance in our age because of the constant danger that any crisis may result in global nuclear warfare. The necessity for study of strategic uses of tension is well stated by Herman Kahn: "Most research analysts believe that any thermonuclear war . . . is likely to be preceded by a very tense crisis. . . . During an intense crisis, possibilities for inadvertent war increase." Kahn adds that there has been too little study of "the intense crisis situation in which it is important to stand firm or even deliberately to risk or threaten strategic war."

In this essay, Mr. Rush studies Soviet behavior in crisis situations, explaining how and why the Soviet leadership seeks to generate crises, and — more important — the limits they set for themselves in determining when to tighten the tension and when to relax it. He sets forth the rationale which establishes both the lower limits of relaxation and the upper limits of military and political tension.

There is some comfort in the indications that Soviet leaders seem eager to avoid general nuclear catastrophe, but no comfort in the realization that an important reason for their choice not to run nuclear risks is their confidence of achieving their goal without general war. According to Mr. Rush, the Soviet bloc has gained and retained the political offensive in the Cold War because their goal is simple and clear, especially as compared to the vagueness and complexity of ours.

This line of reasoning raises the question of whether levels of international tension are reliable indicators of the likelihood of general war. Does relaxation of tension indicate any alteration of Soviet objectives, especially the Soviet determination to communize the world? In short, does a period of relaxation of tension indicate the approach of the end of the Cold War or its basic transformation?

MYRON RUSH

●

SOVIET POLICY
AND
INTERNATIONAL TENSION

THAT MODERN WEAPONS HAVE ALTERED THE CHARACTER OF INTERNA-
tional politics is hardly questioned, but the nature of the change is in
dispute. Many observers believe that nuclear weapons and their
related delivery systems have given rise to acute international tension,
a situation which will almost certainly result finally in a catastrophic
world war. Others believe that by deterring the Communist leaders
the new weapons establish a reliable basis for preserving the present
peace. My object here is not to judge these opposing views, but to
consider an issue that lies near the root of the disagreement: the effect
of modern weapons on tension in the Cold War, and the effect that
tension has had on Soviet policy.

A useful starting point for this inquiry is a remark of Nikita
Khrushchev, which he made to a Communist audience in an improvised talk in mid-1962, when he still ruled in the USSR.[1]

> What kind of international situation do we have? As for our socialist
> countries, we consider it good. You will say: "What is good about it if
> such a row is taking place in the world?" Yes, we shall continue to
> have struggles. The struggle can assume so to speak, the shape of
> high tension, or low tension, but this struggle can stop only when all
> the means of production are in the hands of the working people.
> Taking this into account, then, we have a good situation. They
> frighten us with war, and we frighten them back bit by bit. They
> threaten us with nuclear arms and we tell them: "Listen, now only
> fools can do this, because we have them too. . . . So why do foolish
> things and [try to] frighten us?" This is the situation, and this is why
> we consider the situation to be good[2]

[1]While this essay was written to account for Soviet policy in the period of
Khrushchev's rule, which ended in 1964, it does not appear, six months after his ouster,
that his successors mean to effect a fundamental change in his foreign policy.

[2]Foreign Broadcast Information Service, *Daily Report*, East Europe, May 16, 1962,
p. KK3. The text of this speech, delivered the previous day in Maritsa-East, Bulgaria,
was not published in the Soviet press.

Soviet Policy and International Tension

According to the Soviet leader, despite the ups and downs of tension, the situation is "good." His words do not express deep apprehension about the state of the world, or, in particular, about rises in the level of tension; on the contrary, he shows remarkable equanimity. Khrushchev's apparent composure, at least on this occasion, contrasts strikingly with the widespread belief in the West that nuclear weapons are a principal cause of international tension and with the widespread fear that any sharp rise in tension might be followed by further rises that could well culminate in general war and the destruction of civilization.

This contrast gives rise to several questions. Have Soviet leaders really felt the equanimity that Khrushchev expressed? If so, why this difference between the two sides?

As ordinarily understood, "international tension" refers to the acute concern of nations or leaders who believe the national security to be endangered by other states and their heightened readiness to act to reduce this danger. Before the invention of thermonuclear weapons, the threat to a nation's security was closely associated with the likelihood of war. While the opposing sides might assess the likelihood and the hazards of war differently, both sides were strongly affected by this prospect of war. For the most part, acute international tension resulted from the apprehension of war in the not distant future. Now, however, with the advent of thermonuclear weapons and their possession by the two principal powers in the Cold War, the relation of international tension to the expectation of war has become less direct and more complicated.

Since both sides in the Cold War believe that the destructiveness of modern war has substantially reduced its likelihood, the direct and immediate danger of general war has not been a principal source of international tension during the past decade. Nevertheless, because destructive power of the new weapons has brought in question not only the security but the very existence of the great powers in the event of war, the fear that nuclear war could come about in certain circumstances has strongly affected both sides. The effect has been pervasive, however, influencing actions that were unlikely to *precipitate* war, but might ultimately *lead to* war. Since the effect of nuclear weapons on the two principal powers has been so largely indirect, it has been mediated by the distinctive political character of each. A crucial fact about the present situation, yet one that is sometimes disregarded, is that the advent of nuclear weapons has affected the United States and the Soviet Union quite differently.

The Soviet leaders have been convinced by the advent of thermonuclear weapons that they must avoid actions that appreciably raise the risk of general war. Khrushchev has said this almost in so many words: "We always seek to direct the development of events so as to ensure that, while defending the interests of the socialist camp, we do not provide the imperialist provocateurs with a chance to unleash a new world war."[3] This recognition of the need for restraint has not led the Soviet leaders to conclude that they must give up their goal of a Communist world, but rather to conclude that it can be achieved without a new world war. "In contemporary conditions," according to Khrushchev, "the prospect is opened of achieving peaceful coexistence for the entire period in the course of which the social and political problems that now divide the world must be solved";[4] but for a Communist, the only way to solve these problems is by the world wide victory of Communism.

Acquisition during the 1950's of some capacity to attack the United States directly has given the Soviet leaders a sense of security; it has made them confident that, in the absence of actions on their part which greatly provoked the West, the danger of the outbreak of world war is slight. This is reflected in two new doctrines: that world war is no longer "fatally inevitable," and that the victory of socialism in the USSR is "final."[5] This sense of the *peril* that could result from violent moves, and of the *security* that could be had by abstaining from such moves, has set limits to the levels of tension that are acceptable to the Soviet leaders.[6]

The sense of peril establishes an upper limit, or ceiling, on tension. It is the level at which, it is believed, further Soviet pressure would sharply raise the risk of provoking a response that might significantly increase the likelihood of nuclear war. The Soviet leaders doubtless have no precise notion as to the degree of tension that would bring them close to the ceiling; what matters is that they have

---

[3]*Pravda*, January 19, 1961.

[4]Report of the Central Committee to the XXII Party Congress, October 17, 1961.

[5]Until 1959 it had been thought that the final victory of socialism in the USSR required the disappearance of the imperialist camp, but at the XXI Party Congress, Khrushchev declared that there was no longer a force in the world capable of overturning it.

[6]A sense of these two extremes of *security* and *peril* is conveyed by an editorial in the theoretical journal of Communist Parties: "Imperialism is no longer in a position to change the world balance in its favor.... But it is still able—at the cost of its own destruction—to halt progress and throw humanity back for tens or perhaps hundreds of years by plunging the world into a nuclear holocaust" *(World Marxist Review,* [December 1962], p. 3).

thought this question too dangerous to explore. On the other hand, since they have been confident that there was little likelihood of war resulting from moderate, carefully controlled pressure on the West, the Soviet rulers have seen no need to reduce international tension below a lower limit, or floor. Thus the limits on their pressure against the West have been set by their unwillingness to forego gains that might be had without serious risk and by their unwillingness to raise significantly the likelihood of war. Soviet tactics in the Cold War seem to have been governed by a strategy of restricting fluctuations in international tension to the intermediate range between floor and ceiling.

Two questions arise: What is the evidence for the feeling of confidence among the Soviet leaders that the likelihood of war remains small so long as international tension remains below the ceiling level? And what are the grounds of their confidence?

Premier Khrushchev's expressed equanimity, despite fluctuations in international tension, has already been quoted. Moreover, he has stated on a number of occasions that only a madman would initiate nuclear war and has expressed his confidence, at least since 1959, that the West was deterred from attacking the Communist world. More weighty than these words, however, are Soviet deeds, particularly in the military realm. Although during the past decade the United States has possessed a capacity to devastate the USSR, the Soviet Union did not, at least until recently, give high priority to achieving a comparable capability against the United States.

By the mid-fifties, the Soviet Union had already developed intercontinental means of delivering weapons. Two types of heavy bombers capable of reaching United States territory, the Bison and the Bear, were displayed to the world in 1954 and 1955. They gave rise to fears that the USSR would rapidly acquire a force of hundreds of these bombers which would threaten the United States with complete destruction. Within a few years, however, it appeared that this was not happening, that the USSR was not trying to match SAC's rapidly increasing force of B-52's. By the late fifties a new threat to the United States emerged; the ICBM. This time the Soviet leaders did not actually display the new weapon before the world. However, they claimed in 1957 to have successfully developed an ICBM and proceeded to convince many observers that this was so by launching their Sputniks. Thus was born the famous "missile gap." United States fears, expressed then and subsequently, were not groundless. If the Soviet leaders had given top priority to the production and deployment of

ICBM's, it is reasonable to suppose that they might have had large numbers of operational ICBM's by the early 1960's, in advance of the United States. Whatever the military efficiency of these weapons, they would have posed a serious threat to the United States. As it turned out, however, the Soviet ICBM build-up proceeded far more slowly than it might have. As a result, by 1962, the USSR was faced with the missile gap that we ourselves had feared. Moreover, the inferiority of their ICBM force was aggravated by the continuance of a very substantial bomber gap.

Having early developed vehicles for delivering nuclear weapons to other countries, why did the Soviet leaders allow themselves to fall so far behind the United States in the operational force needed to strike at the main opponent? Whatever the limitations on Soviet resources and capacities, it cannot be said that the USSR has been skimping on defense spending. It has spent huge sums on air defense and on acquiring an overkill capacity against West Europe. The USSR need not have fallen so far behind the United States in intercontinental capabilities if its leaders had feared that this would jeopardize the country's security.

That the Soviet leaders thought it possible to spare themselves the costly effort to reduce the West's overwhelming superiority in intercontinental forces can only mean they did not fear we would attack them without cause; moreover, they were resolved not to give us cause. Evidently the West's great strategic superiority, which reached high points in the mid-fifties and early sixties, did not put the Soviet leaders in a state of acute tension.

Having developed at great cost delivery vehicles which could attack the United States with thermonuclear warheads, the Soviet leaders decided to forgo the substantial additional expense required to make them operational in large numbers. Their confidence that they could obviate war was such that for a time they sought to deceive the West regarding the size of their missile capability instead of actually procuring a large force. Moreover, when their deception, owing to Soviet secrecy and the spectacular Soviet space program, had a measure of success which unintentionally stimulated the United States military effort, the USSR put up (at least for a time) with the adverse missile gap that resulted; their assurance was such that they made no effort to reduce existing tensions by offering concessions, or even by ceasing to threaten the West.[7]

[7]See *Strategic Power and Soviet Foreign Policy,* by Arnold L. Horelick, and Myron Rush, scheduled for publication February, 1966 by the University of Chicago Press.

Soviet Policy and International Tension

More than this, in the face of United States strategic superiority during the past decade, the Soviet leaders have repeatedly shown themselves willing to raise tension sharply by new political offensives, which have in fact been the chief cause of tension in the Cold War. Sharp rises in tension were caused by Soviet actions, for example, on the following occasions:

1. Soviet blockade of Berlin in 1948;
2. The series of moves ("salami tactics") in East Europe, 1945-1950;
3. Communist attack on Korea in 1950;
4. Soviet suppression of popular rebellion in East Germany following Stalin's death in 1953;
5. Soviet suppression of revolt in Hungary in 1956 and threatened action against the Polish regime at about the same time;
6. Soviet termination of disarmament talks in London a few days after announcing that an ICBM had been successfully flight-tested (August, 1957);
7. Soviet establishment of successive deadlines (May, 1959, the end of 1961) for a peace treaty with East Germany;
8. Soviet construction of a wall to prevent East Germans from escaping into West Berlin (August, 1961);
9. Soviet resumption of nuclear testing in September, 1961, which broke a three-year moratorium;
10. Installation of Soviet strategic rockets in Cuba in 1962;
11. Interference with the West's access to Berlin in the fall of 1963 and again in the spring of 1965.

(On several occasions — the 1954 Viet Minh offensive in Indo-China and the Quemoy Crises of 1955 and 1958 — Chinese, rather than Soviet, Communists were probably responsible for rises in tension between the great powers.)

Each of these actions was subsequently followed by an easing of tension, or *détente,* brought about by the USSR either because of the quick success achieved (2, 4, 5, 8, and 9), or because the Soviet leaders believed it unwise to prolong a state of acute tension. On several occasions tension in the Cold War rose because of actions taken, or threatened, by the West, but these are not numerous (see pp. 145-146). In each case, the Soviet response was notably restrained, partly, no doubt, because of a desire to prevent the escalation of tension to a point where, in Khrushchev's phrase, it might be difficult "to direct the development of events."

It should be observed that while tension has most frequently become acute because of Soviet actions, on several occasions these actions were largely *defensive* in character (4, 5, and 8), and not Soviet *initiatives* (1, 2, 3, 6, 7, 9, 10, 11).

From this brief survey it is apparent that the USSR has been the chief source of fluctuation in tension, *both rises and declines,* in the Cold War. While the existence of nuclear weapons, and in particular United States supremacy in them, has induced the Soviet leaders to set a limit on international tension, they have displayed confidence that they could raise tension safely so long as they stayed well short of this limit, controlling the risk of war if necessary by timely retreats or even concessions. When they have underestimated the boldness of the United States response, thus inadvertently raising international tension close to or above the intended ceiling, they have relieved tension by a prudent retreat.

Even when placing great pressure on the West, as in Cuba and Berlin, the Soviet leaders acted less vigorously and provocatively and with greater circumspection than they otherwise might have because of their concern about the ultimate danger of general nuclear war.

Granted Soviet confidence that they could control the tensions they create, how could they be sure that their strategy of limited offensives directed against a power that has possessed great strategic superiority would not suddenly spark nuclear war? They have relied, first, on the lack of bellicosity of the American people and its leaders. Second, they have relied upon secrecy to obscure the full extent of United States strategic superiority. Both expectations appear to have justified themselves; these matters, however, have to do with the effect of nuclear weapons on the United States and are treated in what follows.

Like the Soviet response to the advent of thermonuclear weapons, the response of the United States has been conditioned by its basic political aims. Broadly speaking the United States seeks to maintain the prevailing liberal political system in the West, so far as this can be done, and to preserve the independence of the newly emergent nations while helping them to progress by means of economic aid and other measures. That is to say, the United States (and in varying degree the West as a whole) seeks to preserve the basic structure of the present international system, while trying to reform it. The reforms aim chiefly at increasing the unity of West Europe, at moderating the Communist regimes, and at elevating the role of law in international affairs — all to be achieved at a steady pace and without violence if possible. The Soviet objective, as noted earlier, is much more far-reaching; not the preservation of a modified *status quo,* but the ultimate achievement of a Communist world—the only world, they say, in which peace can be assured.[8] On the part of the West, it seems clear that no serious effort has been made to liberate countries under Communist domination or to deprive the Communist nations of territories that they now occupy.

This basic difference in the aims of the two sides has allowed the USSR to take the political offensive in the Cold War. In some ways, the advent of thermonuclear weapons has amplified the primary differences between the two sides. The Soviet leaders have been confident that they could control the risk of war so long as they kept tension below a certain level. While that level has not been known to them precisely, this has caused no great uncertainty so long as they stay well below it, as has been their intention. The touchstone of Soviet policy has been this confidence; uncertainty, however, has tended to pervade the deliberations of the West.

The United States has been uncertain and concerned about the growth of Soviet strategic capabilities. As a result it has tended to exaggerate the pace and scope of the Soviet program for acquiring delivery vehicles with which to attack the United States, first in the case of heavy bombers (after 1954), then in the case of ICBM's (after 1957). The effect of this uncertainty has been to distort United States perceptions of the strategic balance, largely by obscuring the overwhelming United States superiority and making it appear instead that the USSR would soon achieve parity, if it did not already possess it.

Being uncertain about the strategic nuclear balance, the United States has found it difficult to assess the aims of particular tactical moves made by the Soviet leaders. Moreover, since the USSR has generally had the political initiative, the United States has often been uncertain where the next blow might fall. While Soviet leaders have been confident that war would not result from their particular moves, United States leaders have been uncertain as to the risks involved in alternative countermoves and have therefore tended to respond cautiously. This, in turn, has strengthened Soviet reliance on United States restraint in the Cold War and increased Soviet confidence in its ability to control tension and the risk of war stemming from its actions.

On several occasions, United States *countermoves* have contributed to a rise in tension, as when the United States threatened to intervene against Communist insurgents in Indo-China (1954) and in Laos

[8]"[C]ompromise is admissable only if it furthers the basic *strategic objective* ... the world wide victory of Communism ..." (Editorial. *World Marxist Review,* [December 1962], p. 3).

(1961), moved troops into Lebanon after the revolution in Iraq (1958), and established a partial blockade of Cuba (1962). But the tension declined as it became apparent that the United States had achieved its objective, or was unlikely to do what it threatened. Western *initiatives* have also increased tension on occasion, particularly the basing of the Strategic Air Command overseas, the crossing of the thirty-eighth parallel in Korea, the rearmament of West Germany, and the U-2 flights.

Western actions have generally been designed to cope with some perceived danger and have raised tension only inadvertently. Not infrequently, however, Soviet leaders have deliberately raised tension, as a tactic of pressure to compel the West to make unilateral concessions. This is particularly evident in their policy on Berlin, where they have deliberately maintained tension as a means of eroding the Western position. This tactic has found more general expression in the Soviet policy of nuclear threats against Western Europe, which has had the effect of maintaining tension without seriously risking war. If, as is frequently observed, the Soviet leaders have presented the West with good words more than good deeds, it is also true, paradoxically, that they have been more guilty of bad words (threats) than bad deeds. The relation of words to deeds in the nuclear age is different from what it was formerly, and the difference has yet to be fully explored.

Major Western moves that have raised tension—whether they were initiatives or responses to world developments—have generally been met with Soviet restraint.[9] This is understandable in view of what was said earlier of Soviet fears that tension might rise to a level where it would be difficult to control further developments. Until the mid-sixties, at any rate, lack of preparedness for nuclear war made the Soviet leaders extremely unwilling to accept serious risk of its occurring. For this reason, rises in tension produced by actions of the two sides have *not* tended to reinforce each other, thereby producing an upward spiral. The Soviet desire to maintain a ceiling on international tension has tended to dampen, rather than to amplify, secondary rises in tension. Moreover, even when the USSR has brought about an acute state of tension, as for example over Berlin, the Soviet leaders have been unwilling to prolong it, preferring to abate tension after a time rather than to risk losing control over developments.

Soviet acquistion of nuclear weapons has perhaps encouraged

---

[9]An important exception, of course, was the Soviet reaction to the U-2 flights after May Day, 1960; yet even then, they took care to limit exacerbation of relations with the United States.

the USSR to maintain pressure on the West and to probe for weak spots, but only as long as the probing was unlikely to produce rises in tension of a kind that might rapidly spiral out of control. The nuclear balance effectively discourages Soviet probing of the final limits of the West's forebearance. The Cuban crisis of October 1962, while appearing to challenge this generalization, really provides its strongest support. No doubt the effort to place strategic rockets in Cuba was the boldest Soviet move yet in the Cold War; however, in view of the adverse strategic balance which the rockets in Cuba were to help rectify, the Soviet leaders are unlikely to have undertaken it unless they were virtually certain that the United States would not respond by attacking the USSR. The alacrity with which Khrushchev agreed to withdraw the rockets in the face of strong United States resistance illustrates the extreme Soviet concern to avoid sharp secondary rises in tension.[10] According to the Soviet Central Committee, the USSR refused "to follow in the wake of 'the madmen' ...and *embark upon the road* of unleashing a world thermonuclear war."[11]

Despite the demonstrated readiness of the Soviet leaders to *initiate* rises in tension, then, there is some truth in their declared unwillingness to "accept the challenge of the imperialists to a *competition* in adventurism and aggressiveness";[12] that is, to participate in a series of moves and countermoves that could culminate in war.

To revert to a point made earlier: An important reason why tension has not been a good indicator of the immediate likelihood of general war is simply that the Soviet leaders have sought to avoid any rise in tension that might significantly increase the risk of war. Moreover, since the Soviet leaders for a long time put up with great United States strategic superiority, evidently the tension they have felt has not been due to fear that an attack was imminent, or that developments outside their control might bring about such an attack in the near future. Rather, in so far as United States strategic power has created a problem for the Soviet leaders, it has chiefly done so by confronting them with a great obstacle to the achievement of their strategic objectives and of their final goal which is world communism.

The fact that the United States has maintained a capacity to

---

[10]"It is now perfectly clear that the blockade [of Cuba] was but the first phase and was to be followed by direct intervention with the aim of overthrowing the people's government" *(World Marxist Review,* [December 1962], p. 5).

[11]Open letter of the Central Committee to Party organizations and Communists of the Soviet Union, July 14, 1963. Emphasis supplied.

[12]*Ibid.* Emphasis supplied.

Myron Rush

destroy targets in the Soviet Union far exceeding the Soviet capacity to attack the United States does not necessarily mean that the United States defense effort has been excessive or wasteful. If, despite our great superiority in strategic forces and the consequent need for the USSR to minimize the risk of war, the Soviet leaders have been on the offensive in the Cold War, attacking our interests at many points throughout the world, what might they have done had they not feared our power to destroy the Soviet Union?

The Soviet strategy of maintaining pressure on the West but preserving a ceiling on international tension has been one of the chief sources of disagreement between Soviet and Chinese Communists. They disagree as to how far tension might be increased by Communist initiatives and retaliatory actions without unduly increasing the risk of thermonuclear war.[13] Mao Tse-tung apparently sees no need for the ceiling on international tension established by the Soviet leaders. "I believe none of us [i.e., the Communists] need fear international tension. I personally like international tension. . . . In some countries there exists the prejudice that international tension is unfavorable for the peoples. But in conditions of international tensions, Communist Parties can develop more rapidly, the tempo of their development can be more rapid.[14]

In this polemic Soviet leaders have seemed to argue that the present danger of war is relatively small, in any case it is controllable; moreover, so long as Communist policy does not become more agressive the risk will remain small. Highly provocative Communist actions, such as those demanded by Communist China, however, would cause a great rise in tension and seriously increase the likelihood of war.[15]

Chinese Communists have disagreed on both points. First, they say that the evil nature of imperialism creates a greater risk of war than the Soviet leaders will admit.[16] Next, they argue that no appreciable

---

[13]"The Soviet Central Committee has the impression . . . that the leaders of the C.P.C. [Communist Party of China] regard the preservation and intensification of international tension — especially in the relations between the USSR and the U.S. — to be to their advantage" (*ibid.*).

[14]Quoted by a leader of the Costa Rican Communist Party, E. M. Val' Verde, in *Izvestia,* June 19, 1964.

[15]The Chinese Communist leaders "apparently hold that the Soviet Union should reply to provocations with provocations, fall into traps set by the wild men from the imperialist camp . . ." (*ibid*).

[16]The central committee of the Chinese Communists has asked: "How can war be abolished?" and answered on the authority of Lenin, " 'By abolishing the division of mankind into classes'. . . . However, certain persons [viz., Khrushchev] now actually

increase in the likelihood of war would result from stepped-up pressure on the Western world; rather, the opposite. Any policy other than that of vigorous revolutionary struggle "will only encourage the ambitions of the imperialists and increase the danger of world war." Revolutionary wars do not create sparks that can ignite a world conflagration, but strengthen "the forces which prevent the imperialists from launching a world war." While the Russians believe the stability of mutual deterrence depends upon the avoidance of severe political and military shocks, the Chinese leaders assert that the present strategic balance is proof against shocks administered by Communists. The way to lessen the risk of world war, the Chinese Communists imply, is by accepting the risk of lesser wars. They accuse the Soviet leaders of having ceased to be revolutionaries because of fear of nuclear war.

The Soviet leaders acknowledge that fear of nuclear war has affected the means they have employed on behalf of revolution.[17] They say that the revolutionary process will proceed on its own momentum, assisted by prudent Soviet support; but they argue that "provocative" support for revolution by the USSR would risk thermonuclear war. No doubt their understanding of what is "provocative" was excessively narrow when they made their 1962 decision to place strategic missiles in Cuba, but the resistance they encountered has probably led to a broadening of the Soviet definition of provocative action. While remaining committed to world revolution, then, the Soviet leaders have ruled out the use of means which the Chinese Communists assert, with some reason, to be necessary. The resulting disproportion between means and end is unlikely to endure. It may lead either to the employment of more forceful means or to a further reduction in the fervor with which the Soviet leaders pursue the goal of world revolution.

The dispute with Communist China narrowed somewhat Khrushchev's room for maneuver. Instead of simply threatening the West with Soviet missiles, as he did for several years after Sputnik, Khrushchev was compelled to emphasize the destruction *both* sides would suffer in a world war. This reversal was reinforced by the rapid

---

hold that it is possible to bring about 'a world ... without wars' while the system of imperialism ... still exists. This is sheer illusion" (Letter to the Central Committee of the Soviet Communist Party, June 14, 1963).

[17]"Prevention of nuclear war has become a precondition for carrying out the world socialist revolution in a way that would not jeopardize civilization ..." (B. N. Ponomaryov, "Some Problems of the Revolutionary Movement," *World Marxist Review,* [December 1962], p. 9).

Myron Rush

growth of United States missile capabilities, as well as by the increased United States awareness of its margin of strategic superiority. After Cuba, Khrushchev reluctantly gave up his hopes of making large political gains against the West with inferior strategic forces. He now initiated a policy of *détente,* which must be distinguished from his previously employed *tactic* of reducing tension whenever it threatened to rise too high. The new policy required Khrushchev to cease instigating crises that sharply raised tensions; moreover, the level of tension that he felt obliged to maintain as a sign of revolutionary ardor was reduced.

An important consequence of this new policy of *détente* was the signing in mid-1963 of the treaty banning nuclear tests, excepting those conducted underground, a treaty which the USSR had repeatedly rejected in recent years. Soviet agreement to the treaty was doubtless meant to isolate the Chinese Party within the world Communist movement on the question of "consolidating peace" and lessening the danger to mankind from nuclear weapons. However, it was also designed to ease tensions with the West, and particularly with the United States. Doubtless the Soviet leaders hoped that lessened tension would encourage divisions in the NATO alliance; but this motive was also operable during the years when the USSR rejected the West's terms for a test-ban treaty.[18] The test-ban treaty was not followed by new initiatives; however, the USSR continued to avoid moves that might sharply raise tension.

Whether Khrushchev meant the policy of *détente* to be a lasting one we will never know, inasmuch as he fell from power. How strongly his successors are committed to such a policy remains to be seen.

Programs for reducing tension should begin by taking account of the past, of the justified Soviet assurance of security as long as the USSR does not provoke the United States. To make this one's starting point is not to deny the peril that exists so long as sovereign states possess nuclear weapons, but only to suggest that this state of affairs is not intrinsically intolerable. It may continue for some time without a disaster. This does not absolve us of the obligation to seek ways, together with the USSR, that will help us jointly to escape our common peril. But if the West is not faced with an immediate catastrophe, it need not simply leave the road it is now on to strike out

[18]It might be supposed that the delay was due to the Soviet need to conduct atmospheric nuclear tests. This was doubtless a contributory factor during the period of preparation for the series of nuclear tests in the fall of 1961, but it cannot account for the continuing Soviet rejection of the West's proposals after completion of the series.

on the dubious paths advocated by unilateral disarmers, on one side, and by bellicose cold warriors, on the other.

Were we to change our objectives, were we to decide that "victory" in the Cold War requires putting an end to communism in all the countries where it is now sovereign, then the West might become as great a source of international tension as the Communist world is now. If we believed it necessary to resort to extreme measures of defense and retaliation in defending our interests, this would give rise to new dangers. Indeed, it is by no means certain that the groups in the West who call for "victory" in the Cold War by wiping communism from the face of the earth really desire the strategy of counterpressure that would be required to bring this about, or that they are prepared to accept the risks and attendant dangers which would accompany such a policy. In any case, they are not a dominant political force in the West.

While the "cold warriors" want the West to use its strength in political offensives that would heighten international tension and might substantially increase the risk of war, other groups have opposed efforts to resist Soviet pressure and have urged acceptance of Soviet terms in arms control negotiations in order to achieve a *détente*. Certainly the West, in seeking to abate the Cold War and to eliminate the nuclear peril, must try to bring about a modification of Soviet objectives; but a decline in tension will not of itself alter Soviet objectives. On the contrary, in so far as a reduction in tension stemmed from the West's lack of vigor in defending its interests, the Soviet leaders might begin to doubt that extreme pressure on the West would raise tension close to the ceiling level they have so far tried to avoid. The Soviet leaders would then be encouraged to reinforce their commitment to the goal of a Communist world and to employ more violent means to that end.

Still, we cannot suppose that simply holding the line against communism will of itself assure that Soviet objectives will be modified. In certain circumstances, successfully holding the line could lead to an increased resort to violence to overcome the resistance encountered. For this reason, we should aim at maintaining a margin of strategic superiority over the Soviet Union, with the object of preventing a future resort to violent means for the achievement of Soviet objectives. *We* may need strategic superiority because we seek only to preserve and improve the present international system; *they* can do with less because they have the initiative and are confident that we will not attack them except under the most extreme provocation. At the same time it should be our aim to avoid exacerbating the arms race.

Strategic superiority can probably be maintained without accelerating the race unless Soviet defense policy becomes something different from what is has been.[19]

There are forces working in the Soviet Union and in world communism in general that may help bring about an alteration of the extreme Soviet objectives that generate tension in the world. Soviet society exhibits a great thirst for improved material standards of life; intellectuals stand opposed to arbitrary Party control over the works of the mind; de-Stalinization has given vent to the revulsion of Soviet youth against the Stalinist principle, which made his crimes possible, of abandonment of truth as a fundamental criterion; the technical "intelligentsia," who were increasingly subordinated to the heavy hand of Khrushchev's Party machine, have a considerable political potential which they may yet be able to realize; the minority nationalities, or at least the intellectuals and politicians among them, are still subjected to close control by Russians and are repeatedly purged. These dissident forces exist, but they are unlikely to have great political effect unless certain internal and external preconditions are realized. Internally, there must be a weakening of the cohesion of the Soviet rulers, such as is most likely to occur in a crisis of succession to the dictator's power.[20] Externally, communism must be prevented from expanding, as it was able to do in the half-decade following the last war. Only if containment succeeds (in a flexible, not a literal, sense) are dissident forces likely to bring about an alteration of Soviet objectives.

As regards the *past,* simply because there has been no recent war and no development of the factors that would make for a war in the near future, it could be said that on balance nuclear weapons have been a "good thing." As regards the *future,* on the other hand, we cannot know for certain that war will not come. We cannot even be sure that the Soviet leaders will preserve their equanimity in the face of United States nuclear superiority.[21] Therefore, we cannot suppose that nuclear weapons are a good thing in themselves, to be maintained and increased throughout all time. On the contrary, if we could wish

[19]Circumstances may arise in which the two objectives—strategic supremacy and avoiding an accelerated arms race—are in conflict: This problem cannot be resolved in principle but only by a prudent weighing of pro's and con's.

[20]See Myron Rush, *Political Succession in the USSR* (New York: Columbia University Press, 1965).

[21]Khrushchev's confidence that the United States would not attack the USSR without extreme provocation has not been wholly shared by some top military leaders in the USSR.

them away (along with the knowledge of how to make them) without endangering our security during the period of their disappearance, no reasonable person ought to be against it. But since they cannot be disposed of in this way, the practical question is whether the likelihood of war is so great or so certain that whatever dangers might be involved in getting rid of such weapons pale in comparison. Actually, the danger of unilateral disarmament, or of any agreement to ban the use of nuclear weapons based largely on trust of the Soviet Union, is far greater than the danger we now face. United States nuclear capabilities have deterred the Soviet leaders from pursuing their objectives so forcefully as to appreciably increase the risk of thermonuclear war. The resulting ceiling of tension that has prevailed during the past decade of Cold War may be projected with some measure of confidence into the near future.

EVER SINCE THE END OF WORLD WAR II THERE HAS BEEN CONTROVERSY IN the West about the nature of the Cold War and what our policy should be in relation to it. Some have urged that the West take a hard line, to seek to "win" the Cold War; others have urged that all of our efforts be directed toward ending it on some basis of mutual accommodation, and still others have persistently argued that there really is no Cold War except as we create it by unwarranted attitudes of hostility and suspicion.

But common to all Western positions have been the fervent and impatient desire and aspiration to do away with the Cold War. Our search has been to find some way to end or modify the Cold War. Gregory Grossman, in this essay on the Communist economies, begins by pointing out that the Soviet leadership and population have long been accustomed to the sort of situation we call Cold War, and have not only survived but prospered on it for years.

Mr. Grossman examines questions deeply significant for those who try to see beyond the Cold War. How well do the Communist economies operate to help the Communist bloc move forward toward their great objectives? And what signs are appearing in their economies that indicate an end to or modification of the Cold War?

Judged by the standards of non-Communist economists, the Soviet economy is seen to be in grave trouble, primarily because of the major conflict of centralization and decentralization. As Mr. Grossman ably points out, politics and economics are so inextricably entwined as, alternately, cause and effect that there is always a dire price to pay, hard to evaluate and perhaps even impossible to quantify, for every decision to decentralize some aspect of the Soviet economy — as well as every decision not to.

A political decision to relax Cold War tensions, for whatever international political benefit might be sought, has inevitable and profound effects on the economy, of two kinds, which Grossman calls reallocation effects and institutional effects. Relaxation of tension encourages the "liberalizers" in the Soviet society, which seems inevitably to lead to countermeasures of repression and a return to centralization.

In view of this observed process in the past, Mr. Grossman then considers the prospects of a trend toward a socialist "market economy" in the Soviet bloc. A market economy would not necessarily indicate a significant political alteration, for we know that market economies have often been accompanied by regimes of political oppression. But a major change in the economies of the Soviet bloc in the direction of lessened centralization could indicate a modification in the Cold War.

What are the prospects of basic changes in the Soviet Union such as, for example, the economic changes in Yugoslavia after 1948, the decollectivization of Polish agriculture, and the moderation of the role of the secret police in the Soviet bloc nations since the death of Stalin?

Brief periods of relaxation of tension have not had lasting effects on Soviet society; but might a major détente tend to strengthen the centrifugal forces within the Soviet bloc? There have already been major changes in the economies of other Communist nations. Can they occur in the Soviet Union, too? Our

154

actions can delay or thwart changes in the Soviet economy that could modify the Cold War. Is there a course of strategy we might devise to influence internal Soviet developments and hasten improvements in the international situation?

Gregory Grossman

•

THE SOVIET ECONOMY AND THE WANING OF THE COLD WAR[1]

I

The Cold War is a less unfamiliar and less unhabitual state of things for the Soviet Union, its leaders, and its people, than it is for us. The Communist regime has been in a political and ideological conflict of varying intensity, when not in a shooting war, with most of the rest of the world ever since its advent to power in Russia in 1917. For most of this period the Soviet economy, together with the rest of the Soviet society and polity, has been more centralized and mobilized for the prosecution of national goals than was the American economy even at the height of World War II. Thus, the Cold War necessitated no redefinition of the peace-time role of central government in the economy or of the peace-time pattern of resource use in the USSR, as it did in the United States.

But if the Cold War is not a new problem for the Soviet economy, neither is it a static one. At least as much as in the case of any other major power, there is a complex reciprocal relationship between the dynamics of the Soviet Union's international situation and the growth and systemic evolution of its economy. And since the United States is the USSR's chief politico-military antagonist, its main rival for the attention of other countries, and the reference standard for its own economic success, clearly our foreign policy and the guided and

[1]The author is grateful to Professors Andrzej Brzeski, Robert W. Campbell, and Carl A. Landauer, as well as to the participants of the conference, for valuable comments on this paper.

Gregory Grossman

unguided fortunes of our economy have considerable and far-reaching bearing on the Soviet economy and on Soviet behavior in the international arena. The question to which we address ourselves here is, then, the following: assuming the continued gradual waning of the Cold War, what are the likely effects on the Soviet economy and especially on its institutional structure? If we do not simultaneously inquire into the equally significant converse question—what are the likely effects of internal economic transformation on the USSR's "posture" in foreign relations?—it is not for lack of appreciation of its legitimacy but because it has tended to receive more speculative attention in the West in recent years than the one we are posing.

True, as this essay is being readied to go to press, in May 1965, there is a distinct setback in the improvement of relations between the Soviet Union and the United States owing to the intensification of military action in Viet Nam and the outbreak of the Dominican crisis. Nonetheless, barring a catastrophic turn of events, the gradual waning of the Cold War is not unlikely to resume with time, reinforced as this process has been lately by deep Sino-Soviet differences and the more fluid situation in both Eastern and Western Europe. Our question thus remains topical. More than that: the timeliness of our question is sharply enhanced by the fact that the institutions of the Soviet economy, still essentially Stalinist despite a decade of tinkering by Mr. Khrushchev, have been subjected to a crescendo of serious criticism on many levels and from many directions within the USSR itself in recent years. The Soviet economy may well be on the threshold of major systemic transformations—or at least within sight of them, historically speaking. The removal of Mr. Khrushchev from power in October 1964 does nothing to dispel this impression.

II

LIKE ANY LARGE FORMAL ORGANIZATION ANYWHERE, THE SOVIET economy is continually in search of more effective organizational forms, and especially in search of a better balance between centralization and decentralization. The very growth of the economy and the advance of technology, if nothing else, render the context a highly dynamic and changeable one, while the sheer size of the economy makes the organizational problem particularly acute. On one hand, the great degree of resource mobilization, the urgency of the regime's goals, and the need to maintain a minimal balance in the absence of a market mechanism call for a high degree of central supervision and administration. On the other hand, prompt adjustment to changing conditions, the harnessing of local initiative and ingenuity, effective innovation, and the avoidance of cost and delays of over-centralization require that decision-making be to some degree delegated and dispersed. These considerations are intimately interwoven with the preferences and aspirations of certain groups (such as managers), a variety of vested interests, the exigencies of socio-political control, and the dictates of doctrine and dogma.

Following some limited decentralization in the first five years after Stalin's death, since 1958 the trend has been pronouncedly in the directions of greater re-centralization of all sectors of the economy and greater complexity of the hierarchic organizational structure. At present, the Soviet economy is in most respects no less centralized than at the time of Stalin's death. This is not the place to describe the precise developments,[2] but since the tendency is closely related both to some longer-term forces within the Soviet economy and to the Cold War, a brief look at the underlying factors is in order.

The immediate cause of the continual reorganizations is the very unsatisfactory performance of the Soviet economy in the eyes of the country's leaders. Of the profound disappointment there can be no doubt; nearly every pronouncement by Mr. Khrushchev, his lieutenants, and his successors in recent years has dwelt on economic problems in mordantly critical or sarcastic terms. The flagging growth rate and lagging technical progress are, of course, in the center of attention, but behind these dynamic problems lie numerous "static" defects which range from neglect of state property and of state interests, through bureaucratic inertia, to inept planning and administration. Agriculture contains its own panoply of problems—nearly everything is wrong in that sector—but all the other parts of the economy are by no means paragons of efficiency. For instance, construction causes much concern to the regime, being simultaneously a sector that is crucial for growth but whose performance is difficult to plan and control centrally. Research and development is another such activity. The growing pressure on resources heightens the urgency of greater resource mobilization, starker enforcement of priorities, and avoidance of waste. Lastly, the very growth of the economy and the progress of technology rapidly increase the range of choices to be

---

[2]A brief summary of reforms, as well as the record of Soviet economic growth, during the first post-Stalin decade may be found in Gregory Grossman's essay in William Peterson, ed., *Realities of World Communism* (Englewood Cliffs, N.J.: Prentice-Hall, Inc., 1963).

made, the number of products to be considered, and the multitude of interconnections to be kept in mind and "planned" within the vast bureaucratic hierarchy.

Not surprisingly, the result is a "creeping" recentralization of planning and economic administration, and progressive proliferation of various coordinating, planning, and administering authorities. Consequently, the Soviet economy today is an exceedingly complex and highly centralized hierarchical structure, within which communication is very slow, coordination is very poor, local initiative and consumer interests are repressed, and in whose interstices black markets and illicit private gain thrive despite the threat of heavy penalties. If under these conditions the Soviet economy continues to expand, this is chiefly a tribute to the incessant pressure from above, the enormous resources channeled into growth (investment, training, etc.), and the fact that the growth process itself has been bureaucratically routinized. (The last is probably one of the Soviets' more important social inventions.)

It may be asked: Why then does not the regime radically decentralize the economy? The answers are not hard to find. Substantial further delegation of functions to intermediate levels, as the Kremlin well knows, would result in greatly enhanced regional or sectoral autarky, which is doubtless undesirable both politically and economically. On the other hand, if the decentralization were to delegate large powers all the way down to the factory, mine, retail shop, etc., it would not be effective unless accompanied by drastic institutional reforms and revisions in the price structure — in sum, unless a socialist market mechanism (at least for short-term decisions) were instituted — and this the regime is apparently not yet prepared to "buy" for various ideological and political reasons, nor are certain vested bureaucratic interests prepared to welcome. And economic decentralization raises the specter of socio-political liberalization, which many powerful elements in Soviet society oppose. The Cold War is surely relevant here. So long as the military, economic, and political contest with the West continues, there will be internal pressures and arguments for strong (and stronger) central controls over both the economy and the citizen.

Nonetheless, the issue is far from dormant in the USSR at present. Though it is not yet openly discussed in the press and literature — indeed, the very word is shunned — only the most obtuse of Soviet citizens would fail to recognize far-reaching decentralization as at least a possible remedy to many of the economy's ills. So must have Mr. Khrushchev himself, if he meant even half the uncomplimentary things he said about his bureaucrats; so must his successors, judging by their cautious early steps. Moreover, decentralization has been perhaps the most significant *implicit* policy issue in the intense recent debates among Soviet economists and planners, even if these debates have ostensibly revolved largely around abstruse subjects and are covered by a heavy over-burden of Marxist terminology, scholasticism, and (now increasingly) mathematics. There are those who would arm the central planners with input-output models and electronic computers to allow them to do their work better and faster despite the growing complexity of the economy. Others would furnish rational prices to planners in order to facilitate optimal decisions. This in itself need not have institutional significance, but the appearance of such prices eliminates a major argument against delegating decisions to the periphery, and, with proper institutional facilities, an efficient socialist market economy becomes technically possible. Yet other economists advocate the enlargement of managers' powers, setting up profit as the chief criterion of the enterprise's successful performance, which it now is not, and rendering the price structure more responsive to demand and supply.

The last point of view received much attention in the fall of 1962 with the publication and subsequent wide discussion of an article in *Pravda* by a professor of economics, E. Liberman.[3] A significant "experiment" in the spirit of "Libermanism" was launched in July 1964, still under Mr. Khrushchev, when two garment factories were directed to produce in response to demand from retail stores rather than according to centrally set output quotas and to be guided by profit in doing so. Early in 1965, the practice was extended (by Khrushchev's successors) to some 400 enterprises in the garment and shoe industries, and in industries serving these. Other "experiments," having as their common features some enlargement of the enterprise's autonomy, decentralization of output determination, and greater guiding and stimulating role of profit, have also been started in the Soviet Union and in a number of the Soviet-type economies of Eastern Europe. A rather pragmatic and hard-headed search is on for more supple and effective forms of planning and economic administration, for new stimuli, such as profit and profit-sharing, and for new rules of managerial behavior. While these attempts proceed within the matrix of an otherwise highly centralized and rigid "com-

---

[3]See Alec Nove, "The Liberman Proposals," *Survey,* XX, No. 4 (December 1963), 734-44. Liberman and his followers avoided speaking of decentralization, let alone of the market mechanism. Besides, his proposal seems to us to have been too partial to result in a viable arrangement.

mand economy" that eschews the market mechanism, they are clearly testing the applicability of limited—and eventually perhaps quite extensive—market relations to a state-owned economic machine.

In this connection, two other and far vaster experiments in Eastern Europe are of the greatest significance. One is the Yugoslav experiment, in effect already since the early fifties, on which more presently. The other is the sweeping Czech reform promulgated in January 1965 which has created (at the time of this writing still only on paper) a kind of "socialist market economy": a kind of profit motive, market relations between enterprises (amalgamated into large units for this purpose), prices that are mostly controlled but hopefully responsive to demand and supply, and other features of the market economy. It was a very serious economic crisis that induced the Czech leaders—not without much hesitation and, according to rumor, with a nudge from Mr. Khrushchev—to embark on this radical course. In effect, Czechoslovakia is conducting a kind of laboratory test of the greatest significance for the whole Soviet bloc.[4] Or, perhaps more precisely, it is testing a variant of the Yugoslav model of the socialist market economy, a variant that is stripped of the two politically least palatable features for a Soviet-style dictatorship— namely, autonomous workers' councils (which may erode the Party's power) and decollectivised agriculture.

Thus, the existence of the Yugoslav paradigm, much maligned in the rest of Eastern Europe for over a decade, has already turned out to have influenced institutional developments within the Soviet bloc itself. Yugoslavia's unique economic system has proved itself not only viable but also more consumer-minded, more receptive to innovation, and in many ways more efficient than the Soviet, while at the same time exhibiting rates of growth that compare favorably with those of the USSR and the other Soviet-type economies. The impact of its economic example on its neighbors to the East may be only beginning; how far it may carry will depend on many factors, not the least on the state of Sino-Soviet and Western-Soviet relations.

III

AS FOR THE OTHER COUNTRIES OF EASTERN EUROPE, MUCH OF WHAT HAS just been said about the Soviet economy applies to them as well. Their economic institutions are, on the whole, closely patterned after the Soviet model. (The major exception is, of course, the decollectivized

[4]The Soviet Bloc here denotes the USSR and Eastern Europe (except Albania and Yugoslavia).

agriculture of Poland.) They, too, are feeling heavy pressures on their resources because of ambitious economic goals and lagging productive response (especially in agriculture). Most of them, too, have been experiencing declining growth rates lately. They replicate the inefficiencies and rigidities of the Soviet economy and are also subject to creeping centralization. However, their military outlays are generally smaller in relation to GNP, and their space-exploration costs are nil. (Poland even partly benefits from the Cold War via United States credits and some commercial advantages in comparison with her neighbors.) To the extent that they expand their economic relations with the West and the less-developed countries—as they have been doing in recent years—the individual East European countries enlarge their bargaining powers vis-à-vis the USSR and the whole Soviet bloc, a process that is assisted by the growing divisions and discords within world communism.

It is against this background that the Council for Mutual Economic Assistance (CMEA) has been lately attempting to promote the rational integration of its members' economies in order to improve the utilization of economic resources within the group as a whole. The aim is to bring about an efficient "socialist international division of labor," something that has yet been far from achieved despite the fact that well over half of these countries' trade is with each other. To this major objective are adjoined two others: the "well-rounded" development (industrialization) of each country, and the gradual narrowing of the now large gaps between the less and the more economically advanced members of the group. Clearly, these objectives may at times be mutually inconsistent. For instance, the "well-rounded" and accelerated industrialization of a less developed member may often conflict with the most efficient use of CMEA's aggregate resources (however this might be measured) as well as with the national interest of other member states.

It is necessary to bear in mind that the Council for Mutual Economic Assistance is not a supranational authority but rather a forum for international negotiation and consultation and a collection of technical committees. Its decisions are binding on a member only with the latter's consent. Though the USSR certainly possesses much more influence and power than any other member, its ability to dictate within CMEA is quite limited, as the history of recent years has amply shown. Each of the other states in the organization is sensitive about its politcal sovereignty, jealous of its economic position, and nationalistic.

These political obstacles to economic integration are strongly buttressed by others of a more institutional nature. It seems to be true that centrally administered economies (command economies) of the Soviet type find it most difficult to achieve substantial economic integration with each other *without* a supranational authority. A group of market economies, of course, also encounters many political and economic difficulties on the road to integration. But here, at least, the market mechanism takes over the job of consummating economic integration once the barriers are lowered by international agreement. Not so in Soviet-type economies, where each act of international economic relations, however specific or minor, requires deliberate governmental decision. Besides, planning and administration in these economies is a most arduous task even without the complications introduced by foreign trade, while the chronic shortage of supplies creates a strong tendency toward self-sufficiency at all levels. In sum, we may expect considerable resistance within each country to a high degree of economic dependence on its neighbors, for "bureaucratic" reasons if for not others. The domestic experience of the Soviet Union is quite instructive in this regard: There is little doubt that with its present institutions the Soviet economy would break up into autarkic regional complexes except for the cohesive efforts on the part of the central political and planning authorities. Thus, power politics apart, there is a certain economic or organizational logic to Mr. Khrushchev's cautious proposal (1962) for a single planning entity for the CMEA group of countries, an entity that would presumably possess supranational authority. But, for the reasons just named, its establishment in the near future seems quite unlikely. On the contrary, the only tangible result so far has been a perverse one: Rumania's seizure of relatively greater economic independence.

IV

ONE OF THE MOST SIGNIFICANT FACTS OF LIFE IN THE USSR AND IN THE Soviet bloc as a whole is the contest with the West, the Cold War. It is, therefore, not too much to assume that the conduct of Western, especially American, foreign policy, and the West's response to Soviet behavior in the Cold War, may have substantial influence on economic realities behind the Iron Curtain, as these realities in turn have appreciable effect on the state of international relations. But first, a cautionary note. One would not be justified in supposing that the USSR might be "forced" into better relations with the West, and with the United States especially, by dint of an allegedly crushing economic burden imposed by the Cold War. To be sure, Soviet economic resources are under great pressure, not the least because of the Cold War. No doubt, the Soviet regime would like to be able to devote to other urgent purposes some of the resources now diverted to military and related uses. The defense burden may well be a contributory factor in shaping the Soviets' international posture. But it is hardly the deciding factor, considering how much is at stake in the Cold War (and now in the conflict with China). After all, it was not so long—a decade or less—ago that the USSR bore a relatively much heavier burden of military expenditure than now out of a much smaller national product.

Returning to the implications of a relaxation of tension between the USSR and the West, we should like to distinguish between two possible economic consequences of such a development in the Soviet Union and the East European countries: the reallocation effect and the institutional effect. Both can be evaluated only with the aid of heavy doses of conjecture.

By the reallocation effect we mean the effect on the composition, size, and growth of the national product of a transfer of resources from military and related uses to the civilian sector. This is the type of economic consequence that is usually considered in connection with potential reduction in military expenditure, whether in a Western or an Eastern country. Given the size of the Soviet defense effort and the nature of the economy, it is not to be gainsaid that a substantial transfer of resources in favor of the civilian sector in the USSR will significantly benefit private consumption or social services or invest-ment—and, most likely, all three in some combination. And if the volume of investment is augmented it is also quite likely that the rate of growth—both over-all and in some individual sectors—may be appreciably augmented. *Toutes proportions guardées,* the same applies to the individual East European countries.

And yet, large though it potentially may be, the probable reallo-cation effect of an improvement in Soviet-Western relations should not be overestimated. First, some steps toward an East-West *détente,* such as the nuclear test ban of August 1963, directly entail very little, if any, reduction in military cost and may therefore have hardly any reallocation effect in the economy. Secondly, while further steps in the direction of arms control and disarmament may indeed result in substantial reductions in military and related expenditures, it is likely —especially now in view of the Soviet conflict with China and the latter's efforts to become a nuclear power—that the USSR (as well as Western powers) would spread them over several years and would carry them considerably short of Mr. Khrushchev's "complete dis-

armament." Since 1962, the Soviet defense budget has been running
at some 13 to 14 billion rubles per annum. And while the total defense
effort, broadly defined, is presumably higher, even under politically
very favorable circumstances the cutback in Soviet defense outlay may
turn out to be no more than 2 to 3 billion rubles per year, if and when
it comes. An amount of resources of this magnitude additionally
injected into the civilian economy every year for several years is
certainly not insignificant. But is also not strikingly large. We may
compare it with following aggregate magnitudes in the Soviet economy in 1963 (round figures in "new" rubles): a GNP (western
concept, factor cost) of something like 155 billion rubles, total expenditure in the consolidated state budget of 90 billion rubles, gross
fixed investment (all sectors of the economy) of over 40 billion rubles,
and an increase in inventories and stockpiles of 14 billion rubles.[5] The
postulated 2 to 3 billion rubles released annually by the transfer, or
even the 10 billion rubles or so that may be released over several years
under favorable international and internal conditions, do not loom
very large by comparison.

But we must not restrict our attention to aggregates. The particulars may be more instructive. To the Soviet planner, ever in search of
resources to break bottlenecks or to spur investment, the "mere" few
billion may be an enormous windfall. We may surmise that the bulk of
the resources released from military use would be channeled into
investment, because of the physical nature of such resources and
because of the serious lag in construction and other investment
activity under the Seven Year Plan. Hence, there may be a boost to the
rate of economic growth, but hardly a very large one on this account
alone. Some of the additional investment may well be in consumer-
goods producing sectors, such as agriculture and housing, or in
industries working for them, such as chemical fertilizers and synthet-
ics.[6] Even so, the rate of growth would be favorably affected, at least
for a while, and over the longer run possibly as well via beneficial
effects on work incentives, to give but one example.

If some of the rechanneled resources serve to break bottlenecks,
of which there are quite a few in the USSR, the positive effect on the
economy may be disproportionately large. But the breaking of some

[5]Except for the GNP, the data are from official Soviet sources. The GNP figure
has been crudely estimated by the author on the basis of the official Soviet national
income figures.

[6]These indeed are the main directions in which resources were being rechanneled
by Mr. Khrushchev's successors in the first months of their rule. At this writing,
however, it is not yet clear at the expense of which sectors this was being done.

bottlenecks will no doubt create others, given the general pressure on resources. Also, many of the bottlenecks probably owe less to scarcity or immobility of physical resources than to various institutional factors: bad planning, faulty incentives, bureaucratic rigidities, and so forth. These may not be much helped by a release of resources from military use. Witness that despite a near-doubling of the GNP and a marked reduction in its proportion devoted to defense since Stalin's death, the Soviet economy is no less ridden by bottlenecks and shortages now than it was then.

An important resource that is very heavily committed to the military and space programs is scientific and technological "brainpower." But the extent to which it may be released for other employment, thanks to a substantial improvement in the international climate, is moot. How much, if at all, would the space program be curtailed? It may even be bolstered by a shift of resources from military use proper in the event of partial disarmament. Will weapons research and development be cut back in proportion to the reduction in over-all defense expenditures? This hardly seems likely, though it would, of course, depend on the extent and nature of the defense cutback and on the type of international inspection system (if any). How much good to the civilian economy would a substantial infusion of scientific and technological "brainpower" do? Past Soviet experience gives no easy clues to this puzzle, and the answer in any case depends on whether or not there would be significant institutional changes in the economy (to which we presently turn).

It is often presumed that a substantial release of resources from defense may lead to greatly expanded Soviet economic aid to underdeveloped non-Communist countries. This may well happen, but if it does, the reason is more likely to be political than the sheer freeing of resources from military use. Soviet foreign aid represents a very small claim on that country's resources (as is also true of the United States) and probably can be expanded considerably in any case without releasing large resources from military use. On the other hand, the cutback in defense spending would be associated with a major change in the international atmosphere and a major shift in the nature of "competition" between East and West, which may in turn create the political rationale for much larger foreign aid on the part of the USSR (and then also probably on the part of the West).

In sum, the reallocation effects of even a major reduction in Soviet military (and related) expenditures are likely to be favorable to consumption, investment, and growth. The extent of the effect or effects is highly conjectural and quite possibly rather modest. The institutional effect, as we have already noted, is even more conjectural, and if we raise the problem at all it is not out of excessive boldness but because of its potentially great importance.

V

ANY MAJOR RELAXATION OF TENSION WITH THE WEST CONTAINS A potential for far-reaching political and institutional consequences within the Soviet Union, within the individual East European countries, and in relations among the members of the Soviet bloc. Inside the USSR a likely consequence would be generally to encourage and embolden those varied and at times mutually incompatible groups that in the West tend to be thrown under the single, broad rubric of "liberalizers." If these groups have anything in common it is their desire to reduce the power and control exercised by the central authorities; otherwise their goals and aspirations may be very diverse. They include those who would expand the scope of intellectual and artistic freedom, those who yearn for broader civil liberties and stronger "socialist legality," those who desire greater regional or departmental autonomy (though they may have no intention of granting larger powers to *their* subordinates), those who would impart some measure of independence to the individual factory or farm, and possibly those (as yet silent) who would come out for autonomous workers' councils. At a certain propitious moment the pressure from all these directions against the central authorities may become rather great. We may expect from past experience that the regime would begin taking countermeasures at an early point in order to prevent the situation from getting out of hand. In fact, on the propaganda front, countermeasures have already begun in the form of emphasizing that "peaceful co-existence" does not mean "ideological co-existence."

Yet, the countermeasures need not be entirely successful in containing all the pressures for "liberalization." A major *détente* with the West may well give Soviet society a push in some or all of the various directions enumerated in the preceding paragraph, especially if the more reactionary forces are at the same time inhibited by the conflict with Communist China. The crucial question in this context is whether the liberalizing mood will carry with it *economic* decentralization—an issue which, as we have seen, is already very much in the air —and carry it far enough. The last is most important. A partial decentralization would only bring about serious imbalances in the economy, or strong regional autarky, or both, and would thus be short-lived. The reform will not discredit itself only if it gives substantial autonomy to the lowest economic level and is supplemented by appropriate and ample institutional arrangements so as to create, in effect, a socialist market economy. At that juncture, the fortunes of the Czech experiment of 1965 and the existence of the Yugoslav model may be of crucial significance.

We leave aside the discussion of the socio-political consequences of a transformation of the Soviet economy into a market economy, albeit a socialist and planned one, an event that itself would presuppose some slippage in the dictatorial regime's power. Suffice it to mention that simple and easy inferences are to be avoided: Obviously, many a market economy has existed along with political oppression, cultural stagnation, and social inequities—as well as the opposite—and the qualifier "socialist" is no guarantee against these conditions. In the limited space here at our disposal, we restrict our attention to a few general remarks about the economic consequences. These, in our opinion, would be significant and possibly great indeed.

No one who follows the current Soviet economic scene can fail to be impressed by what may be called a basic structural incoherence in that economy, which, at once, severely impairs the economy's efficiency, depresses consumer satisfaction, and inhibits the rate of growth with the given rate of investment. To explain: That there is an enormous pent-up demand for consumer goods in the USSR (and in all Communist countries) is obvious; Mr. Khrushchev's own indefatigable pronouncements were eloquent evidence thereof. The housing shortage alone is likely to last well into the twenty-first century, considering the nature of the present stock of dwellings and its rapid obsolescence. Secondly, there is in being a large productive capacity that is now very ineffectively utilized even for the regime's high-priority purposes. At the same time, the marked unevenness in its technological level, its many imbalances, and its inadequate orientation to consumer needs suggest also a vast and sustained potential investment demand even (in large measure, especially) after a thorough decentralization of decision-making. Lastly, but equally impressively, there is an enormous pool of skilled and trained manpower, much of it talented as well, whose creative potential is now repressed by overcentralization and bureaucratization, or misdirected by faulty incentives. Most imperfectly as these three elements—demand, capital plant, and human resources—are brought together at the present time, the threat is that this basic incoherence will become aggravated rather than alleviated as the resources grow and the economy's complexity mounts. It is difficult to escape the impression that a properly instituted market mechanism, even without a shift away from the public ownership of the means of production, would tend to bring the pent-up demand, the capital plant, and the human resources much closer together and that the results would be on balance beneficial to the Soviet economy.

We may note that a thorough decentralization of the economy need not also entail the decollectivization of agriculture, as it has not in the Czech experiment (at least so far). The "liberation" of managers may well arrive without, and certainly before, that of the peasants. For one, it is conceivable that economic decisions are decentralized to the level of the collective farm (or state farm) without any major loosening of the bonds between the peasant and the collective. Secondly, and in any case, decollectivization in the sense of the setting up on family-sized independent cultivating units faces serious technical obstacles (shortage of suitable equipment, too small a size of operating unit), which the decentralization of industry does not face. Nonetheless, any major decentralization in the rest of the economy would have a profound impact on the collective farm sector and would ever more sharply pose the question of institutional reforms in agriculture.

Thanks to the likely dishoarding of resources and greater efficiency in their use, under proper institutional arrangements a thoroughgoing decentralization of the Soviet economy would quite likely be followed, at least for some time, by a substantial boost to the rate of over-all growth and, especially, by rapidly improving satisfaction of consumer needs. It is not even impossible that the ensuing economic upsurge would—at least for a while—exceed quantitively anything the Soviet economy has yet experienced since Stalin's death, and the qualitative improvements in both consumer and producer goods may be even more notable. Of course, much depends on the impact on other significant variables of the same train of events that might bring about the market mechanism and particularly on what happens to the rate of investment. That command economies do not have a monopoly on high investment rates is clear from recent experience. The socialist market economy of Yugoslavia, by dint of planned allocation of the national product, has a rate that is comparable to the USSR's, as have several capitalist market economies in Western Europe, while the Japanese investment rate is even considerably higher than the Soviet. Decentralization of day-to-day production decisions and of many specific investment decisions would not necessarily mean, for the Soviets, renunciation of central determination of the basic division of the national product between total consumption and total investment. And even a somewhat lower investment rate need not dampen growth if resources are more efficiently utilized:

So much for the possible institutional effect and its economic consequences that might be triggered by a decisive improvement in Soviet-Western relations. To outline is not to predict. We do not wish to exaggerate the chances of a "marketization" of the Soviet economy or to belittle the internal obstacles facing it. Any major economic decentralization—as any major socio-political liberalization—will no doubt be tenaciously resisted by many and powerful elements in the Soviet society: by the millions who have a vested interest in present arrangements, by those managers who would rather obey orders than face market competition, by the lower- and middle-party bosses who today partly function as a substitute for the market and its rules, by many higher functionaries and party leaders who would certainly lose status and power as a result of the reform, by the Party as such that may fear losing control of the country, by the ideologues with their mental rigidities and their own vested interests, and by all those who fear any change or simply cannot conceive of alternative arrangements. The dice are loaded against a thoroughgoing economic decentralization, if they are not already loaded against the antecedent Soviet-Western *rapprochement.* If the decentralization comes at all, it may come only after one or more succession crises; indeed it may be a major issue in such crises. But to reject its very possibility is to underestimate the potential for evolution in Soviet society in the coming decades, as well as the lessons of such major changes in the Communist world as those in Yugoslavia following 1948, the decollectivization of Polish agriculture, the Czech reform of 1965 (true, as yet to be realized) and the moderation of police terror almost immediately after the tyrant's death in the Soviet Union itself.

Moreover, a major East-West *détente* is likely to strengthen centrifugal tendencies within the Soviet bloc, as it is likely to promote the further alienation of China from Russia and growing "polycentrism" in the world Communist movement. What then of the economic integration of the CMEA countries? Though the centrifugal tendencies would work against it, paradoxically it may in a sense gain substance should things go far enough, that is, should the CMEA countries transform themselves into a group of socialist market economies. What we may see then is less mutual economic dependence among them (as measured, say, by the ratio of intrabloc trade to their aggregate trade), but a more efficient economic interrelationship thanks to the "marketization" of the individual countries and more meaningful prices in them. At the same time we may also expect considerable enlargement of economic ties between Eastern and Western Europe.

The picture that we have just sketched is of a politically much less cohesive "socialist camp" — if any longer a "camp" at all — with internal economic arrangements and economic relations with the rest of the world very different from those we have become accustomed to in the postwar era. It also a picture of a "socialist camp" that is economically much stronger, more efficient, and more prosperous than it is now or is otherwise likely to be in the near future. As such it would represent an economically more formidable competitor to the West on the commercial plane and in the rivalry for the attention of the "third world," although in an East-West setting that is, by assumption, politically, and probably also ideologically, more relaxed. To reiterate, this is only a possible, long-run consequence of a major diminution of the Cold War, but one of such magnitude and importance that we can hardly afford to dismiss it as we think ahead.

Is it, for us, an attractive prospect or not? The answer surely depends on many complex factors which we cannot stop to examine here, as well as on one's own values and predilections. Attractive or no, this prospect surely cannot be brought about by the West at will, although the West can probably thwart — or at least seriously postpone — its realization by restraining or delaying significant improvement in the international atmosphere. On the other hand, there may be quite a few instruments at the disposal of American foreign policy and that of its allies. Obviously, relaxation of East-West tension, and especially major arms control and disarmament agreements, would tend to work in this direction. So would the encouragement of large-scale contacts between individuals and groups in the East and the West, of greater flow of information between the two parts of the world, of diversity within the Communist world, and of the loosening of ties between the USSR and what today may still be its satellites but which are straining hard for greater freedom of action. In this we have rather substantial assets at our disposal because, generally speaking, the peoples and the governments of Communist countries, at times jointly and at times at cross purposes, want very much more from us, the West, than we want from them: capital goods and consumer goods, credits, science and technology, ideas, esthetic values, international respect and the sense of belonging to the world community; in the case of some of the East European countries, re-establishment of traditional cultural and religious ties. (Yet, we should also bear in mind that some of our assets may be subject to attrition and obsolescence in the future.) And, of course, they—as we—desire to avoid nuclear war.

It is easy to list our assets for dealing with the East; it is hard to employ them imaginatively and effectively. But it may help us to put them to better use if we also realize that, despite a rigid façade, the economic institutions of the individual Communist countries and of the CMEA are in flux, that substantial and possibly even radical transformations are not at all impossible, much as the regimes and the vested interests may resist them, and that the West's behavior may bear significantly on the issue.

While the waning of the Cold War would inevitably affect all parties, large and small, to the Grand Confrontation, the West's own policies to this end are likely to be more effective if they recognize the essentially different interests and positions of the *individual* East European countries and of the USSR. With regard to the former, our most effective tools are likely to be economic ones, as indeed the history of the first half of the sixties shows. By proferring to these countries valuable economic alternatives to their inward orientation within the bloc, the West can look forward to the further loosening of the bloc's cohesion and possibly to a series of internal institutional reforms on the Czech—if not the Yugoslav—pattern. Vis-à-vis the Soviet Union, however, economic instruments, though not unimportant, are likely to be overshadowed by agreements or tacit understandings in the politico-military sphere, especially with the United States, as landmarks in the continued waning of the Cold War. Similarly, if the kinds of systemic economic reforms that we have sketched out come at all within the USSR, they are likely to come only as the end result of a very complex interplay of internal forces—probably punctuated by a series of succession crises—against the background of evolving relations with the West, the changing positions of East European countries and the possible structural reforms in *their* economies, and, of course, relations with China. Most probable, however, is that so long as the Soviet economy remains highly centralized, waste and inefficiency will persist on a grand scale, the consumer will continue to feel slighted, and internal pressures for radical decentralization will not disappear.

To reiterate, any thoroughgoing decentralization of the Soviet economy, such as the establishment of a socialist market economy, will undoubtedly be tenaciously resisted by various interests within the country, which will see in it threats to both personal position and ideological canons. In fact, this resistance may itself place definite limits on the improvement of relations with the West. But it should also not be forgotten that the present Soviet economic system was specifically designed by Stalin to bring about extremely rapid growth in a technologically backward and little-educated country with an undemanding population and in the face of (allegedly) hostile encirclement. As these conditions lose their appositeness, will not Stalinist economic institutions be placed increasingly on the defensive? Herein lies a great challenge to Western—and especially American—foreign policy as it looks into the future, "beyond the Cold War."

ADDENDUM (OCTOBER, 1965)

At the end of September, 1965, the Soviet regime announced a new economic reform. This is *not* the kind of reform discussed above. Rather, it is a relatively conservative reorganization with some very modest steps in the direction of greater enterprise autonomy. The reorganization consists essentially of the scrapping of the regional industrial authorities (*sovnarkhozy*) introduced by Mr. Khrushchev in 1957 and their replacement by "traditional" industrial ministries. The simultaneous extension of the power of individual enterprise is so limited that there is serious doubt of the viability of the arrangement. An early recentralization is quite likely for reasons spelled out in the text of this article. This impression is reinforced by lack of any indication that the proposed price reform—now postponed to 1967-68—will adequately reflect the interplay of supply and demand, and by the emphatic retention of the elaborate system of physical material allocation. In the same way, the immediately preceding international situation was not at all the equivalent of the East-West *détente* postulated in the above discussion.

THE GREAT CUBAN MISSILE BASE CONFRONTATION IN OCTOBER, 1962, *was only the most dramatic event in the continuing Cuban role in the Cold War, but it may not be the one from which we can draw the greatest instruction. Because of its obvious, and even visible, thermonuclear aspects, all the world was able to see and experience how a moment of armed crisis in the Cold War between the two greatest nuclear powers, regardless of the ultimate intentions of the participants, increases to an almost unbearable level the possibilities of inadvertent nuclear war. And even should such a crisis be considered, in itself, not unbearable, the prospect of such confrontations occuring repeatedly over an indefinite period into the future is unbearable, and so induces men of forethought to seek an end to, or some modification of, the Cold War.*

The Cuban crisis was a classic example of the Soviet leadership's manipulation of international tension, as described previously by Myron Rush, for the Soviet Union sought to gain in the Cold War both by the sudden increase of tension and also by the subsequent sudden relaxation. The net effect of the Soviet moves was to leave the Soviet Union with thousands of military personnel and great quantities of materiel firmly established in Cuba, unchallenged by the United States.

But Robert Alexander, in this essay, is more concerned to examine domestic and international political factors before and after 1962, to put that most dramatic crisis in perspective, so that we may understand Cuba's true role in the Cold War, the attitudes and errors that led to the communizing of Cuba, the future prospects, and what future policies and attitudes are most appropriate for the United States, based on understanding rather than on ignorance and emotion.

Mr. Alexander poses the most difficult questions and seeks to answer them: What is the true danger to the United States in the Cuban situation? How should the United States face it? To answer these questions, he raises and considers prior questions: Why did Batista fall? Was Castro always a Communist? If not, when did he choose the course of Communism, and why? Now that "Cuba has evolved into a thorough-going Communist regime," what is Cuba's position among the Communist nations?

Mr. Alexander shows the dilemma of the Cuban position now, with Castro caught in the middle of the Sino-Soviet conflict, leaning to the doctrine of the Chinese Communists because of his desperate need to spread Castroism to the rest of Latin America, but hampered by his utter economic dependence on the Soviet Union. "Castro's heart is in China, but his stomach is in the Soviet Union."

If all of these factors are well understood and taken into account, United States policy-makers will judge and act in accord with this developing situation. The Cuban problem is not simple, but it can be analyzed and grasped. It does not suffice simply to seek the overthrow of Castro. We must consider how this is to be done, what the effect will be on the rest of Latin America and the rest of the world, by whom he is to be overthrown, and especially by whom he is to be replaced. Our soundest guide, Mr. Alexander suggests, in formulating our

Cuban policy, will be the answer to one last question: What are the essential characteristics of a Cuban regime with which we can cooperate? The answer to that question also provides the strongest clue to United States relations with Cuba and Latin America beyond the Cold War.

ROBERT J. ALEXANDER

•

CASTRO, LATIN AMERICA AND UNITED STATES POLICY

THE ADVENT OF THE FIDEL CASTRO REGIME IN CUBA HAS PRESENTED the United States with one of the most difficult foreign relations problems which it has encountered in all of its history. Some of the difficulty lies in the confusion concerning the nature of the danger presented by the Castro government; the rest in basic disagreements concerning how this danger should best be confronted.

BACKGROUND OF CASTRO'S COMING TO POWER

CUBA WAS NOT THE COUNTRY WHICH MOST OBSERVERS WOULD HAVE picked as the scene of the American hemisphere's first successful Communist revolution. The island had one of the most advanced economies to be found in the New World. Its per capita income was higher than that of two-thirds of the other Latin American nations. Its sugar industry brought in a foreign exchange income which was the envy of most of the other nations of the region. It was the fifth most heavily industralized country south of the United States.

Standards of living of a large part of the Cuban population were high. The island had one of the largest middle classes of the hemisphere. Television sets, electric refrigerators, and other consumers' appliances were commonplace even in many of the more humble homes of Havana and other principal cities. It was by no means

Castro, Latin America and United States Policy

unusual for an industrial worker or office employee to own a second- or third-hand automobile.

In a word, the economic situation of Cuba was considerably better than that of most of its neighbors. The cause of the Castro regime, and the turn which it took, must be sought elsewhere than in the economic sphere.

It seems to us that one of the keys to the question of why a Communist regime came to power in Cuba is its political history. From the time that Cuba gained its independence in 1902, the country was plagued by a dictatorial tradition. Some of the tyrannical regimes were more intense than others, but only a handful could qualify as democratic. Those which were succeeded in discrediting themselves on other grounds.

Two dictatorial regimes were particularly bad, those of Gerardo Machado and Fulgencio Batista. Machado came to power in 1924 with wide popular support, but as his avarice for power and pelf became increasingly obvious, his popular backing declined. When in 1928 he amended the constitution in order to keep himself in power, he became highly unpopular.

The resistance to the Machado regime took on heroic proportions. It was led particularly by university students, who used personal terrorism as one of their principal weapons. They had support from urban organized workers and much of the middle class. Soon after Machado was overthrown in August 1933, there came to power a revolutionary regime headed by Dr. Ramón Grau San Martín, a professor of the University of Havana Medical School. It consisted mainly of students of the same university. They were backed by the armed forces, the leadership of which had been seized by a sergeant, Fulgencio Batista.

The 1933 Revolution is an important antecedent to that of Castro. It aroused widespread enthusiasm for its program of economic nationalism and social welfare. Although the Grau government lasted for only four months, the young men associated with it continued to be the hope of a large part of the humble citizenry for more than a decade.

The Batista dictatorship came in two installments. The first part of it began in January, 1934, when the ex-sergeant ousted President Grau San Martín in the face of refusal by the State Department to recognize his regime. During the following six years, he made and unmade presidents at will, and during much of this period his regime ruthlessly suppressed all opposition.

175

Robert J. Alexander

In the late 1930's Batista sought to democratize his regime. As part of this effort, he made an alliance with the Communist Party, according to which Batista assured them of control of the labor movement in return for their support for his regime. This alliance lasted until a few months before Castro came to power.

Batista became president in 1940 and remained in office until the middle of 1944. At that time, his candidate in election was defeated by ex-President Ramón Grau San Martín, nominee of the Partido Revolucionario Cubano (Autentico), which had been organized under Grau's leadership a decade earlier.

Between 1944 and 1952 the Autentico Party remained in power, during the administrations of Grau San Martín and Carlos Prío Socarras.These eight years were the most democratic which the country had experienced. There was virtually complete freedom of press, assembly, and speech. There was a high degree of economic prosperity, which included at least appreciable segments of the working classes.

However, two factors tended to discredit the Autentico regime, and it was this process of discrediting which constitutes a second key to the advent of the Castro regime. First, the Autenticos proved to be if anything even more corrupt than their dictatorial predecessors. Ramón Grau San Martín was indicted after leaving office for allegedly stealing $180 million, which was a measure of the extent of the corruption of the Autenticos. Few of the ministers or other high officials of the regime left office as poor men.

The second weakness of the Autentico regimes was their failure to carry out their own economic and social program. During the first six years, the Autenticos did virtually nothing to diversify agriculture, foster industrialization, or bring about a greater degree of economic independence for the island. Although in his last two years, Prío Socarras began to put into effect the Party's program in these fields, his action came too late to rescue the reputation of the Autenticos.

The discrediting of the Autenticos paved the way for the return of Batista to power. Batista's second installment of dictatorship commenced on March 10, 1952, when he organized a *coup d'état* with the help of young officers of the Camp Columbia garrison near Havana. In the face of recognized inability to win a presidential election scheduled for less than three months later, Batista took power once again by the method he had first used almost two decades before.

During his first years back in power, Batista governed with a relatively light hand. However, resistance to him began immediately, and in the face of mounting opposition he became increasingly tyrannical. During the last two years of his government, Batista presided over a regime which equalled that of Machado in its terrorism and violence and outdid it by far in its corruption.

There is now a myth to the effect that Batista was overthrown because of a combination of treachery in his own camp and conspiracy in the State Department. This can only be labelled "poppycock." Batista fell because his regime so alienated all elements of the population that it collapsed of its own weight. Batista's armed forces were only defeated in the field in one major battle, but by the end of the struggle against Castro—and most of the rest of the Cuban population— his soldiers were refusing to fight and were virtually melting away.

The opposition included all ranks of the population. The country's richest sugar producer was said to have contributed $1 million to Castro. This author talked with the Secretary of the Cuban National Association of Manufacturers soon after Batista's fall and was informed by him of the way in which that class had been completely alienated from Batista during the last six months of his regime. The middle class, the urban workers, and many peasants also participated to a greated or lesser extent in the opposition.

Until the penultimate moment, the United States supported Batista. The Truman Administration took only eight days to recognize the Batista regime in 1952. In subsequent years the United States sold and granted arms and military advice to Batista's army. We gave honors to leaders of the Cuban government, including an Order of Merit to the commander of Batista's air force, which was granted only a few months before Batista's regime disappeared.

It is true that in March, 1958, about eight months before Batista fell, the United States officially ended shipments of arms to Batista. However, material already "in the pipeline" went even after that. Furthermore, a United States military mission was training Batista's troops until the day they stopped fighting. Little or no public criticism was made by leaders of the American government of the Batista regime or its behavior, until after it was overthrown.

It seems to us absurd to argue that the Batista regime fell as a result of anything except the general repudiation of it by virtually all elements of Cuban society. Until December 31, 1958, it had overwhelming superiority in weapons, soldiers, and all outward evidences of power. However, it was thoroughly rotten at its core and was hated by the general populace, and it was these facts which resulted in its overthrow.

Robert J. Alexander

WHAT HAPPENED AFTER JANUARY 1, 1959?

THERE ARE SEVERAL EXPLANATIONS FOR WHAT HAPPENED ONCE CASTRO came to power on January 1, 1959. It is very important to try to get a clear picture of the events during the first year or so of Fidel's period in power if one is to attempt to decide on the efficacy of the Eisenhower, Kennedy, and Johnson Administrations' handling of the Cuban problem, and if one is to make any judgments about what the future holds.

One very popular point of view is that Fidel Castro and his closest associates were all Communists when they came to power and had been for a matter of years before that date. It is even argued that Castro was an international Communist agent as early as April, 1948, the evidence for this being his presence in Bogota, Colombia, during the insurrection there which is widely known as the *bogotazo*. Apparent vacillation in Castro's own behavior during his first months in power are explained away as mere maneuvers designed to cover up Fidel's Communist commitments.

The author feels this explanation of events of the first few months of Castro's regime to be erroneous. The Bogota evidence makes it necessary to believe that the *bogotazo* was a Communist-led insurrection, and even that the Communists killed Liberal leader Jorge Eliecer Gaitán, thus setting off the uprising.

This author does not accept this interpretation of the *bogotazo*. If the Communists had organized it, they could have seized power in a city which had only two hundred soldiers on hand. Rather, the *bogotazo* was an unorganized, spontaneous uprising of the Liberal population of the city, outraged by the murder of their idol, Gaitán. It seems more likely that Gaitán was murdered by Conservatives, who knew full well that he would be elected president if he continued as leader of the Liberal Party. In any case, Castro was only about nineteen years of age at the time of the *bogotazo*, hardly old enough to be an important Comintern agent; and his presence in the city can be explained very well by the fact that there were hundreds of delegations from all over Latin America there to present arguments to delegates at the Inter-American Conference then meeting in the Colombian capital.

Nor does Castro's behavior during most of 1959 bear out the argument as to his politics at that time. During these months, this writer had occasion to visit Cuba three times, and to look particularly at the labor movement, and is therefore fully aware of the fact that

Castro supported those of his followers in organized labor who fought the Communists in the trade unions.

Finally, during these months Castro had very little need to maneuver or cover his tracks. After January 1, 1959, Castro was absolute master of Cuba. During the first few months, the vast majority of the people would have followed Castro in virtually any direction he decided to go. As he subsequently showed, he had little regard for those among his associates or followers who disagreed with him, so he was not trying to respect their sensibilities by appearing not to be a Communist if he really was one.

An alternative argument is that Castro never really wanted to go down the Communist path and was only forced to do so because of the policy of the United States. This is the argument of one of the most intelligent apologists for the Castro regime, Professor William Appleman Williams of the University of Wisconsin.

This point of view also seems mistaken, although it has somewhat more to recommend it than the first one. Rather, it appears that the basic attitude of the State Department and of most other elements in the executive part of the United States government during this period was one of "wait and see." There was widespread recognition of the fact that the United States had erred gravely in maintaining its support of Batista as long as it did, and Castro and his associates must have been made aware of this when they were here in April, 1959.

If one accepts, as does this author, the idea that Castro did not definitely make up his mind which way to lead the Revolution until late in 1959, one may well feel that a forthright and public offer of aid by the United States to the rebuilding and transformation of the Cuban economy might have been the factor which would have made Fidel decide against a pro-Communist policy. However, this writer finds it hard to believe that the kind of policy the United States followed in 1959 was sufficient to drive a leader such as Castro into the kind of all-out embracing of Communism which he undertook at the end of 1959. It, rather, appears that it was national and not international considerations which finally made Castro decide as he did.

A somewhat more naive explanation for why the Castro regime went the way it did is that offered by Fidelista apologists Huberman and Sweezy, and J. P. Morray. They would have it that some metaphysical force, "the Revolution" or "the forces of history," took Castro inexorably down the Communist road. To prove this they rely heavily on parallels with the French and Russian revolutions.

However, this is as untenable as the "Communist before, during, and after the Revolution" argument. Again, we would stress that in the early months Fidel was unchallenged chief of the revolutionary movement and could have taken it in virtually any direction he had wished. He was not prisoner of any metaphysical forces.

THE MOST BELIEVABLE EXPLANATION

THE BEST EXPLANATION, THE ONE WHICH MAKES MOST SENSE, AND WHICH leaves fewest questions unanswered, is that Castro himself did not make up his mind in the first months of the Revolution where he wanted to take the country. He was torn in two directions during this period, and his state of indecision was reflected in the zigzags of his policy. This is basically the explanation offered by Theodore Draper, and this author agrees with it.

The 26th of July Movement was very heterogeneous politically. Aside from conservative elements outside of the Movement who supported the Revolution because of their objections to Batista, the active members of the 26th of July were basically split into two factions.

The first faction may be labelled Democratic Leftist. It favored a fundamental agrarian reform to put the land in the hands of those who cultivated it, putting emphasis on establishment of small and medium sized holdings, but also experimenting with cooperative farming where that was appropriate. It favored a mixed economy, in which the State would have a large role in establishing and running the economic infrastructure and stimulating industrialization and agricultural diversification. It also backed the idea of removing foreign-owned firms from such key spheres as public utilities, railroads, and perhaps sugar mills.

The Democratic Leftist element favored a much more independent attitude toward the United States than had prevailed since 1898. At most, they were in favor of a neutralist policy, but were opposed to any alignment with the Soviet Bloc in international affairs.

Finally, this element supported the re-establishment of democratic government. This had been a fundamental promise of the 26th of July from its inception. Of course, the Democratic Leftists did not demand elections immediately, but did feel that they should be called after a reasonable period of provisional government, during which basic reforms could be gotten under way. Meanwhile, it opposed all cooperation with the Cuban Communist Party.

The most outspoken representative of this element in the 26th of July was Major Huber Matos, commander of the Rebel Army in the

Province of Camaguey. However, it also included most of the 26th of July trade union leaders, as well as Felipe Pazos, Manuel Ray, and other leading figures in the first Castro government. In all probability, the commander-in-chief of the armed forces, Major Camilo Cienfuegos, also sympathized with this group.

The second faction in the 26th of July Movement may best be labelled Jacobin Leftist. Like the Jacobins of the French Revolution, it favored drastic social change at any cost; it was xenophobic nationalist; and it had contempt for political democracy. More specifically, it favored an agrarian reform patterned after that of the Soviet Union. It foresaw a virtually completely socialized economy with all economic development being undertaken by the State. It favored cooperation with the Cuban Communists and opposed the restoration of the democratic constitution of 1940. Finally, it supported alignment of Cuba in the anti-United States camp, which inevitably meant joining the Soviet Bloc.

The leaders of this group were Raúl Castro, brother of the top leader of the Revolution, and Ernesto Guevara, probably the most outstanding military leader of the 26th of July. The leaders also included Antonio Nuñez Jiménez, head of the National Institute of Agrarian Reform, a small minority of trade unionists, and various other important figures in the new regime.

Until the end of October, 1959, Fidel Castro did not make a definitive decision in favor of either of these two groups or of the alternative policies which they advocated. He apparently sought a *rapprochement* with the United States, although strictly on the basis of conditions which he laid down—an attitude which very much worried his brother Raúl. The text of the agrarian reform law, enacted early in June, 1959, was more closely patterned after the ideas of the Democratic Leftists than after those of the Jacobins. Castro supported the anti-Communist attitude of most of his supporters in the labor movement. He continued to talk about elections, although getting increasingly vague on the question of when they would be held.

On the other hand, he allowed the administration of the agrarian law to conform to the model advocated by the Jacobin Leftists, in defiance of the letter of the law. He summarily dismissed President Manuel Urrutia when Urrutia protested against increasing penetration of the administration by Communists, a development which Fidel refused to halt.

It seems to the author that the moment of decision came for Fidel with the attempt of Major Huber Matos to resign from the Rebel Army at the end of October, 1959. Matos did so as a means of protesting against Communist infiltration in both the Rebel Army and the civil administration. Instead of allowing Matos to retire, Castro had him arrested, charged him with subversion, and appeared as star witness against Matos at his court martial.

Concurrently with the arrest of Matos came the disappearance of Cienfuegos. He had gone with Fidel to Camaguey to help arrest Matos, but reportedly had assured the latter that he would not be subject to a kangaroo court, but would get a fair trial. Cienfuegos reportedly disappeared on an airplane flight from Camaguey to Havana. There is good reason to believe that he was done away with purposely, by Fidel Castro or someone closely associated with him.

Cienfuegos and Matos were probably the only 26th of July leaders who had wide popular backing of their own, rather than merely reflecting that of Fidel Castro. They were therefore potential dangers to the megalomaniacal Castro. Cienfuegos came from an old anarchosyndicalist family and reportedly had been a Trotskyite in his teens. He had refused to allow the distribution of the Communist daily paper "Hoy" among the troops in Camp Columbia. If fully aware of Castro's determination to go with the Jacobin Leftists, Cienfuegos might well have been able to offer embarrassing and perhaps dangerous opposition.

Whatever are the facts about Cienfuegos' disappearance, it seems that there is no doubt that Castro's decision, in October, 1959, to join forces with his Jacobin Leftist followers was deliberate, definitive, and irreversible. From it, everything else that occured in subsequent months follows logically.

After October there was a 180 degree change in Castro's policy in both internal and international affairs. The wide degree of freedom of press, speech, organization, and assembly which had existed until that time disappeared. By May, 1960, all open criticism of the government in the press had become impossible; leaders of opposition groups which had participated in the fight against Batista—the Autenticos, Triple A Organization, 2nd Front of Escambray, and Directorio Revolucionario—had been jailed, forced into exile, or driven underground.

In international affairs, too, there was a basic change. Fidel Castro began an unremitting series of violent attacks upon the United States, culminating in his oration in February, 1960, at the funeral of workers killed when a Belgian munitions ship blew up in Havana Harbor. At that time Castro said "we have reason to believe" that the Americans had the ship blown up, although admitting that he had no evidence to support his charge.

Castro, Latin America and United States Policy

There seem to be two fundamental reasons for Castro's decision concerning the direction his regime would take. First is the fact that the leaders of the Jacobin Leftist faction were his closest associates. Raúl Castro was his own brother and the member of his family who had always been closest to Fidel. Che Guevara was the intellectual mentor of Fidel, an exceedingly intelligent man, very well read in economics and politics, a good administrator, and, as he proved in the civil war, a military man of competence. He had a dynamic personality, but was shrewd enough not to challenge Castro's points of view openly, a mistake which Matos and others had made.

The second basic reason for Fidel Castro's decision was his megalomania. He had a degree of absolute power which had seldom been matched in recent times and during these first months was idolized by the great majority of the Cuban population. It would have taken a man with an exceedingly powerful character to resist the attraction of such power and adulation. Fidel Castro had no such strength of character. The road of revolutionary dictatorship advocated by the Jacobin Leftists promised Fidel an indefinite continuation of his unchallenged position as boss of Cuba.

THE PRESENT CUBAN SITUATION

DURING THE YEARS SINCE OCTOBER, 1959, CUBA HAS EVOLVED INTO A thoroughgoing Communist regime. All of those in the 26th of July who opposed this evolution were purged. The Democratic Leftists were removed from the cabinet and from other leading posts in the government. Subsequently most of them were jailed, exiled, or driven into the underground. The same thing occurred to a large part of the leadership of the labor movement.

At the same time that the democratic elements were driven out of the 26th of July, the Communists of the orthodox Partido Socialista Popular entered in droves into government positions. After Fidel's decision of late October, 1959, there were no barriers at all to their penetration of the regime.

Castro's own thinking evolved drastically in 1960 and early 1961. He declared, as early as December, 1959, that to be anti-Communist was to be against the Revolution. He ceased describing the Cuban Revolution as "humanist." Finally, a couple of weeks before the so-called Bay of Pigs invasion of April, 1961, he proclaimed that Cuba was a "Socialist" country in a context which equated it with the Soviet Union and other Communist-controlled nations. He reiterated this statement on May Day, 1961.

Robert J. Alexander

On the July 26th anniversary in 1961 Castro went further. He announced that the remnants of the 26th of July and what remained of the Directorio Revolucionario would merge with the Partido Socialista Popular (Communist Party) to form a new Partido Unico de la Revolución Socialista. As a first step, the so-called Integrated Revolutionary Organizations (ORI) would be established immediately. An old Communist, Aníbal Escalante, was put in charge of organizing the new party.

In the last months of 1961 and the first two of 1962 the orthodox Communists seemed well on the way to taking complete control of the Cuban regime. Lazaro Peña, one-time Communist deputy, who had first become Secretar General of the Confederación de Trabajadores de Cuba when the Communists made their deal with Batista in the late 1930's, returned to this post in November 1961. Almost simultaneously, Juan Marinello, former President of the Partido Socialista Popular, became Rector of the University of Havana. Even more important, old Communist leader Carlos Rafael Rodríguez—like Marinello, a former member of Batista's cabinet—succeeded Fidel Castro as head of the very powerful National Institute of Agrarian Reform. He also succeeded Ernesto Guevara as head of the country's national planning agency.

However, rivalry between those who had come from the 26th of July and members of the orthodox Communists continued. It came out into the open in March, 1962. At that time, Fidel Castro reasserted the control of himself and his closest associates over Cuba and its Revolution. After first announcing a list of the Executive Committee members of the new united Party, in which there were fifteen 26th of July people and only ten orthodox Communists, Castro delivered a series of blistering speeches in which he denounced the orthodox Communist leaders. He accused them of doing just exactly what they were doing—trying to seize control of the government. Since then, there has been little doubt concerning who is still boss in Cuba.

The political evolution toward a Communist regime has been accompanied by similar developments in the economy. Between July and October, 1960, virtually all Cuban industry—both foreign- and domestic-owned firms—was nationalized. A government foreign trade monopoly was established. Although thirty thousand peasants were reportedly given individual landholdings, they were subjected to extensive government control over all aspects of their use of the land, and the vast majority of the holdings confiscated from large landlords were organized into collective and state farms. In the summer of 1962

Castro announced the abolition of all collective farms and their conversion into state ones.

From 1960 on, the Cuban economy suffered a profound crisis. Sugar production fell from six million tons to under four million; coffee production also fell. Locally consumed crops which had always been in abundant supply before, such as citrus fruits and malangas, became scarce and most were rationed or virtually unavailable.

The industrial side of the economy suffered almost as much. The Soviet Bloc made very bold promises concerning new industrial establishments which it would provide for Cuba. However, actual accomplishments have so far been extremely meager. Furthermore, many of the industries which existed in 1959 are either unable to function or are functioning poorly, due in large part to inability to obtain spare parts from the United States.

However, there is another fundamental factor in both the agricultural and industrial crisis. This is the attitude of the workers. Complaints by Castro and others about absenteeism, unwillingness to work, and other misbehavior by both rural and urban workers are sufficiently frequent to indicate that the regime has serious problems in this direction. It seems likely that there is serious passive resistance by workers both in the countryside and in the cities. It is not probable that this is due to the organized underground, but there seems little doubt that it exists.

One other aspect of the contemporary economy should be mentioned, its international relations. Whereas Cuba formerly depended for about two-thirds of its exports and imports on the United States, today it depends for about 80 per cent of its foreign trade on the Soviet Union and the East European satellites. Much of this trade is political. It came into existence to win and hold Cuba to the Communist Bloc, rather than to provide the European Communist countries with products which they vitally needed.

CASTRO'S INTERNATIONAL POSITION

FOR THOSE WHO SEE INTERNATIONAL POLITICS IN SIMPLE TERMS OF GOOD guys and bad guys, or black and white, the position of Castro is clear and uncomplicated. He is a tool of the Soviet Union and is as much a "satellite" of Moscow as is any leader of Eastern Europe. However, to this author his position does not appear by any means so clear-cut.

Castro's position in Latin America certainly is not a completely favorable one. Furthermore, his situation within the Communist camp is becoming increasingly complicated and cannot be separated from the disintegration of that once monolithic bloc.

There is good reason to believe that Castro and other top leaders of the Cuban regime are convinced that in the long—or medium—run the success of their government depends on the spread of similar revolutions to other Latin American countries. The Castro regime has from the beginning undertaken the training of potential guerrilla fighters from most other Latin American republics. They have likewise poured considerable money into revolutionary movements in these countries. Guevara's pamphlet on guerrilla warfare has become virtually a Bible for revolutionists or potential revolutionists elsewhere in Latin America.

However, in the many years they have been in power, Castro and his associates have not been able to foment successfully any other revolution in Latin America. The supporters of Castro outside of the orthodox Communist parties in the other countries of the hemisphere are confined almost solely to high school and university students. They have virtually no following in the organized labor movement, and, except for Francisco Julião's leagues in Northeastern Brazil (which have been decimated since the April 1, 1964 *coup d'état*) they have very little more among the organized peasantry.

It would certainly be rash to predict that there will be no further Castro-like revolutions in Latin America. However, the fact remains that so far the Cuban Revolution is unique, and all efforts to foment similar movements in other countries have failed. Furthermore, the very widespread support which Castro had among democratic political leaders during the first year-and-a-half of his regime has entirely disappeared.

Castro's lack of success in extending his revolution outside of his island complicates his situation within the international Communist movement. It reduces his bargaining power within the movement and makes him more subject than he might otherwise be to pressure from the contending Communist giants.

Castro's position in the Sino-Soviet struggle is not an enviable one. His natural inclinations and to a certain degree his interests would tend to put him in the Chinese camp. Yet, economically his regime depends almost totally on the Soviet Union and its East European allies.

Fidel is the natural leader of the pro-Chinese Communists in Latin America as a whole. This is so because he seized power in exactly the way which the Chinese are arguing is the only orthodox Communist method of doing so; and he is seeking to foment revolutions patterned after his own—and to a large degree on that of China—elsewhere in Latin America. He has been highly critical of "those elements" who think that the revolution in the Western Hemisphere can come in any way other than through terror and guerrilla war.

Taken together with Fidel's own temperament, these facts would impel him sentimentally to sympathize with China in the world Communist feud. Furthermore, his need for further violent upheavals in Latin America gives him a good deal more than mere sentimental reasons for favoring the Chinese over the Soviet approach to revolution.

Finally, Castro and his associates have good personal reasons for disliking the Russian leadership. They were humiliated, and to their way of thinking betrayed, by Khrushchev's decision, in October, 1962, to withdraw his missiles from Cuba. All attempts by the Russians to flatter and cajole Castro since then have been something less than completely successful.

However, the Cuban leaders are faced with one basic and unchangeable fact which perforce must restrain their enthusiasm for the Chinese Communists. This is that China cannot possibly substitute for the Soviet Union in providing the close to $500 million a year in trade and aid which now comes to Cuba. Someone has summed up this problem of Castro's by saying that his heart is in China, but his stomach is in the Soviet Union.

CASTRO'S FUTURE RELATIONS WITH LATIN AMERICAN COMMUNISTS

THE EXISTENCE OF THE CASTRO REGIME HAS HELPED TO PRECIPITATE A growing schism within the extreme Left in Latin America. Probably such a split would have been inevitable in view of the Russo-Chinese divergence. However, the presence of the Castro government, with its constant urging of revolutionary violence in other Latin American countries, has probably hastened it.

The advent to power of Castro served as a catalyst for the Jacobin Left in other Latin American countries. Factions which had become disillusioned with democracy and had come to the conclusion that the social changes needed in their countries could come only through a violent revolution saw in him their natural leader. These same factions shared the xenophobic nationalism which he preached. They also felt that the orthodox Communist parties were too cautious and conservative in their approach.

It is these factions who are principally responsible for preparing for violence and guerrilla warfare in Latin America. However, they

Robert J. Alexander

are being joined by young and more militant elements of the orthodox Communist parties. In several countries, there have been splits by
or expulsions of extreme Leftists from the national Communist
parties. In Brazil, opponents of party leader Luiz Carlos Prestes have
formed a rival organization. There have also been splits in the
Peruvian and Ecuadorean Communist Parties. In Mexico and Chile,
dissident factions have been expelled.

The situation is probably most serious of all in the Venezuelan
Communist Party. There, since early 1962, the Communists and
Jacobin Leftist elements, including the Movimiento de Izquierda
Revolucionaria and a faction which early in 1964 was expelled from
the Unión Republicana Democrática, have been mounting a campaign of terror in the cities, while attempting to launch a guerrilla
war in the interior of the country.

The effect of this campaign of violence has been disastrous on the
Communist Party. It has lost the position of prestige and respectabil-
ity which it had during the year or two following the overthrow of the
Pérez Jiménez dictatorship in January, 1958. It has lost all but a
fraction of the considerable influence which it had had in the labor
movement. It has seen a widespread purge of its members from the
press, government employment, and other key areas where they
wielded considerable influence a few years ago.

As a result of the losses the Party has suffered, many older
Communist leaders have sought to abandon the violence tactic. Such a
proposal was reportedly made to a party conference in January, 1963,
and the meeting broke up in fist-fights. One well informed Venezuelan politician told this author that at least some older party leaders
fear that if they push through a resolution ending the violence
campaign they themselves may be murdered by some of the young
hotheads.

This kind of conflict, between orthodox Communist leaders on
the one hand, and more extreme members of their own parties and
Jacobin Leftist groups on the other, is likely to become more extensive. It may well extend to Cuba itself. It is certain that there was some
disagreement, in October, 1962, between the Fidelistas and some
orthodox Communist leaders over the attitude to be adopted toward
Khrushchev's decision to withdraw his missiles. In the last months of
1963 Castro began a purge of old-line Communists from key posts in
the regime.

Outside of Cuba, Castro is likely to support the more extreme
elements when such conflicts arise. There was a concrete case of this
during the summer of 1963. The Brazilian peasant leader Francisco

Julião and Luiz Carlos Prestes, chief of the orthodox Brazilian Communists and a severe critic of Julião, were in Cuba at the same time, both apparently seeking the support of Castro. Reportedly, Prestes went back home empty-handed, while Julião was promised full support by Fidel.

Ultimately, this dissidence on the extreme Left in Latin America will become involved in the world-wide Communist split. It is this writer's opinion that when the situation becomes such that each Communist Party has to make a definitive choice between the Soviet Union and China, virtually all of the Latin American Communist parties will take their stand with the USSR. It will be among the Jacobin Leftists and the elements expelled from the orthodox Communist parties that the Chinese will find their supporters.

It is against this developing situation in Latin America and in the world Communist movement that the position of Castro and his government must be judged. It presents Castro with a great many problems and both democratic-minded Cubans and the United States with great opportunities.

United States Policy and Castro's Cuba

Generally speaking, there are three alternative policies which the United States might adopt toward the Castro regime. In the first place, it might accept suggestions that efforts be made to "lessen tensions" between the United States and Cuba. In practice, this would mean renewal of diplomatic relations with Castro's regime, restoration of trade with Cuba, and possibly discussions to settle issues arising from confiscation of United States-owned property there.

Such a policy would be a mistake. It would not only vastly increase the prestige of the Castro government while making the United States look ridiculous, but would be rank betrayal of democratic elements in Cuba and throughout Latin America.

The extreme alternative to such a policy of appeasement of Castro would be a policy of frankly using armed force against the Cuban regime. This seems to be what critics of the Kennedy and Johnson regimes were calling for when they asked for "action to get rid of Castro." It seems to me highly unlikely that any action of this sort which would be short of a large-scale invasion by United States troops could be effective.

What the advocates of such a policy are asking is that the United States violate a long series of treaties and agreements in which she has recognized the juridical equality of the other American states and has promised not to intervene militarily in their affairs. An overt attack by the United States on Cuba would undoubtedly serve to seriously undermine what is after all one of the main advantages which the United States has in the Cold War: its moral position as a democratic power respectful of the rights of others not only internally but in international affairs.

Aside from these arguments, which undoubtedly would not impress a believer in a purely "practical" approach to world affairs, there are others which might be more understandable to such a person. An invasion of Cuba by the United States would be a major political blunder, and, as a result of it, we might "win" Cuba, but lose one or more much more important Latin American states on the mainland.

The political impact elsewhere in Latin America of a United States invasion of Cuba would depend to a very considerable degree on the swiftness with which it would succeed. It is probably true that if the United States could overthrow Castro in a forty-eight hour campaign, it would arouse violent protest and demonstrations throughout the hemisphere, but it would soon be accepted as a *fait accompli* and might well not have any further serious repercussions.

However, it is unlikely that the United States could oust Castro in any such lightning move today. He has the second largest and best equipped armed force in the Western Hemisphere, which, although it is certainly no match for the United States, might well be able to put up resistance for several weeks. Indeed, Castro might be able to mount a guerrilla war for months or perhaps longer. We might well find ourselves bogged down in another Viet Nam.

Such a long, drawn-out conflict, in addition to being costly in the lives of our troops, would constitute a virtually insurmountable obstacle to our maintaining friendly relations with most of the rest of Latin America, particularly with the major nations of the area, such as Argentina, Brazil, Chile, and Mexico. The scene of United States soldiers in combat with Latin Americans would serve to revive all of the latent fear of "interventionism" which still exists among our neighbors. It would present both the orthodox Communists and the Jacobin Leftists throughout Latin America with opportunities which they could not possibly create for themselves.

KENNEDY AND JOHNSON POLICY TOWARD CUBA

THE KENNEDY AND JOHNSON ADMINISTRATIONS HAVE OFFERED AN alternative to these two extreme policies for dealing with the problem of the Castro regime. Like all policies which seek to follow a middle path, this one does not completely suit anyone. However, this author belongs to that apparently small minority — at least among those who speak and write about the matter — who feel that the Kennedy-Johnson policy is the only one which makes sense under current conditions.

In order to understand why the Kennedy-Johnson policy is an appropriate one, it is first necessary to define just what that policy is. Perhaps this seems too rudimentary, since it has been so widely debated. However, it appears to me that much of the discussion of the Administration's attitude toward Cuba, even by some of its defenders, has served to misrepresent and distort it, largely for reasons of internal United States policies.

First of all, the Kennedy-Johnson policy seeks to isolate the Castro regime as completely as possible from economic, diplomatic, and other contact with the rest of America and generally with all of the non-Communist world. Thus, we ourselves have ceased virtually all trade with the island, creating major difficulties for Castro to obtain replacement parts for his country's disintegrating capital equipment. The United States has also used diplomatic pressure to convince its West European and Latin American friends to cut off their commercial relations with Cuba.

We have also maintained the rupture in diplomatic relations with Castro and have convinced all Latin American nations but Mexico to break theirs. At the same time, we have sought to reduce to an absolute minimum the means by which the Cubans can export printed propaganda, political organizers, and potential guerrilla fighters and terrorists to other Latin American countries. The only remaining exit for these in the Western Hemisphere is through Mexico, but there we have close collaboration with Mexican authorities, who have confiscated many tons of Castro propaganda and refuse to allow anyone to travel to and from Cuba who does not have properly accredited passports.

One aspect of this policy which has been overlooked by virtually all disputants is the fact that it is presenting the Soviet Union with a serious question of policy of its own. As Cuba's ability to earn free foreign exchange and, therefore, to purchase goods in the international market is limited, the supply of needed goods and services to Cuba becomes increasingly the responsibility of the Soviet Union. It is now reported to be costing the USSR and its satellites at least $1 million a day to supply Cuba.

Inevitably, the Soviet leaders must be asking themselves whether this expenditure is worth it. Since October, 1962, they have known that Cuba cannot be used as a major military base against the United States. On the other hand, if Cuba is to be useful to the Communists as a showplace for their kind of society, the Soviet Union will have to spend a great deal more than it now is to bring this to pass. Current expenditures are merely serving to soften somewhat the decline of Cuba's economy and the levels of living of its people.

The Soviet Union's willingness to make such added expenditure is not yet evident. Furthermore, the long continued expenditure even at the present level must be conditioned by the unreliability of Castro as an ally, which we have previously discussed. In recent months there has been vocal protest from the Soviet Union's East European allies, who have been called upon to share the cost of aid to Cuba, against pouring good money after bad.

A second major element in the Kennedy policy toward Cuba was the Alliance for Progress. The Administration took the view, which the author fully supports, that the only way in which the danger of further Castro-like revolutions elsewhere in Latin America can be avoided, even in the short run, is to end the conditions which make the area ripe for such revolutions. This can be done by bringing about needed social reforms in these countries through democratic processes, while pushing forward more rapidly the economic development of the region.

The Alliance was not designed specifically to counter Fidel Castro and his influence in the hemisphere. Senator John F. Kennedy was very concerned with the deterioration of United States relations with Latin America well before the advent of Castro to power, and he had already outlined the major elements of a new United States policy toward the area by the time Fidel came victoriously into Havana.

However, the success of the Alliance as originally conceived by Kennedy would be the surest way of short-circuiting Castro's efforts to foment uprisings elsewhere. If agrarian reform can be started by a non-Communist regime and can give hope to the great mass of the landless peasants that they will receive land, and if some progress is being made in providing them with schools, electricity, housing, etc., the supporters of Fidel will find it very difficult to get them to join a guerrilla war. This has been amply demonstrated in Venezuela during the last couple of years. If economic development is rapid enough to provide even very modest increases in living levels, labor unions are not likely to substitute Communist or Jacobin Leftist leaders for democratic ones. Finally, if it becomes clear that the United States is willing and anxious to support democratic social reform and rapid economic development in the area, this will serve to contradict the xenophobic anti-Yankeeism of the Jacobin Leftists and Communists, who argue that the United States is against all progress in the area.

There are indications that the Johnson Administration has taken a somewhat different attitude towards the Alliance for Progress than did its predecessor. It has tended to downgrade the reform and political aspects of the Alliance, and to concentrate on its function as an aid to the economic development of Latin America. Continuation of this emphasis will greatly reduce the effectiveness of the Alliance as a means of confronting the Castro regime or using it as a tool for establishing a solid basis for political democracy in the hemisphere.

There is one final element which the author presumes to be part of the Kennedy-Johnson policy toward Cuba, but about which he has no positive information, and about which the United States government in the nature of the case cannot advertise. This is aid to the underground opposition to the Castro regime. There certainly is moral support in terms of radio and other propaganda. But this writer, for one, cannot say to what degree there is also backing given the anti-Castroites in terms of money, equipment, and arms.

In this connection, it seems quite understandable and correct that the Administration should not allow raids to be made upon Soviet ships and personnel in Cuba from United States soil. They are not worth the dangers of a further Soviet-American confrontation. However, it is hoped that more discreet help is being given to those elements which are actively engaged in trying to overthrow Castro.

However, one last word should be said concerning the opposition. One of the fundamental errors in the Bay of Pigs invasion, it seems, was the fact that those principally involved in it were ex-Batista supporters and very conservative anti-Batistianos. It is highly unlikely that people of this type will be able to overthrow Castro, if he is overthrown. The *status quo ante* 1959 is not going to be restored, and we should not wish to see it restored. It is the more radical opponents of Castro, those who accept the basic need for a revolution in Cuba but who wish it to be democratic, who are likely to be the effective opponents of Castro.

THE FUTURE

IT WOULD BE EXCEEDINGLY RASH TO PREDICT WHETHER OR NOT CURrent United States policy toward Cuba will be effective in securing the ouster sooner or later of the Castro regime. There are certain factors, however, which should be kept in mind by anyone who is really concerned about this problem rather than about making political debating points against the present Administration.

The first factor is that the problem of Castro is not a simple one. It cannot be dealt with in isolation. It involves our relations with the rest of Latin America. It is closely intertwined with the growing split in the international Communist movement. It may well also have repercussions on United States relations with the uncommitted countries of Asia and Africa.

The second point is that the overthrow of Castro is not something which can be accomplished easily or quickly. Anyone who argues that it can is either guilty of demagoguery or is advocating large-scale United States invasion of Cuba, which would be successful but would in all likelihood exchange one Communist regime on an island in the Caribbean for several on the mainland of Latin America.

Third is the fact that in all likelihood if Castro is overthrown his downfall will be brought about by elements within his regime. These elements are not likely to establish in its place a regime completely committed to the kind of extreme free enterprise system which does not exist in the United States but is advocated by many people in this country.

Hence, it is important for those in the United States government and outside of it who are concerned with this problem to be clear in their own minds what the essential prerequisites are for a Cuban regime with which we could cooperate. These, it seems, are three in number: that it be democratic; that it not be under the control of any foreign regime, Soviet, Chinese, or any other; and that it not ally itself in the world scene with the national enemies of the United States.

All other issues should be negotiable. Particularly, the future of formerly United States-owned property in the island should be subject to conversations between the Cuban successor government and the United States. The particular degree of mixture between government and private enterprise in the future mixed economy of the island should be the business of the people and government of post-Castro Cuba.

Finally, it is necessary to have both patience and flexibility in dealing with Cuba. The worst possible thing would be for the Cuban issue to become so much a political football that very short-run considerations would force this country into taking rash measures which would strengthen Castro or would involve us in a military adventure in Cuba which might result in his overthrow, but would also bring similar governments to power in other Latin American countries and might even involve us in World War III.

A MAJOR THEME OF THE PRECEDING ESSAY IS THAT DOMESTIC CUBAN *factors have been more important than international factors in the development of the Castro regime and its subsequent behavior in the Cold War. Similarly, in this essay, Leonard Binder presents the thesis that the viewpoints and prejudices of the policy-makers of the New Nations are more powerful determinants in guiding their role in the Cold War than objective outside forces. Mr. Binder seeks to impress us with the severe limitations on our powers to influence the international policies of the New Nations. Ignorance of these limitations could lead to futility and serious setbacks for Western diplomacy.*

Mr. Binder examines the level of "maturity" of New Nations' leaders, their grasp of their own nations' material limitations, their understanding of the effect their policies may have on the bipolar Cold War balance, whether they truly desire to see agreements between the United States and the Soviet Union, whether they display the flexible diplomacy and inclination toward peaceful accommodation that alone can move us toward an end or modification of the Cold War, whether they truly want to see the Cold War ended, and what caliber of international leadership can come from the New Nations.

His instructive answers to these many questions derive from his description of how the world looks to these leaders of relatively weak nations, which struggle to survive on the fringes of the Cold War. From this account we learn what, if anything, the New Nations may contribute to the task of building a world beyond the Cold War.

LEONARD BINDER

•

THE NEW STATES IN INTERNATIONAL AFFAIRS[1]

I

IN THE COMPARATIVE STUDY OF FOREIGN POLICIES A GREAT DEAL OF emphasis is placed upon the view that each individual government takes of the international system. These views will differ from country

[1]I would like to acknowledge the assistance of the Committee for the Comparative Study of New Nations at the University of Chicago in the working out of the ideas presented herein.

The term "new states" or "new nations" is the newest euphemism for non-Western and underdeveloped countries. It refers to the fact that these countries have been newly admitted into the society of states as that society was defined by the historical community of European states.

to country. They will be rooted in the attitudes of the policy-making elites within each country. When we start with a single analytical scheme, we impose our own framework on the international scene. When we, on the other hand, look at foreign policies, we are trying to conjure with a multiplicity of analytical approaches to the under-standing of international politics, and we must try to put these together in some kind of a framework.

There is an overlapping between the two approaches in that, in the second, you rely upon individual countries or the leaders of individual countries, to produce the analytical scheme. There can be even more overlapping in that occasionally, perhaps more than occasionally, we find that the conception of international politics that will dominate the thinking of a particular national elite will be a reaction to the point of view held by another elite. This, I think is helpful to us in establishing a frame by which we can understand, somewhat analytically, the diverse views that are taken by the leader-ships of underdeveloped countries. Their views regarding interna-tional politics are, to a very great extent, reactions to dominant views regarding international politics held in the West and among the former imperialist countries. They tend to be rejections of Western ways of viewing the international order. They are frequently counter-arguments, denials that our ways of viewing the international scene are at all correct.

It might be argued (with some justification) that the fact that the Western and developed countries *share* a more or less unified attitude toward international relations is a sign of intellectual maturity. These Western, developed countries, having grown up in the Western international system as it developed in Western Europe particularly during the post-Reformation period, have gained a common experi-ence through this history and have a more or less objective attitude toward international relations. Of course, they are imbued with nationalism, they seek their own self-interest, and so on, but they are capable of viewing those with whom they relate in international relations as being more or less of the same nature as they are. That is, the same interests will motivate them. They will have a parallel nationalism. They will seek economic welfare, and so on. It is possible to see, in one's antagonist or in one's ally, very much the same as one sees in oneself. In other words, it is sensible to extrapolate by means of introspection in approaching problems of policy.

This, it might be argued, is a kind of mature political view. It recognizes that there may be ideological differences, that ideological differences may lead us to distort our understanding of international relations, but if we are careful we will see that all nations want about the same thing and act the same way (given disparities of power and geographical position, etc., in international relations), but that one nation or another nation does not have a monopoly of right and justice.

Even if we argue that we have right and justice on our side and the Soviets and the Chinese have evil and injustice on their side, we attempt to establish this claim in terms of some kind of objective evidence, and we try to avoid, insofar as we can, the use of loaded terminology. We always accuse our antagonists of twisting words, or of using words in the wrong meaning, and we seek to establish the firm meaning of words. Hence, we might say that, in our understanding of international relations, intellectuals who are more or less uncommitted to set policy positions and to the institutional frame of policy-making in the United States are capable of exerting some kind of influence over the terminology that is used to describe international relations. It might be argued that the new nations are immature in this regard. In the main, they are concerned with acting against the dominant views of the Western powers, and the terminology they use will be borrowed as easily from the East as from the West. Very often the language they employ will be a debauching of the true meaning of the words that they choose, and they will even create catchwords of their own in an attempt to create the symbols that will serve to unify their own people behind them.

There is not anything very startling about remarking the disparity in economic capacity and in military power between the industralized countries of the West and the newly independent countries of Asia, Africa, and the Middle East. It is somewhat more rare, and certainly less acceptable to the leaders of the new nations, that attention be called to the disparity in the level of intellectual maturity with which the problems of international relations are faced. This is not to argue that our pursuit of self-interest is intellectually mature while theirs is not, or to use the notion of intellectual maturity in place of simple goodness.

Essentially, by intellectual maturity is meant the intellectual and emotional capacity to sustain a set of principles of behavior which will allow the possibility that occasionally alter is correct and ego at fault. The really critical aspect of such a position for international politics is not that it permits more effective policy-making in the simple senses of means-ends rationality and ideology as reality testing. Certain characteristics of the present international situation may preclude the possibility of ultimately testing out which of the views of the international scene is truly "realistic." The balance of terror and the neutralist power vacuum are situations which suggest that many issues will never be brought to a solution. We shall probably never learn by experience whether our view, the Soviet view, or the neutralist view of these issues is the correct one. The really important problem of international relations is not who can or how to best exploit these issues. If the essence of the interaction system known as "international" is purposeful negotiation and compromise, then a common set of assumptions about those relations is more important than one that is more empirically true in a descriptive sense. Descriptive empiricism would be in conflict with operative pragmatism. Correctly understanding existing predicaments is less important than discerning the means by which we will pass from existing situations to new ones. At least we are sure that things will change; they always have. The question then becomes whether the changes in the structure of international relations will be brought about by purposeful diplomacy, or whether they will emerge in an instable context of mutual misunderstanding and lack of effective communication.

The ideological is not the only dimension of a mature approach to international politics. Another dimension involves a realistic grasp of one's own material limitations. Even if goals are not determined by capabilities, the interdependence of capabilities and policy goals has to be recognized under ordinary conditions. Ordinary conditions are not prevailing conditions, however. The prevailing international situation is one in which the possibilities for interdiction are high but the possibilities for successful diplomatic, political, or military action correspondingly low. These prevailing conditions suit the leaders of most of the new nations very well. Under such conditions ideologically compelling prejudices about the international system need never be tested; under conditions of easy interdiction the differences between great powers and smaller ones are minimized; finally, under these conditions certain cultural preferences for verbalization over decision-making may be satisfied and a predominantly affective-oriented leadership maintained in power.

The prejudices of the new nations regarding contemporary international relations are ideological in the sense that they are derived from the need to react against Western views of the international system and from the need to respond to a domestic political environment about which they have very little real information.

In attempting to develop these two themes we shall proceed to examine some of the attitudes toward international relations which appear to be widely shared among the new nations. We shall refer to these attitudes as prejudices only in order to emphasize that they are counter-arguments and not to suggest that they are necessarily incorrect.

II

THE FIRST TOPIC INVOLVES A SET OF PREJUDICES RATHER THAN A SINGLE one. This is the problem of understanding bipolarity. The concepts "loose" and "tight" bipolarity, as used by M. Kaplan in his *System and Process in International Relations* permit us to distinguish, in a preliminary fashion, between the views of the new nations and those of the great powers at the onset of the Cold War. It would appear that the great powers conceived of the emerging structure of the international system as one characterized by tight bipolarity. It might even be argued that they thought such a system the one that *ought* to exist.

Gradually, as new nations came into being through decolonization, they proffered views which stressed the importance of a loose bipolar system which would permit non-aligned countries to withdraw from this struggle. We, and others, rejected, for a very long time, the possibility that there could be any such thing as loose bipolarity. The United States expended great efforts in seeking tight bipolarity. The Brussels Pact and NATO following that, together with the sprucing up of the Organization of American States, and other manifestations of pactomania all reflect an attempt to tighten the bipolar structure of the international system.

The Soviet Union, during the early post-World War II phase, in rejecting the tactics of working with the national bourgeoisie, did the same thing. The USSR rejected the possibility of working together with non-Communist countries and in a sense was pushing all of the neutralist countries into the arms of the United States. It was the reaction to colonialism and to Western imperialism that prevented them from falling into our arms.

In a sense, the neutralist view, or the non-aligned view, or the view of the new nations, has come to predominate in the international scene in this matter of bipolarity. The kind of bipolar structure we have is a loose one and not a tight one. Indeed, both of the superpowers are trying to enhance the looseness of the bipolar system in the sense of permitting and encouraging neutralism. They are not trying to encourage the looseness of their own blocs, but they have been unable to discourage the loosening of either the Eastern or the Western blocs. These blocs have loosened.

The view that loose bipolarity is an appropriate structure for the

199

international system has been encouraged by the occurrence of middle-power aggression. Technically, middle power means non-super power, but it has special reference to Britain and France going into Suez in 1956. That invasion raised the question of whether it is possible under a system of a loose bipolarity for middle-power aggression to be successful. This question in turn raises the further question as to whether or not the new nations are right when they say that they are afraid of the renewal of Western imperialism. The events of 1956 have been diversely interpreted. We can only ask the question, does 1956 prove that we will have middle-power aggression because we had it in 1956, or does 1956 prove that we will not have middle-power aggression because that aggression failed in 1956.

Among the elites of the new nations, politically informed people continue to insist upon the possibility of middle-power aggression. In their view, the possibility of renewed middle-power aggression can best be coped with by enhancing the looseness of the great power blocs and by the organizational blocs among the new nations. They are encouraged in this view by the propaganda efforts of the Soviet Union. In encouraging this view the USSR has been able to exploit the greater looseness of the Western alliance and subsequently might dissociate itself from Chinese aggression in India. To India's chagrin, most of the new nations still find it difficult to attribute a tendency toward middle-power aggression to any but the declining imperialist members of the Western bloc.

A third difference of attitude between the great powers and the new nations concerns the role of the new nations under existing conditions of bipolarity. To put the matter concisely, the question is whether the new nations can influence international affairs by other than moral means. The great powers act as though they believed that the material capabilities of the new nations might be significant factors in resolving the bipolar conflict. The leaders of the new nations tend toward the belief that their own attachment to either bloc will not significantly alter the bipolar balance.

Theoretically, the issue is one of the measurement of power in international relations. The very meaning of the term bipolarity is involved, for the stability and continuity of a bipolar system must be related to certain assumptions about the distribution of power in that system. Assumptions are not the same thing as knowledge, and it may be further acknowledged that we have no sure way of determining the power differential between the United States and the Soviet Union. Under the circumstances, there is room for more than one opinion; there may be a reasonable justification of both the demand that the new nations align with the blocs of their choice and of the insistence that non-alignment can do no harm and may do some good. More importantly, those who are convinced that they cannot materially alter the bipolar balance are easily convinced that demands for total alignment are expressions of a renewed imperialism unrelated to the bipolar struggle.

The view of the new nations is in part sustained by the difficulty we face in attempting to measure power comparatively. Despite efforts of rival intelligence agencies to count the hardware in the possession of all possible opponents, this sort of intelligence product will tell us nothing about the conditions under which hostilities might be initiated. The new nations would be quite correct about their own inability to alter the bipolar balance only if we could be absolutely sure that the balance rests upon the balance of terror. To put the point even more directly, the condition under which the position of the new nations is correct is that the great powers would be willing to use nuclear weapons in other than the most extreme circumstances.

It is most difficult to attempt to define the conditions under which any of the great powers might use nuclear weapons, but conceivably issues relating to the disposition of the new nations with regard to both regional politics and bipolar politics might be considered of less than extreme moment. Though it is not necessary to this argument, I would go even further and assert that it is at least conceivable that the leaders of both the United States and the Soviet Union could not be brought to use nuclear weapons unless first attacked by the other.

If we can call the situation just described a balance of terror, what are the consequences of this nuclear stalemate for the possible role of the new nations in international relations? Clearly, under these conditions, the role of the new nations may no longer be determined by the results of power measurement or our inability to measure power. The actions of the new nations will manifest themselves in regionally particularized strategies which may radically alter the existing structure of the international system. It might be going too far to argue the possibility that the Cold War might be won or lost in the developing areas, but we can argue that substantial changes can take place which may provide a distinct advantage for one side or the other.

The balance of terror and the strong likelihood that nuclear weapons will not be used increase the opportunities and the responsibilities of the new nations. The great powers tend to be most sensitive to the new responsibilities of the new nations, while the leaders of the new nations are more aware of their opportunities.

Insistence upon the collective moral responsibility of the new nations to end the Cold War glosses over the empirical consequences of specific allocations of their material capacities. There is good reason to gloss over this aspect of the foreign policies of the new nations, too, for their leaders believe that the nuclear stalemate absolves them of responsibility for the material disposition of the bipolar conflict. This conviction leads them to the further assumption that no use of their own material power within their own regions can have serious consequences for the bipolar system.

It is these views which have helped to define several regional international systems which have become more or less independent of the major bipolar system. These regional systems are primarily culture areas in which certain languages predominate. It is easier for intellectuals and political leaders to communicate with one another than with the representatives of the great powers. It is also relatively easier for political leaders in these regions to communicate directly with all of the urban populations of the region. In a sense, subordinate international systems are propaganda systems. Most of the members of these systems have little power and cannot exert much of what power they do possess beyond their own boundaries. Nevertheless, a little strength goes a long way in these regions because they are relatively well insulated from the influence of the great powers.

The reasons for this insulation are doubtlessly as variable as is the degree of insulation itself. Still, the limited influence of extra-regional powers is adequately demonstrated in pointing to the difficulty outside powers have in attempting to sustain governments which are uncongenial to neighboring regional powers. Illustrations may be drawn from the Indo-Chinese peninsula, from the Middle East, and from Africa to bear out this point. The situation described represents a decided reversal of the condition which permitted the scramble for colonies outside Europe. Thus it is the decline of imperialism as well as the bipolar conflict which contributes to the partial independence of these regional systems.

But these systems are independent in only a limited sense. The great powers do intervene, although they find it most effective to do so through an area power. More significant than that, however, is the possibility (already discussed) that changes in the regional systems may ultimately affect the dominant bipolar system. If the latter is true, the only way in which the great powers may control their own destinies is to come to an agreement about the disposition of these regional systems. Obviously, such an agreement is precisely the most feared outcome of the Cold War as far as the leaders of the new nations are concerned.

The second prejudice is that the policy of populist regimes is always moral, by nationalist definition. By nationalist definition, we mean here that the nation-state is thought to represent the sovereignty of the people as a whole, and a populist regime is one which claims to derive its legitimacy from the people. Since there is no higher authority than the sovereign people, then anything which the sovereign people requires or demands is, *ipso facto*, moral. This definition applies especially within the framework of international relations that has been accepted by the new nations. Each of these nations sees itself as one of a host of independent sovereignties, no one of which has the power to insist upon that which is moral or ethically correct above any other independent sovereignty. As a consequence, then, of nationalist definition, the policies of populist regimes are always just. There is no higher justice than that which is demanded by a populist regime in a nation-state.

Third, a great many leaders of new nations believe that economic development depends upon skillful international maneuvering. In the few cases where a sufficiency of domestic resources may be found for economic development this may not apply. Nevertheless, even the best endowed of the new nations need ready capital and technical skills which they must somehow move from the more advanced countries to their own. The close links which have evolved between development assistance policies and Cold War policies have rendered international boundaries less of a barrier to economic development than they were before World War II. On the other hand, the mechanism which moves development resources in international exchange is not so much comparative advantage as it is diplomatic advantage. This diplomatic advantage is often based, in turn, upon a favorable geographical position within a region.

From the point of view of the new nations, the Cold War may be recognized as the existential source of the goods and services so desperately needed for development, but the willing acceptance of these things is justified by the argument that the country has been exploited by imperialist powers and native resources have been drawn away to Europe or to the Western hemisphere.

What is more significant is that the limits on economic development are unknown and the possible scope of development aspirations unbounded. Neither domestic resources nor some agreed notion of what is due from the more developed countries serve to set rational limits. The only real limitation upon development is in the limited diplomatic ability of the new nations to extract resources from the international system as a whole.

Fourth, the pattern of the international system permits the establishment of asymmetrical relationships with the great powers. Many leaders of new nations believe that international relations in modern times permits and justifies a way of playing the diplomatic game whereby the new nation gives less than the new nation takes in dealings with the great powers. That is to say, one does not have to think in terms that have been made famous by George Kennan and Professor Morgenthau. One does not have to think of diplomacy in terms of accommodation, of give and take on more or less equal terms. Exactly what the measure of the exchange must be is not at all clear. That depends again on the skills that may be brought to bear on the game. The basis of this view is partly ideological, depending upon a particular interpretation of the moral consequences of imperialism, and partly political, depending upon assumptions about the nature of bipolarity which we have already discussed.

Fifth, intra-area relations are or ought to be insulated from extra-area influences. It is characteristic of the thinking of many of the leaders of new nations, if not all, that somehow or other the whole purpose of bipolarity and of setting up new nations over and against the former colonial powers, weaker nations over and against stronger nations is to establish an ethical barrier which sustains the barrier, created by a nuclear stalemate, against the intervention of the super-powers in the regions of the world outside the developed areas of Western Europe and the North American continent. They either hold that American, Soviet, and Western European power cannot be intruded into the underdeveloped areas or that it ought not be intruded, and they maintain that somehow or other the pattern of the international system as it has developed in post-colonial times and in the nuclear age permits the insulation of these areas from great power influence.

Sixth, they believe that the boundaries which are the heritage of imperialism are illegitimate and ought to be changed. All governments want to keep the territory that they now have, but there is precious little legitimacy attached to boundaries anywhere that have been established by imperial powers which are alien to these regions. A great many leaders of the new nations are interested in altering these boundaries so that they may conform to their own notions of legitimacy. Often, these notions barely disguise a kind of neo-irredentism which results in an instability further aggravated by tendencies toward regional integration.

The seventh prejudice is that regional integration or federation can resolve many domestic problems and provide the necessary power for full entry into the major system of international relations. Not all leaders share these views, but when certain leaders of underdeveloped countries come up against what appear to be irresolvable problems of development or of unifying ethnically diverse peoples within a certain territory, they find that they can change the nature of their situation by thumping for regional integration or for federation with neighboring countries. They hope this will change the pattern, either the ethnic pattern, the pattern of resources, the pattern of external threat, or perhaps even the pattern of foreign trade.

By increasing the territory and the number of people that are associated under a single government, the power and influence of the particular underdeveloped state may be increased. If the power of an underdeveloped country can thus be increased by adding territory and population, and not only by adding military equipment and military capacity, then it may be possible—just barely possible—that the new nation can enter the dominant international system. It might be able to get a veto in the Security Council. This would be symbolic of becoming a truly great power. Despite their rejection of the attitudes and assumptions of the Western nations toward international relations, the ultimate goal of at least the larger and more powerful of the new nations is to be included within that framework of dominant nations. But it is a matter of tactics, also, to reject the great power view of international politics until such time as the nation may have a chance of entering into that great power arrangement.

Some states will have the chance to do that. Certainly India will have some opportunity at sometime in the future of entering into the major international system. Doubtlessly at sometime in the future China will have a similar opportunity. Perhaps Brazil will be able to do this. Whether any African state can become a world power is questionable. Certainly it would be impossible to conceive of a present-day African state entering into the major international system, or becoming a veto power in the Security Council, unless a widespread federative movement takes place.

And the last of the prejudices attributed to leaders of new nations is that they often feel that the foreign policies of great and small powers are fixed ideologically and hence may be easily comprehended. They tend to believe that foreign policies do not vary with

situations and that they do not vary with opportunity. They will call
their enemies opportunists and they will use the epithet of Machiavel-
ism, but in the main they tend to approach their own domestic and
external problems in terms of a nationalist ideology, and they will
attribute a similar view to the leaders of other countries. Perhaps this
is because most of the leaders of the underdeveloped countries are
intellectuals of one sort or another.

While the prejudices of the leaders of the new nations regarding
international affairs are not necessarily incorrect, they have certain
consequences for the diplomatic performance of the new nations.
These consequences are negative from the point of view of those who
prefer flexible diplomacy and peaceful accommodation. If we re-
examine our list of prejudices, we find that few of them encourage
compromise: If the balance of terror prevents the great powers from
acting, if the policies of populist states are moral by definition, if
relationships with great powers may be asymmetrical, and if foreign
policies are ideologically fixed, why should any state be encouraged to
negotiate toward a compromise? The same tendency prevails in
regional relations as well as in relations with the great powers. The
illegitimacy of local boundaries and the domestic basis of the desire
for regional integration create an atmosphere of distrust that weakens
regional diplomatic processes.

A second consequence of these prejudices is that the foreign
policies of the new nations will not be adjusted to their material
capabilities. For the leaders of the new nations, achievement of
international goals will depend primarily upon matters of ideology
and verbal cunning. It may be doubted that great successes will attend
the implementation of such policy, but the prospect that failure will
not be attributed to lack of resources portends even more extremism
as the pattern of frustration develops.

A third consequence, which depends on the first two, will be a
continuation of the presently low incentive to train good diplomats
and to give such men important responsibilities. There is, after all,
little sense in training men to gather the facts and report on the
background of important international issues if the facts do not
matter. Area specialists need not be trained if the only countries that
count are those visited by contemporary leaders during their school
days.

III

IT IS CLEAR THAT THE DIPLOMATIC PERFORMANCE OF THE NEW NATIONS
will not reduce the difficulties of the great powers in getting along

with one another, nor will they be very effective in ironing out their own problems with neighboring regional powers. Our consideration of the attitudes and prejudices of new nation leaders has led us to this conclusion, but it is further sustained by the extremely weak institutional base for foreign policy formulation and administration in the underdeveloped countries and by the vague "operational code" of neutralism which has been derived from the new nations' view of the structure of the international system. In examining these two additional bases for pessimism regarding the international political role of the developing nations, some effort will be made to distinguish among the countries. In terms of general orientation as described above, most new nations are similar, but they see themselves somewhat differently in their own regional contexts. They also have varying institutional arrangements which give rise to different kinds of policy limitations.

The major weaknesses of the new nations in policy-making and administration are organizational. There is little understanding of what an organization dedicated to the carrying on of foreign affairs, such as a foreign ministry, is supposed to do, and few facilities, either human or mechanical, are provided for doing anything besides maintaining ceremonial representation. In general, foreign ministries are like armies in that they are manifestations of national sovereignty; but unlike armies they tend to have little influence in making foreign policy. Most of the new nations have instituted cabinet systems, but the minister of foreign affairs is usually a dependent of the king or president or prime minister. His prestige within the cabinet is usually lower than that of the minister of defense or the minister of interior or even of the minister of national economy. The foreign minister will often be a party crony, a wealthy aristocrat, a relative of the head of the state, or perhaps a technician of fairly low political prestige. The tasks assigned to the ministry will be mostly routine, such as case-making on a day-to-day basis at the United Nations, checking up on students studying in foreign countries, advertising for tourists, and carrying on routine economic services such as issuing import licenses and settling tax problems. The most significant part of the duties of the ministry will be maintaining ceremonial representation and dealing with the representatives of foreign countries, most of whom will similarly be from underdeveloped countries.

The recruitment of diplomatic personnel for the ministry as well as for the overseas posts usually differs somewhat from the recruitment of ordinary civil servants. Foreign ministry posts are prestige positions preferred above most other sub-cabinet positions, but they are reserved for the most loyal, the most highly educated, and usually for members of the dominant ethnic community. Qualifications for such positions, besides the expected university degree, are knowledge of languages and of international law. Specialized area knowledge is not required.

If the foreign service differs in composition from the rest of the civil service, the conception of its method of working does not. Most foreign service officers sit at desks, read and note files that pass around offices, and conceive of their jobs as the carrying out of routine tasks. Even this kind of administrative arrangement suffers from all the ills of administrative underdevelopment: There is an excess of formalism in office relations, responsibility is avoided and the "buck passed" whenever possible, records are kept poorly and are hard to find, and channels of internal communication are very poor.

The consequence of this type of institutional arrangement is that the foreign ministries of the new nations can provide little infrastructural support for the serious study and rational determination of foreign policy problems. Foreign policy decisions are not related to staff work in the ministry, but are primarily general positions taken as a result of direct contact between heads of state or based upon the advice of a few influential insiders who may be more ideologues than foreign affairs specialists. Where the organizational machinery is even weaker, the great bulk of foreign policy may simply be taken over from a neighboring state.

In a most general way, these weaknesses characterize foreign policy organization in all of the new nations, but the impact of these weaknesses does vary with particular institutional arrangements. We cannot go into a detailed description of all the varied institutional patterns of the new nations, so in order to illustrate the differential impact of the difficulties described we will employ a simple analytical typology of five kinds of regimes.

First is party governments, governments where the political elite is essentially that of a political party. As examples we will choose Turkey, India, Ceylon, and Nigeria. Parliamentarism may be just as important as party activity, and the number of active parties is not an important criterion here. The critical factor is party organization. Political leaders are designated by the party or act through the party and within a parliamentary framework.

The second group will be the military regimes which are bent on radical reform. Here we have Egypt, Pakistan, Burma, and the Sudan as examples.

A third would be one led by a single national party, the head of which is a charismatic leader or one who tries to develop his own charisma. We take Ghana, Indonesia, Guinea, and possibly the Ivory Coast as examples of this third kind of institutional pattern.

Fourth, are mixed traditional regimes in which you may have a monarch, in which you may have an aristocratic oligarchy, but in which you also have modern military units, a modern bureaucracy, modern taxation systems, or modern entrepreneurship, not as characteristic features but as adjuncts to traditional institutions. Thailand, Iran, Libya, and Morocco are mixed traditional regimes.

Fifth are traditional, monarchical regimes. Ethiopia, Saudi Arabia, Cambodia, and Afghanistan are examples.

In the first of our categories, under party governments, there is some semblance of popular participation and influence in policy-making. Such popular participation is limited to the educated classes only and may only manifest itself in parliamentary debates and editorials rather than through permanently organized voluntary associations or rank-and-file party member activity. Nevertheless, the possibility of debate and criticism encourages the accumulation of accurate information, the assessment of consequences, and the proposal of alternatives. Where party government has worked reasonably well within a parliamentary framework we usually find a firm foreign policy consensus and a degree of policy stability and responsibility which is all too rare among the new nations.

In the first two of our categories, under party governments and under military radical-reform governments, a trained professional bureaucracy plays a relatively important part in foreign policy-making. Both types of regime depend heavily, for all political and administrative tasks, upon a modern educated class which was in most cases developed under foreign occupation. Foreign service officers will not make the most important of foreign policy decisions, but as in the case of much domestic policy the initiative in bringing up problems for decision rests with the bureaucrat. The prestige of bureaucracies is high in these countries, and efficient administration, even if routine in nature, is commonly associated with the concept of modernity. It is, therefore, among these countries that the administrative strictures described above have their greatest impact.

The second group of countries, i.e., the military-radical-reform regimes, are occasionally the source of some anxiety to their neighbors because of the expectation that a government of militarists will tend toward an aggressive foreign policy. Such fears have not been much borne out by experience, which rather demonstrates the persistence of the inefficient bureaucracy syndrome.

Leonard Binder

There have been, perhaps, two outstanding occasions in which military force has been exported by new nations in very recent times. One of these is the export of Egyptian troops to the Yemen. There was a much smaller group of Egyptian troops sent to the Congo, and some Ghanaian troops, too, but it was obvious that these movements were not undertaken solely under the resources of those countries themselves but that there was an infrastructural base that was provided by the United Nations and by the United States.

In the Yemen, we could say that Egypt managed to pull off an export of military force wholly on its own that was not entirely ineffective. Another example is the use of military force by the Indonesian government, first to put down a rebellion in Sumatra and then in preparation for the forcing of the Dutch out of West Irian. It was apparent that the demonstrated ability of the Indonesian government in using force against the rebellion in Sumatra proved their potential for the export of military force to West Irian. In other words, they could have given the Dutch some trouble. How much trouble, we can not tell, but evidently enough trouble that the Dutch were not willing to suffer that discomfort and withdrew from West Irian.

Here are two examples of the possibility of the export of military force by new nations. They do not encourage us to believe that this can be done very effectively or that the use of force by new nations will become a more frequent occurrence in international relations or area international relations despite the dominance of military leaders in so many of these governments. It may be concluded that the continued dominance of the military is significant for the maintenance of domestic control rather than as a factor in international relations.

In the last three types of regime, party-charismatic, mixed traditional, and traditional-monarchical, professional bureaucracies play a very small part in the determination of foreign policy. In all three, foreign policy-making is the prerogative of a small group of political insiders. They differ greatly, however, in the degree of importance attributed to foreign relations. The party-charismatic regimes consider foreign policy, and particularly positions taken on Cold War issues, as highly important. Foreign policy is made by the leader and a small group of confidants. The methods are often more conspiratorial than formal and administrative. Nevertheless, foreign policy tends to be declaratory rather than operative.

In the mixed traditional regimes, the major outline of foreign policy is produced by the head of the state and mechanically pursued by the foreign minister. Usually, there will be found a small group of

landed and influential persons who have recently entered into commercial activities. One of the most important parts of the foreign
relations of such countries is the devious process by which these
persons exert influence over economic policy. By contrast, Cold War
policy or development policy may not stand out as such controversial
issues. With these regimes, too, policy tends to be declaratory rather
than operative.

In the last group, the truly traditional monarchies, foreign policy
is the prerogative of the king, but it is often made by a special adviser
who may even be a foreign resident. Foreign powers generally have
great influence over the policies of these monarchies, but the moral
bond between highly traditional regimes and others is so weak that
the pattern of their relations with others most nearly resembles the
pragmatic bargaining ideal. Surprising as it may seem, even these
governments tend to follow the prevailing method of voicing neutralist platitudes about grave international questions in order to
strengthen the impression that they, too, are "new" nations.

All three of these groups of states, despite the important differences among them, illustrate the paradoxical disparity between the
ease of implementing declaratory policy externally and the difficulty
of implementing development policy internally. The paradox has
little operational significance for the two traditional types of regime
because we are not at all convinced that their rulers desire economic
development. Their international declarations are made simply because that is the thing to do. In some cases declarations may be made
in order to avoid more effective means of dealing with internal
development. For the party-charismatic regimes there is a closer
connection between foreign policy declarations and internal policy.
The former is not so much a substitute for the latter as it may be
thought of as a means of acquiring the resources needed for the
latter. Nevertheless, one cannot forebear the suggestion that some
governments have found it more pleasant to concentrate upon making foreign policy declarations than in actually moving ahead with
development. Some of them hope, through such symbolic manipulation as may be involved in declaratory efforts on the international
scene, to creat solidarity, unity, support for the government; to break
down ethnic barriers within their own country; and to overcome what
appear to be cultural and social obstacles to economic development.
They do this because they cannot come to grips with the problems of
development in a direct technical and administrative manner.

Finally, we distinguish the policies of the new nations in terms of
two additional factors: (1) policy stability and (2) initiative. These two

are, in this author's opinion, relatively contrary to one another. Policy stability refers essentially to continuity in the pursuit of declared goals or in positions vis-à-vis other countries. Initiative means showing maneuverability, flexibility, and the ability to switch from one kind of arrangement to another kind of arrangement, from friendship with a country to hostility and back again to friendship as tactical requirements may demand.

This is not an arbitrary or formalistic distinction, but one that is closely dependent upon the prejudices of the new nations about the international system. We have described those prejudices, and we have discussed some of the problems which affect the performance of the new nations in international politics. The role of the new nations is in part determined by both, and we shall define it in terms of a neutralist operational code. It will be noted that effective role performance as defined by the operational code requires a degree of policy initiative that cannot be sustained by all new nations. Those new nations that are capable of demonstrating initiative are not only bound to benefit from the persistence of a distinctive new nations' view of international relations; they will also be the ones who will most threaten the stability of great power relations. Manifestly, such incentive and the possible resultant threats will occur within the underdeveloped regions.

The rules of neutralist policy are as follows:

First, that non-alignment is restricted only to Cold War issues. On all other issues, especially those relating to either the relations between the West and the underdeveloped areas, the East and underdeveloped areas, or underdeveloped areas among themselves, one does take a position.

Second, that it is up to the neutrals to derive maximum benefit from either side in the Cold War.

Third, that everything possible must be done to prevent either side from winning the Cold War. By preventing this victory, the new nations will have time to catch up. If they will ever catch up, they must have time to do so. By preventing a victory in the Cold War, they will also prevent a renewed imperialism. Finally, by preventing such victory in the Cold War, they will manage to continue to insulate the power of the great powers from being intruded into their own areas of the world. And, lastly, once the great powers are firmly excluded, a new relationship among regional powers, one that is unaffected by imperialism, must be brought about.

If the foregoing interpretation of the neutralist role is correct, then it follows that policy flexibility and the ability to hit upon new policy initiative within, at least the region, are essential to adequate performance. Performance may be hindered by lack of objectivity, and it may be hindered by inadequate organizational and institutional facilities. Here, however, we are more concerned with situational factors which permit some new nations to benefit greatly from the existing structure of the international system while other states, not much different in terms of the topics already discussed, are prevented from so doing. Needless to add, the new nations which are so favorably situated are a minority, but it is they who have been able to perpetuate the new nations' perspective of the international system.

Policy stability or initiative do not appear to depend very much upon institutional factors or even upon the level of development of the country itself, but rather upon the geographical position of the country and upon the attitudes and ideology of the political elite. Let us look first at some of the new nations whose foreign policies are relatively stable. The first group refutes our assertion that policy stability has little to do with institutional arrangements, for our party government group of Turkey, India, Ceylon, and Nigeria all have fairly stable policies. It may be possible that parliamentary restraints upon rapid shifts in foreign policy as might be determined by an unhampered executive are operative in these cases. On the other hand, other matters may also come into the picture.

Pakistan, until permitted greater flexibility as a consequence of the Chinese attack on India, pursued a very consistent policy. For a long while, the Pakistani position was determined more or less by what the United States would permit and by how much the United States would give. While this has changed to some extent, it is apparent that Pakistan is unwilling to sever her connections with the West. Pakistan's greatest concern remains fear of India and the future of Kashmir.

Burma has had a relatively stable policy. Friendly with the West in a vague way and fearful of Communist China in a most immediate manner, Burma has attempted to pursue a neutralist policy of the purest type in order to keep out of trouble. The Sudan with a similarly stable policy has been more friendly with the West, but retains a policy of non-alignment because this ambivalent position best deters the UAR from interfering in Sudanese affairs. Thailand has had a similarly stable policy resulting from fear of China, a willingness to accept American assistance, and a desire to protect established privilege domestically. Iran is similarly fearful of the Soviet Union, willing to accept American assistance, and desirous of preserving elements of political tradition. Libya, Saudi-Arabia, and

Ethiopia all combine fear of neighbors with a desire to preserve tradition and all have stable, consistent, foreign policies.

The flexible countries are far fewer. Egypt is one of them. Ghana, Indonesia, Guinea have also shown some initiative. Morocco apparently has shown some ability to switch back and forth, but it is probably going to be backed into a position of stable dependence upon the West if there is a movement for unification of Arab North Africa. Cambodia has also seen a little switching back and forth by a skillful king, and this is attributable to uncertainty over which neighbor to fear most.

Afghanistan has shown some amazing flexibility in balancing its position among its neighbors, but one wonders whether this is really flexibility and initiative on the part of Afghanistan and/or a kind of passive acceptance of assistance from both sides and a rejection of any attachment in a very passive way. On the other hand Afghanistan has attacked Pakistan. The Afghans have manipulated the tribesmen. They have tried to make deals with Iran. They have sent delegations to Egypt and have allied with India.

These few examples suggest certain tentative conclusions. The first of these is that policy stability is fairly closely correlated with either parliamentary institutions or an association (sympathetic or material) with the Western bloc. In too many of the cases the institutional pattern that is most closely associated with stability is a traditional monarchical pattern or a mixed traditional one. But the most outstanding characteristic uniting all of the new nations with fairly stable foreign policies is their fear of powerful and hostile neighbors. It does not seem to matter much whether these neighbors are neutral countries or members of the Soviet bloc. We have further made no distinction between those countries of stable policy which are formally allied with the West and those which are not. For purposes of analyzing the role of the new nations in world politics it would appear that neither institutional patterns nor Cold War associations can serve as really useful analytical tools. Given prevailing attitudes among the new nations about the bipolar conflict, and given their performance weaknesses, the really critical questions become which of the new nations can take advantage of the resultant situation in their own regions and what effect will their action have on the bipolar struggle if we assume the likely possibility that nuclear weapons will not be used by either side.

THE UNITED NATIONS WAS FOUNDED BEFORE THE COLD WAR BEGAN, and its Charter assumes co-operation among the great powers as the necessary foundation of an effective international organization. Termination of the Cold War is, therefore, a logical goal of the United Nations, for cold war is alien to the nature of the UN. At the same time, the existence of the Cold War among the great powers robs the organization of its strength and thus is the chief reason that the world cannot rely on the peace-keeping power of the UN. The Cold War is also the underlying cause of many of the transformations which have occurred in the institutional character of the UN, as its members have sought, one way or another, to make it an effective peace-keeping agency.

Since the Cold War began, the UN has been looked to hopefully as the instrument by which the new world beyond the Cold War might be reached. What are the prospects? Erich Hula begins with the assumption that the survival of the UN depends on the continuing strong support of the United States; that, in turn, depends on whether the UN deserves our support. Are the interests of the United Nations and the United States in accord?

To answer this sovereign question, Mr. Hula first takes us back to the founding of the UN, to consider its original design and how its subsequent history has affected the form and course of the Cold War. This reconsideration of the UN and its Charter also shows how the Cold War has affected the form and workings of the organization.

Mr. Hula shows how the United Nations Charter reflected the controversy within the United States between the internationlists and the isolationists, why we insisted on the extraordinary powers of the Security Council in 1945, why we led the movement to alter the distribution of power that gave more of the peace-keeping function to the General Assembly in 1950, and what the consequences of this and other changes are now for the United Nations and the United States.

The growth of neutralism and anticolonialism, in intensity and extension, and the proliferation of new Asian and African members of the General Assembly, have operated to change drastically the appearance, the temperament, the character, and the functions of the United Nations. These and other factors are shown by Mr. Hula to explain why the UN has not succeeded and cannot now be successful as an international peace-keeping force.

It can and should be stated that as an agency of mediation and conciliation, the UN's performance, though uneven, has been "far from poor." And this must be balanced against the negative findings that African and Asian nations are using the UN to achieve their own ends, which, as Leonard Binder has shown, will not necessarily be in accord with the interests of the United States. Perhaps a more persuasive negative finding is, as Mr. Hula points out, that "it is no accident that the Charter outlaws war but not revolution," and so-called revolutions, exploiting the sentiments of anticolonialism, are being used throughout the world to promote the interests of the Communist camp and to endanger the position of the United States in the Cold War.

Mr. Hula thus comes to the inevitable question: Does the United States

215

serve its cause better by continuing its membership or withdrawing from the United Nations? Consideration of that question raises prior questions: What can we reasonably expect to be able to make the United Nations do? What can we reasonably expect to be able to prevent the United Nations from doing? What are the most likely, and most dangerous, possible areas of conflict between the interests of the United States and the United Nations?

Mr. Hula's conclusions of what we should do are based on realistic appraisals of past and future gains and losses. What we will do will depend very much on our understanding of what the United Nations is and is not. For example, if we continue to encourage or tolerate efforts to extend further the powers of the General Assembly, not anticipating a future day when "the General Assembly might engage . . . in peace-keeping operations of which we could not approve, to which, in fact, we would be opposed," that lack of understanding and foresight might make a decision to withdraw from the United Nations advantageous and even imperative.

Mr. Hula urges us and guides us to judge the United Nations for what it is and will be, not what it might have been or what we wish it were. Only thus can we know what role it may play hereafter.

ERICH HULA

●

THE UNITED STATES AND
THE UNITED NATIONS

THE UNITED NATIONS POLICY OF THE UNITED STATES HAS BEEN A matter of increasing concern in recent years. This concern has become manifest especially in the national debate, inside and outside the United States Congress, over the United Nations bond issue. Several participants in the discussion, men whose public record qualifies them as sincere supporters of the world organization, have asked for, or undertaken themselves, a reconsideration of the United Nations

216

and of the policy that the United States should pursue toward and in the world body.[1]

A sober reappraisal of the United Nations, as it is today, in the light of the foreign policy interests of the United States, is indeed well warranted. Admittedly, the United Nations owes its existence primarily to American efforts; the United Nations Charter is largely the product of American planning, and the actual development of the Organization *praeter* and *contra legem* has been decisively influenced by United States actions. But all this does not deprive us of the right to ask whether and to what extent the United Nations still deserves American support. The special relationship of the United States to the United Nations merely obligates us, when reassessing our United Nations policy, to be duly conscious of the special responsibility which the United States has assumed toward the Organization.

I

THERE ARE A GREAT MANY VARIANTS OF CRITICISM IN THIS COUNTRY OF the United Nations and its policies. There are in fact about as many as there are cases in which the United Nations has, or has not, taken action and as there are views, valid and invalid, on what the United Nations can, and what it should, do. The criticism ranges from the charge that the Organization has no practical relevancy in the real world of international politics, to the accusation that it is a serious threat to the sovereignty and security of the United States. These extreme contentions are suggestive of the two main trends of criticism to which the United Nations has been, and is, subjected.

During the first decade of its existence the United Nations was chiefly reproached for not doing things, for not going far enough in what it was supposed to do, for not making full use of the legal powers conferred on it. Complaints of this type were probably strongest in the Greek case, but were leveled at the Organization also in the Indonesian, the Palestine, the Kashmir, and, last but not least the Korean case. True, as the United Nations, contrary to what this criticism would seem to suggest, took in general a rather broad view of its legal authority, even in those earlier years, it was occasionally also blamed for exceeding its powers. But the trend favoring a loose construction of the Charter definitely prevailed in American public opinion during the initial period of the United Nations.

[1]See the collection of essays on the United Nations in Raymond A. Moore, Jr., ed. *The United Nations Reconsidered* (New York: Columbia Univ. Press, 1963).

Erich Hula

Owing to the emergence and the growing influence of new political forces in the United Nations, still another type of criticism gained momentum in American public opinion during the second decade of the Organization's existence. More and more often the United Nations was reproached not for what it did not do but, on the contrary, for what it did do, for going too far in its actions, for arrogating and exercising powers that under the Charter it did not possess, particularly for intruding into the domestic jurisdiction of member states, expressly recognized by the Charter as falling outside United Nations control. These complaints were, and are, chiefly related to the activities of the world body in the rapidly shrinking colonial field and were vehement in the cases of the Congo, West New Guinea, South Africa, Southern Rhodesia, and the Portuguese African territories.

This criticism of United Nations policies poses the problem of the current policy and position of the United States in the world Organization. Insofar as the United States government wholeheartedly supported, or even initiated, those policies, it clearly shares in the responsibility for them, as is the case in the issues of the Congo and West New Guinea. If, as in the other cases mentioned, the United States obviously only yielded to political pressures brought to bear upon its decisions, the question arises as to how strong the United States still is in the councils of the United Nations. How long, critical voices ask, will it still be possible to assume more or less dogmatically that the interests of the United Nations and the United States are necessarily identical? In fact, has not the assumption already been invalidated by trends and events beginning with the Suez crisis in 1956, if not earlier?

II

THE ASSUMPTION UNDERLIES THE UNITING FOR PEACE RESOLUTION OF 1950 rather than the United Nations Charter of 1945. Since the essentials of both instruments are of American origin, the difference indicates a significant change during those five years in the attitude of the United States toward the United Nations.

Harley A. Notter, the official historian of United States *Postwar Foreign Policy Preparation,* vividly describes the dilemma that confronted the planners in the State Department when they set out to draft the constitution of the peace organization that was to replace the defunct League of Nations. The prospective constitution had to win the approval of the internationalist wing of American public opinion and

The United States and the United Nations

had to be acceptable to the isolationist wing as well. "Uncertainty," remarks Notter, "regarding Senate consent to ratification of any proposed agreement in this field was ever present."[2] In other words, the future organization was to be more akin to genuine international government than the League of Nations, but the restrictions on United States sovereignty less far reaching than supposedly they would have been under the Covenant. The only solution of this dilemma was a constitutional construction that would provide the nucleus of a supranational world government and at the same time assure the United States, and necessarily other major powers as well, a special privileged status within the system. The United Nations Charter fully meets these requirements. The Security Council was to have supranational powers, though only as peace-enforcing agency acting under Chapter VII of the Charter. Moreover, the United Nations' procedures were to be governed by the majority instead of the unanimity principle which prevailed in the League. But thanks to the rule of the Charter that majority decisions of the Security Council shall require the concurrent votes of the five permanent members of the Council, which implies their veto right, the United States would virtually be exempt from the supranational authority of the Council. It could not be compelled to participate in any sort of enforcement measures and, by the same token, could prevent their application against itself. In regard to the very questions of war and peace that affect its interests most closely, the United States, together with the other major powers and contrary to all other United Nations members, would retain the traditional right of sovereign nations to be their own judges of their rights and obligations under international law, including those under the Charter. As Senator Arthur H. Vandenberg, when advocating the ratification of the Charter, assured his colleagues, the flag would stay on the dome of the Capitol.

The grant to some members of a privileged position in the United Nations was hardly consistent with the idea of equality of states, affirmed in the Charter, or, for that matter, of collective security as a generally applicable system. The device of a built-in concert of the leading powers in an otherwise democratic organization is reminiscent, in fact, of the European Concert of Powers in the nineteenth century, though this was a purely aristocratic model of international government. The ingenious construction, however, not

[2]U. S. Department of State, General Foreign Policy Series 15, *Postwar Foreign Policy Preparation 1939-1945* (Washington: U. S. Government Printing Office, 1949), p. 113. For the following see also Erich Hula, "The Evolution of Collective Security under the United Nations Charter," *Alliance Policy in the Cold War,* ed. Arnold Wolfers (Baltimore, 1959), pp. 88ff.

only was apt to assuage isolationist fears but recommended itself and was justifiable on other grounds as well. In the first place, to require for the operation of the United Nations peace system agreement among its most powerful members was only a formal recognition of the fact that the maintenance of international peace depends ultimately upon their cooperation. Secondly, to rule out the application of the enforcement system against one of the great powers, and particularly one of the two then emerging superpowers, was intended not to burden the United Nations with a task that would most certainly go beyond its physical capacity. Moreover, such enforcement action would practically mean the very kind of global war that the United Nations was founded to avert.

The rapidly unfolding Cold War made it soon clear that the political assumption on which the Charter system of collective security was based did not stand the test of reality. The very powers that were expected to cooperate in the direction of United Nations affairs were pitted against one another in and outside the United Nations and began to look upon each other as potential adversaries in another world holocaust. It soon also became clear that the veto shielded not only the great powers themselves but also their allies and satellites against United Nations intervention. But if we thus found out to our dismay that the Security Council would not be able to cope with the very questions that affected us most closely, we also discovered that we had overrated the risk of United States membership in the world body.

The hegemonic position that had fallen to the United States as a result of World War II secured it the leading role also in the United Nations. In fact, we commanded in all of its councils sweeping majorities in practically all important issues that were raised in them. The feeling that United States interests were in need of protection by constitutional devices against United Nations policies, therefore, began to yield to the belief in a preordained harmony of the United States and United Nations interests. Ironically, the protective shield of the great-power veto proved to be the only obstacle we encountered in trying to make full use of United Nations procedures for furthering American interests. Thus we forgot that only a short time ago we considered the veto an indispensable guarantee of "our perpetuated independence of international dictation," as Senator Vandenberg put it in 1945, and disparaged with its alleged abuse by the Soviet Union the device itself. In order to circumvent the Soviet veto in the Security Council, we now favored, and became instrumental in effecting, a gradual shift of the constitutional center from the Council to the General Assembly. Finally, in 1950, at the height of the Korean crisis, we sponsored the Uniting for Peace resolution which terminated the monopoly of the council in dealing with threats to the peace, breaches of the peace, and acts of aggression.

By initiating a constitutional reform that was intended to circumvent the Soviet veto in the Council and subject the Soviet Union in the last instance to majority decisions of the General Assembly, we also implicitly submitted our own policies to the ultimate control of the Assembly. In strictly legal terms, admittedly, we thereby did not extend our obligations beyond what they were under the Charter, for, unlike the Security Council, the General Assembly has no compulsory but only recommendatory powers. But such distinctions do not weigh very heavily in United Nations politics. Moreover, what the Assembly is lacking in legal authority it makes up for by the greater prestige it enjoys as the democratic organ of the United Nations. It was, in fact, part of our own policy, both for reasons of ideological predilection and of expediency relating to the Cold War, to extol the Assembly and attribute to it a democratic legitimacy and moral authority that it actually does not possess, either by its composition or by the spirit of its proceedings. The risk we ran thus by sponsoring the Uniting for Peace resolution was not altogether negligible. However, it seemed inconceivable then that we would ever be unable to sway the deliberations and decisions of the world parliament.

Just as the collective security scheme of the Charter was patterned on the model of the Grand Alliance of World War II, the system of the Uniting for Peace resolution was based on the assumption that the political alignments in the initial period of the Korean War would continue beyond its termination. But the second assumption proved as faulty as the first. The political constellation of 1950 tended to change even before the Korean hostilities ended.

The Assembly system of the Uniting for Peace resolution, as we never tried to conceal, was designed as a means of strengthening the Western defense position against the East; it was aimed at the Soviet Union. To all practical intents and purposes it was an attempt to span and tighten our particular alliances by an all-embracing American-led alliance in the legal form of an abstract collective-security system. The tendency of the members of a collective security organization to use the abstract system, contrived as a protection of all against each and every other state, for the purpose of building and cementing an alliance against a concrete state or group of states, will always be very strong indeed. But, given the complexity of international relations, the use of the system for such purpose is also likely to be strongly resisted, as the United States soon found out. The Uniting for Peace resolution provided for military means, similar to those envisaged in Chapter VII of the Charter, which were to assure the effectiveness of the new system. However, the General Assembly persistently refused to implement the military provisions of the resolution. The latter remained a dead letter no less than the corresponding provisions of the Charter.

The result of the reform of 1950 differed from the expectations of its sponsors in still another respect. The authors of the Uniting for Peace resolution found satisfaction in seeing it applied to cases to which it had been tailored, as to the case of Chinese Communist intervention in Korea and to the case of Hungary. The Suez and the Lebanon cases, however, showed that the new system was a double-edged weapon that could be used against the West as well. Moreover, the reluctance of the smaller member nations to become involved in the power struggle of the giant members—traces of this reluctance were already discernible prior to and during the Korean War— strongly increased with the rapid growth of United Nations membership and the formation of a neutralist fraction in the latter half of the fifties. We soon also realized that we had underrated the impact of the other Cold War, the one between the colonial and anticolonial powers, both on the operations of the Assembly and on the political dynamics of the Organization in general. Ever since the middle of the fifties the colonial issue, in one form or another, has been in the center of United Nations politics, and the tendency of the anticolonial members to view and use the United Nations primarily as an instrument for terminating the colonial system has become ever stronger.

III

THE FAILURE OF THE UNITED NATIONS MEMBERS TO IMPLEMENT THE military provisions of Chapter VII of the Charter and of the Uniting for Peace Resolution has so far not been understood to imply the abandonment of the very principle of collective security that to prevent and repel aggression, if necessary by armed force, is the most significant task of the world body. Rather, the assumption was that the principle itself was still valid, though its application would have to be improvised in each case of need. The validity of the principle was recently contested, however, by none other than Secretary-General U Thant in his Harvard address of June 13, 1963,[3] and in later statements as well. "There has been," the Secretary-General said, "a tacit transi-

---

[3]See *United Nations Review*, X (July, 1963), pp. 54ff.

tion from the concept of collective security, as set out in Chapter VII of the United Nations Charter, to a more realistic idea of peace-keeping. The idea that conventional military methods—or, to put it bluntly, war—can be used by or on behalf of the United Nations to counter aggression and secure the peace seems now to be rather impractical." As the Secretary-General emphasized, the peace-keeping forces of the United Nations in the Middle East and in the Congo are essentially different from the military forces envisaged in the Charter and the Uniting for Peace resolution. Their task was not to enforce peace, but to support the Council and the Assembly in attempts to terminate an international conflict by the pacific procedures outlined in Chapter VI of the Charter. "They are essentially peace and not fighting forces, and they operate only with the consent of the parties directly concerned." They also are composed of military forces supplied by the smaller nations and not, as the Charter provided, by the great powers, "which has the advantage of not entangling United Nations actions in the antagonisms of the cold war."

The Secretary-General's statement undoubtedly was motivated by his neutralist leanings, but it would be difficult to deny that it is a realistic appraisal of current trends in the United Nations. We had better accept the fact that the emergence in the General Assembly of a strong neutralist faction has undone what the United States tried to accomplish by initiating the Uniting for Peace resolution. At any rate, it is most unlikely that in case of Soviet aggression the two-thirds majority required for recommending or authorizing military enforcement measures could be attained. It is doubtful, in fact, whether sufficient votes might be available in the Assembly for recommending economic or diplomatic sanctions or even for a mere condemnation of the aggression. At best, the Assembly might agree on a colorless, politically meaningless resolution.

The situation is not likely to be different, as the experience of the Goa case has taught us, if a colonial power, or, for that matter, a state pursuing domestic policies giving offense to anticolonialist members, should become the victim of aggression; for instance, to put it bluntly, if African or Asian member states, in violation of the Charter, should resort to force for the purpose of securing the independence of the few remaining colonial possessions or the termination of South Africa's discriminatory domestic policies. The situation might be about the same in case of Arab aggression against Israel, which in Arab eyes is a colonial power. The balance of physical forces in Africa being what it is today, the immediate danger to peace on that continent is not so much direct as indirect aggression by the time-honored method of subversion from outside. But even direct aggression is within the realm of possibility.

The sweep in and outside the United Nations of the anticolonialist movement is due to a combination of several favorable factors. The movement has benefited, and still does, by the competition of the two superpowers for influence and power in the uncommitted areas of the world. Anxious to maintain and possibly improve the global balance of power to its own advantage, each of them began to woo the smaller nations, unborn as well as born. Currying their favor, from 1955 onward, they promoted and supported rather than obstructed the admission of new members to the United Nations. The pertinent Charter provisions notwithstanding, the admission procedures have become a mere formality. The notion that membership implies obligations toward the Organization which applicants for admission have to prove to be willing and capable of meeting has become obsolete.

Both superpowers, moreover, for reasons of their political traditions, are morally committed to an anticolonialist course, which, of course, is not to say that their ideas of self-determination of peoples under colonial rule have the same meaning and practical implications. At any rate, the Soviet Union and the United States, in pursuing their anticolonialist policies, find themselves in almost opposite positions. The one is as fortunate for the former as the other unfortunate for the latter. For while the Soviet Union can always be certain that its policy is not only compatible with but actually furthering its national interest, the United States is always plagued by doubts about the effect of its policy on the strength of the Western world, with which it is bound by common interests and ties of a military-political alliance. Long-range interests seem to suggest full support of decolonization, but more immediate interests relating to the West-East conflict pull in the other direction. This accounts for the Hamlet-like attitude of the United States in colonial questions that has manifested itself as far back as the Conference of San Francisco. It was not the United States but the Soviet Union that proposed to the Conference to make it an express purpose of the United Nations "to develop friendly relations among nations based on respect for the principle of equal rights and self-determination of peoples" (Article 1, paragraph 2).

The endorsement by the Charter of the principle of self-determination has proved a powerful ideological weapon in the anticolonialist struggle. So has the fact that the Charter proclaims as another purpose of the United Nations "to achieve international cooperation . . . in promoting and encouraging respect for human rights and for fundamental freedoms for all without distinction as to race, sex, language, or religion" (Article 1, paragraph 3). The very provisions of the Charter which deal directly with colonial matters have been no less effective in strenthening the cause of colonial emancipation. Both Chapters XI and XII envisaged a radical transformation and the final termination of the colonial system, with the United Nations assisting in the process.

Article 1 of the Charter establishes a hierarchy of the purposes that the United Nations is to pursue. The purposes stated in the second and third paragraph are clearly subordinate to the purpose "to maintain international peace and security" stated in the first paragraph of Article 1. In fact, one can speak of a Hobbesian tendency among the fathers of the Charter to absolutize the value of peace. When at San Francisco some smaller nations proposed to make, in addition to the maintenance of international peace and security, the maintenance of international law and justice an express United Nations purpose, the conferees, following the lead of the United States, rejected the proposal. According to the intention of its founders, the United Nations, in promoting self-determination of peoples and human rights, must go no farther than is conducive to the cause of peace.

But whatever the original intention might have been, the very endorsement by the Charter of these principles tends to cast a shadow of doubt on the legitimacy of any conditions that are inconsistent with them. It lends itself to the interpretation and, in fact, has been interpreted to imply that only a political order, international or national, founded on those principles is legitimate. Or, in negative terms, states, governments, possessions, boundaries, or international treaties that supposedly do not conform to them are lacking in legitimacy. The solemn affirmation of these principles, by the same token, does seem to sanction policies and actions, including revolutionary policies and actions, that try to reshape the world according to those political maxims. It is no accident that the Charter outlaws war but not revolution.

Admittedly, the fact that the Charter lends support to the anticolonialist cause cannot be understood to imply a qualification of the obligation of United Nations members, stated in Article 2, paragraph 4 of the Charter, to "refrain in their international relations from the threat or use of force." The prohibition of force, often called the most essential provision of the Charter, is meant to be absolute and leaves no room for a legally permissible "war of liberation" of any kind. But the very fact that the Charter favors so strongly the end, liberation (if liberation it is), cannot but lessen the effectiveness of the limitations it places on means for attaining that end. Nor is it likely that the United Nations will take strong action against aggression if it considers the cause for which it has been undertaken legitimate, as we know from the attitude of United Nations members in the Goa case.

The contingency of Goa need not actually repeat itself, however. What we have experienced so far, and must expect to meet with more and more often in the near future, is the exploitation by African and Asian members of our fear that they will use force unless we help them to mobilize the machinery of the United Nations for the attainment of their particular ends. The threat to the peace, caused by those states, is used by them as an argument in urging the United Nations to take collective action against the very states they themselves are threatening. The pressure brought to bear by African and Asian members both on the Security Council and the General Assembly to take coercive punitive measures of one kind or another against Portugal and South Africa has been mounting in recent years, and indications that we are yielding to the pressure have been multiplying. One wonders whether the time has not come for the United States to reassert the primacy of peace in the hierarchy of United Nations purposes, recognized in the Charter, thanks primarily to its own efforts. True, our national traditions are not apt to arouse in us sympathies for historic rights, but prudence and forbearance in applying abstract principles *are* part of our national heritage.

One can think still of another type of international conflict with which the United Nations might have to deal in the future; conflicts between the emancipated heirs to the former empires. The tensions between Indonesia and the Federation of Malaya and border disputes between African states are cases in point. The fluidity of the political constellations in the Council and the Assembly can in such cases be expected to be greater than in those relating to the two cold wars. It is also possible that the rift within the formerly monolithic world Communist movement will have similar effects on the dynamics of United Nations politics. The structure, the political capacity, and the functions of the United Nations are likely to be subject to rapid changes in the future as much as they have been in the past.

IV

THE FAILURE OF THE UNITED NATIONS TO DEVELOP AN EFFECTIVE system of collective peace-enforcement, on the pattern either of Chapter VII of the Charter or of the Uniting for Peace resolution, was bound to affect the members' conceptions of their rights and obligations under the Charter.[4] They probably were still more powerfully influenced by the prospect of nuclear aggression, which was not yet anticipated at the time the Charter was drafted. Both factors combined to revive the notions of self-help that were dominant in international society prior to its institutionalization and lingering on still in the Covenant of the League of Nations, but exorcised from the United Nations Charter. Thrown back on their own resources and facing the possibility of a type of aggression which could spell their very annihilation, United Nations members in general and the nuclear powers among them in particular have increasingly tended to apply to their rights under the Charter, and especially "the inherent right of individual or collective self-defense" recognized in Article 51, an extensive interpretation and to interpret restrictively. their obligations, particularly the obligation of Article 2, paragraph 4, to refrain from the threat or use of force. The experience of the League is repeating itself in the United Nations: Members of a political society are ready to recognize limitations on their right to judge for themselves and assert their own cause only as long and to the extent that the public authorities are willing and able to afford them protection.

It would be difficult to say whether the erosion of Article 51 or that of Article 2, paragraph 4, set in first, and which of the two processes is more advanced today. At any rate, the erosion has progressed pretty far in either case, although the United Nations has not yet reached, and perhaps never will reach, the stage the League of Nations entered in the second half of the thirties, when the members began to deny officially the validity of the most important provisions of the Covenant. United Nations members so far try rather to present their deviations from the Charter as consistent with its spirit, if not its letter. The reinterpretation to which the Charter has been subjected since 1945 is the more ominous as the United States, too, which can claim to be second to none in devotion to the ideals of the Charter, has substantially contributed to the modification of its original meaning.

The reinterpretation of Article 51 was begun by the Security Council itself. By accepting in 1947 the First Report of the Atomic Energy Commission, it recognized implicitly that the strict interpretation of the words, which seem to limit the permissible exercise of the right of self-defense to the case of an actual armed attack, was not

[4]See Hula, *op. cit.* pp. 99ff.

justified in view of the conditions of nuclear warfare. In other words, preventive action against an imminent nuclear attack, the Security Council implied, was to be considered as lawful. Soon there also developed among United Nations members a trend to claim that the term "armed attack" must be understood to cover indirect aggression as well, in the form, for instance, of foreign support for domestic subversion. Thus, in spite of Article 51, self-defense again tends, as was the case in former times, to be held legitimate in practically any case in which a nation feels seriously wronged by the policy of another nation. United Nations members, moreover, did not hesitate to tell the Security Council that it had no right to control their exercise of self-defense unless the Council could assure them of effective protection by its own means of their vital interests.

The reinterpretation of Article 2, paragraph 4, also began at an early date. It was encouraged by the wording of the provision which seems to imply a qualification of the no-force rule that actually, however, was not intended by the fathers of the Charter. Mention was already made of the doctrine of the justness of wars of national liberation. Before it was adopted by anticolonialist members and applied by India in the Goa case, the doctrine was advocated by the Soviet Union and put to use by the Soviet bloc in the Korean War. Ineffectiveness of the United Nations as a reason warranting disregard of the prohibition of force played a great role particularly in the Suez crisis. "If the United Nations proves ineffective," the Australian Premier declared, "we must, in the absence of willing and proper negotiations, be ready to impose sanctions ourselves. The doctrine that force can never be employed except pursuant to a decision of the Security Council is a suicidal doctrine."[5] The most dramatic case involving the interpretation of the Charter's rules on the use of force and the right of self-defense was, of course, the Cuban crisis of October 1962. The legality of the United States quarantine against Cuba is still a matter of heated controversy among American international lawyers. It is indeed most difficult to prove the legality of the American action in terms of the Charter as it was originally understood and as the United States itself repeatedly interpreted it. But this makes the Cuban case yet more significant as an indication of current interpretations of the law of the United Nations. The case suggests most impressively indeed the persistency of the notion, supposedly discarded a long time ago, that resort to force for the purpose of maintaining the balance of power is legitimate. United States policies

[5]Quoted by B. V. A. Roeling, "The Question of Defining Aggression," *Symbolae Verzijl,* ed. (La Haye, 1958), p. 325.

in Viet Nam and in the Dominican crisis are more recent manifestations of the process of erosion suggested above.

V

TESTED BY THE MOST AMBITIOUS INTENTIONS OF ITS FOUNDERS, THE United Nations undeniably is in default. It has failed to create an effective system of peace enforcement and, therefore, has also failed to secure unqualified acceptance of legal principles meant to eliminate from international society recourse to self-help and thus approximate the relations among its members to those among members of a national community. But the League of Nations and the United Nations have both also been assigned tasks that were performed in international society before. Moreover, not all legal principles of the Covenant and the Charter are novel principles, untried prior to the establishment of these organizations. The rules of Chapter VI of the Charter governing the pacific settlement of disputes by the Security Council and the General Assembly are in fact of a rather conservative nature. What, then, is the record of the United Nations as an agency of mediation and conciliation?

There seems to be almost general agreement that on the whole the performance of the world body in this field has been far from poor. Needless to say, the record at the same time has been rather uneven, the success of the United Nations in resolving disputes and terminating armed conflicts necessarily depending upon the character of the issues involved in each case. There are intractable issues that even the most skillful mediator cannot settle. Moreover, he can only advise the parties but not compel them to comply with his advice. Mediation and conciliation are procedures based on the principle of consent.

The most intractable issues that the United Nations have faced have been those relating to the Cold War between East and West. The Organization certainly was not able to resolve them, but its mediatory efforts have nonetheless been useful, at least in some cases. The United Nations admittedly played in the Cuban crisis of October 1962 only a minor role, but there can be no doubt that its very existence and the services it actually offered facilitated the resolution of the conflict. It was in areas outside the orbit of the Cold War, however, where what the late Secretary-General Dag Hammarskjold called "preventive United Nations diplomacy" scored its greatest successes. True, even in such cases as Suez and Gaza, Lebanon and Jordan, Laos and the Congo, the effectiveness of the United Nations depended ultimately upon the attitude of the two superpowers. If they were not ready to support the policy of the United Nations, they had at least to acquiesce in it.

The successes of the United Nations in these cases were also due to the political and constitutional development of the Organization itself. The emergence of a tripartite, instead of the bipolaristic structure that prevailed in the first decade of United Nations history, prepared the ground for the rise in the Organization of the Secretary-General to the position of a leading diplomatic figure and powerful executive. Mr. Hammarskjold could claim ever more forcefully, even vis-à-vis the great powers, that, owing his office to election by both the Security Council and the General Assembly, he was set apart by the Charter itself as "an independent opinion factor" able to speak and act on behalf of the entire Organization as long as he had the confidence of the member states. Making full use of the moral and legal authority he had acquired, the Secretary-General organized in the Suez and Congo cases what in the diplomatic language of the nineteenth century can be called armed mediation. While the United Nations is generally given credit for its armed mediation in the Middle East, its action in the Congo, especially in its later stages, aroused much criticism.

The usual kind of criticism any mediator, individual or collective, must expect to be subjected to is that he has yielded to the power realities and disregarded the rights and wrongs in the conflict he has tried to resolve. This criticism was leveled, for example, at the settlement by the United Nations of the conflict between the Netherlands and Indonesia over West New Guinea. The criticism of United Nations policy in the Congo went much farther. It consists in fact of three indictments: first, that the United Nations enforced a settlement of the internal conflict in the Congo, though the mediator is only entitled to advise and recommend; second, that the settlement was unjust because it violated the right of Katanga to self-determination, a right which is affirmed in the Charter; third, that the enforcement of the settlement, regardless of its content, violated another basic principle, recognized in Article 2, paragraph 7, of the Charter, according to which the United Nations has no authority "to intervene in matters which are essentially within the domestic jurisdiction of any state."

It is, indeed, true that the United Nations overstepped the limits set to the mediator. Its action in the Congo began as armed mediation, but ended as armed intervention. The experience of former times repeated itself in the Congo: The line of distinction between armed mediation and armed intervention is very thin and likely to be disregarded when mediation of a conflict runs into insuperable difficulties. This must be expected to happen particularly in the case of a collective mediator such as the United Nations. But one may seriously doubt whether the charge of a violation of the principle of self-determination is equally well founded, or, rather, whether the principle was applicable to the Katanga case at all. The principle of self-determination makes no sense where, as in Katanga, there is no homogeneous collectivity recognizable as the subject of the right. Moreover, is the policy of most African states to recognize the boundary lines established during the colonial era not more likely to conduce to the stabilization and consolidation of the continent than the application of the abstract principle of self-determination? "The circumstances," Edmund Burke has wisely remarked, "are what render every civil and political scheme beneficial or noxious to mankind."

There is, on the other hand, again some truth in the third indictment of United Nations policy in the Congo. In terms of Article 2, paragraph 7, of the Charter, as originally conceived, the exception to the nonintervention principle hardly applied in the Congo case for the very reason that the action of the United Nations was meant to be mediation under Chapter VI, but not enforcement under Chapter VII, of the Charter. In fact, the United Nations action in the Congo is difficult to fit in with the original scheme of the Charter in general.

When the newly founded Republic of the Congo turned to the United Nations with the request for military assistance, it claimed that it was the victim of external aggression. In actual fact, the dispatch of Belgian armed forces when public peace and order broke down in the infant republic was intended to serve no other purpose than the urgently required protection of life and property of Belgian citizens. It was none other than Mr. Hammarskjold who frankly recognized that it might be doubtful whether "the United Nations faced a conflict between two parties." The Secretary-General held that the question was not legally essential for the justification of the United Nations action. He saw its legal basis in the explicit request of the Congolese Government for military assistance and in the implied finding of the Security Council that the consequences of the breakdown of internal law and order in the Republic constituted a threat to international peace and security. The restoration of domestic law and order was thus from the beginning one of the objectives, if not the primary objective, of the United Nations action.

In trying to define the legal and political nature of the Congo case, one is reminded of the suggestion General Smuts made in 1918 that the future League of Nations should assume the guidance and control of the new states that were then arising from the breakup of the Austrian, Russian, and Turkish empires. The same idea that the ordering hand of an international organization should, if need be, assist formerly dependent peoples in the early days of statehood inspired Secretary-General Hammarskjold when he proposed the United Nations action in the Congo.

The record of the United Nations as an essentially diplomatic body, charged with the traditional functions of mediation and conciliation, thus shows a picture that is the very opposite of its record as a collective security system proper. It is at least prior to the financial crisis that incapacitated the Organization, a picture of expansion and not of retraction. From the mere conference type of international organization the United Nations has developed into a body capable of "executive action, undertaken on behalf of all members, and aiming at forestalling conflicts and resolving them, once they have arisen, by appropriate diplomatic or political means," to describe this transformation in the words of Mr. Hammarskjold's last annual report to the General Assembly. Admittedly, the concomitant of this development has been an increasingly loose interpretation of the pertinent powers of the Organization. The limitation on the authority of the United Nations in Article 2, paragraph 7, of the Charter has been exposed to the same process of erosion as the limitations on the rights of United Nations members in Article 2, paragraphs 4 and 51. No sooner had the Organization started to operate than a restrictive interpretation of the nonintervention principle came into use. This tendency was the stronger as the Charter principles of self-determination and human rights actually invite United Nations intervention in domestic affairs. But the chief reason for this development was political. The boundary line between domestic and international matters is always difficult to draw with precision and is bound to be even more so in a revolutionary age when the front lines of ideological warfare are cutting across all geographical and political boundaries and acts of indirect aggression are a daily occurrence in international politics.

If we complain today about the tendency of the United Nations to arrogate and exercise powers that under the Charter it does not possess, we should also remember the record of the founding Conference at San Francisco. It shows that the United States was foremost among those conferees who rejected the legal guarantees for which smaller nations were pleading as a protection against the virtually unlimited powers of the Security Council under Chapter VII of the Charter. Such restrictions on the Council's authority, the United States felt, would lessen its effectiveness as an instrument of peace.

The United States and the United Nations

VI

THAT WE ARE TODAY INCREASINGLY CONCERNED ABOUT LOOSE INTER-pretations of the Charter is, of course, an expression of our growing uneasiness about our diminishing strength in the councils of the United Nations. But do we actually need to be alarmed about our position in the Organization?

Undoubtedly, the ease with which the United States influenced and controlled United Nations policies during the first decade of its history is a matter of the irretrievable past, as much as is the commanding position the United States held outside the United Nations during those years. But, speaking in general terms, one is entitled to say that ours is still the most influential voice of any single nation in the halls of the world organization. With equal assurance one may assert that the Soviet Union has no chance to attain in the United Nations a hegemonic position similar to that of the United States in the first postwar years. The Soviet Union has not gained as much as the United States has lost through the recent evolution of the United Nations. The chief beneficiaries of the ascendancy of the General Assembly and of the open-door policy in matters of admission have been the small and smallest nations of Asia and Africa. "The fact is," as Ambassador Adlai E. Stevenson remarked in 1963, "that in 17 years the Soviet Union has never once—never once—succeeded in building a majority for any proposition of substance against the opposition of the United States."[6] The statement is as valid today as it was in 1963. Nor must we judge the voting chances in the General Assembly exclusively by the numerical strength of the several blocs. In actual fact, the voting pattern is surprisingly flexible today, owing to the curious way in which the two cold wars are intertwined and to the resulting complexity of loyalties and interests that bear on the policies of United Nations members. Both the Western and the Afro-Asian blocs are likely to fall apart when they vote on questions that, from their point of view, are related to the other cold war, and there are often even defections from the Western bloc on issues of the West-East conflict and from the Afro-Asian bloc on questions of colonialism. Only the coherence of the Soviet bloc has so far been absolute.

To judge from the voting record, there is thus no reason for being alarmed about our position in the United Nations. The voting record, however, does not tell the whole story about our actual weight

[6]The statement was made before the Subcommittee on International Organization Affairs of the Senate Committee on Foreign Relations on March 13, 1963. See *The Department of State Bulletin*, XLVIII, No. 1241 (April 8, 1963), p. 527.

in the Organization. The record does not cover the cases in which we refrained, as we did in the Goa case, from submitting a question to the General Assembly, or, for that matter, to the Security Council. Nor does it reveal the scruples we might in many cases have felt in going along with the majority for reasons of expediency. If we want to find out whether and to what extent United States and United Nations interests are still running parallel, we, rather, must ask and answer the questions: What can we reasonably expect to be able to make the United Nations do; what can we reasonably expect to be able to prevent it from doing, in matters that are of vital concern to us?

If we ever had illusions about the contribution the United Nations could make to our military security, they were soon dissipated by the stark facts of postwar international politics. Since the end of the forties we have been relying exclusively on our system of alliances and on our armaments as means for protecting our national interest. This policy has so far not been seriously impaired by the United Nations. Is there any danger that it will in the future? Two possibilities, in particular, immediately come to mind; mounting pressure of the United Nations in questions of disarmament, exerted in a direction which seems to us to run counter to the requirements of our national safety, and opposition in the United Nations to actions we might feel compelled to take in the Western hemisphere. If need be, the one would have to be resisted as the other disregarded. The more difficult case for us to handle would be the second, as we know from recent experience in the Cuban and Dominican cases. Assuming armed intervention in some part of the Western hemisphere once more would become necessary in our view, the hostile reactions to it in the United Nations might very well be formidable. But this prospect would hardly be decisive in deterring us from taking the action. The decisive consideration in weighing the pros and cons of the measure undoubtedly would be the likely reaction to it of the Soviet Union; our second consideration would be its effect on our Latin American allies; and the attitude of the United Nations would be our third concern only. In other words, the United Nations would not and could not prevent us from doing what we, rightly or wrongly, hold to be absolutely essential for the protection of our vital interests; it would operate only as a restraining influence on our decision. But, then, is not the exercise of restraining influence on the actions of its members the most significant task of the United Nations?

What about the policies we would like the United Nations to pursue? The preceding discussion on the United Nations as a novel system of collective security and as a diplomatic body, applying and developing traditional methods of mediation and conciliation, has shown the range and the limits within which the United Nations can reasonably be expected to be useful, within which, in fact, it is indispensable. To improvise in each and every case of international crisis the methods and procedures of mediation and conciliation might have satisfied the simpler needs of international society in former times. But the deficiencies of this system, or, rather, lack of system, were felt strongly already in the nineteenth century and led to the formation of the European Concert of Powers, the first modern model of international government. But the Concert still was an occasional rather than a permanent institution. In the complex conditions of world society in the twentieth century, the need for permanent global international institutions of mediation and conciliation has become imperative. It is inconceivable that the United States could, nor is there any reason why it should, discontinue its cooperation in such institutions within the United Nations and withdraw its support from the Organization.

But in view of possible divergencies today between United States and United Nations interests, the United States would do well to reconsider the constitutional policy it has been pursuing during the last fifteen years. Admittedly, we cannot return to the conceptions we advocated at Dumbarton Oaks and San Francisco. Equalitarian tendencies within the international community are today too strong to make the reversion of the constitutional development which has transformed the United Nations feasible, even if we felt it to be desirable. But one wonders whether it would be wise on our part to try to extend the powers of the General Assembly still further. Our attempt, stubbornly pursued during recent years, to secure the recognition of the Assembly's budgetary authority in peace-keeping operations is a case in point. Considering the strength of the political forces opposed to its objective, the attempt was bound to be futile. But it also was ill-advised from the point of view of United States interests. It cannot be ruled out, after all, that the General Assembly one day might engage in peace-keeping operations of which we could not approve, to which, in fact, we might be opposed. The risk of United States membership in the world body cannot any longer be taken lightly.

Printed in U.S.A.